SELF-DEVELOPING AMERICA

SELF-DEVELOPING
AMERICA

HAROLD J. RUTTENBERG

HARPER & BROTHERS, PUBLISHERS
NEW YORK

TO RUSSELL W. DAVENPORT
(1899-1954)
Poet, Journalist, and Philosopher

I dedicate this book to Russell W. Davenport, whose premature death (and what man does not die prematurely) kept him from completing his self-appointed task of precipitating "in words, from the limitless flux of American life, the special meaning and mission of his country." He died on April 19, 1954, while writing *The Dignity of Man*, published posthumously, in which he treated the spiritual content of America as a foundation for the succeeding volumes that he planned in his series of books, *Studies in Freedom*. This book is a continuation of his work in which I respond to his challenge: "Only if we can give the word 'spiritual' a real and self-evident content, can we hope, in turn, to give meaning to the political principles on which our system is based."

CONTENTS

ACKNOWLEDGMENTS

This book is a collaborative effort with my wife, Katherine Monori Ruttenberg, extending over a period of fifteen years. After a dozen years in the labor movement (1934-1946) we left the United Steelworkers of America just as its position had become strong and secure. With pain in our hearts we risked our deep friendships with fellow workers in the cause of man who might become disillusioned with me when I joined the Cleveland financier, Cyrus S. Eaton, to form the Portsmouth Steel Corporation (Ohio) of which I became executive vice-president. Kató felt that we were leaving the happiest years of our lives behind us—an unfounded fear that I too shared. She was opposed to the move. But I was driven by a compulsion to acquire at firsthand a detailed knowledge of industry and finance to match the firsthand, detailed intuitive knowledge that I had acquired in organized labor and in government (War Production Board and War Labor Board, 1942-1945). We would not have left all for which we had worked just to earn money, although materialistically oriented friends wrote us off for this reason with those few exceptions who still are our dear friends. Such is life.

Within thirty months (January, 1949) I left Portsmouth Steel and went out on my own. I was able to exercise my stock purchases and move the family—now three boys and a girl on the way—back to Pittsburgh, which is our home, with my six-figure bundle of cash (after taxes) and my integrity still intact. For two years I wandered in the wilderness, a lonely but persisting man in search of the central meaning of America, the land of the brave and the home of the free, your country and mine. In March, 1951, I acquired a sixty-nine-year-old well-drilling machinery company; rebuilt its declining business; revolutionized the method of drilling water wells in hard and abrasive rock formations in the United States; and sold and delivered drill rigs to fifty separate countries throughout the world, in my last year (1958) as being president-owner. Kató and I traveled extensively abroad and in this country during these years, since we develop together and I would not want to have a rich travel experience that we did not share. A European by birth, Kató never truly understood America until we traveled Texas together, and I, in turn, never comprehended the United States until she made me go to Europe to celebrate our fortieth birthdays.

My original purpose in going into industry was put to its full test in January, 1959. Stephen Raushenbush patiently let me make up my own mind. When we returned home after the directors' meeting that completed the sale, Steve said to Kató, "Harold has made a wise decision." My personal timetable of choice was 1964 when I would be fifty and might be financially independent. But I had already found my answer to What is America? The moral obligation to pass it on to my fellow countrymen determined my course. My decision was reinforced by the death of our friend David S. Osler, a businessman whom cancer cut down in the prime of life in July, 1958. When I had my last chance to say No to the Koehring Company to whom I sold, another intimate friend, Dr. Irving Hartmann, was being eaten up by cancer and died on the last day that I owned the Stardrill-Keystone Company, January 31, 1959. His story merits a separate book; this significant scientist in the U.S. Bureau of Mines achieved an excellence—not lopsided growth in one specialty, but well-rounded development in all the basic disciplines—in his too-brief life and work that is rare in twentieth-century America but has a good chance of becoming the norm in the United States of the twenty-first century. Throughout the writing of the final drafts of this book I have felt the presence of Dave and Irv with whom I had argued out so many facets of the universe.

My mother-in-law, Helen Monori, who wanted so much to see the results of our long labors, died while the manuscript was nearing completion. Her spirit has been a continuing inspiration, and I am also indebted to Emil Monori for his many helpfulnesses.

Stephen Raushenbush, whom I had first met a few months after my father died in 1933 and adopted as my stepfather before I was twenty years old, has critically read the several drafts of this book over the years. His continued living presence has been indispensable, all the more so because he has different views of some of the matters discussed in the final draft. If there were an ultimate in eternity, what would heaven be but a place where we communed with kindred spirits? This it has been my privilege to do repeatedly with the man who, among other things, helped me to see that I could not find as meaningful an answer to What Is America? if I confined my career to a lopsided growth confined to the labor movement.

My brother Stanley H. Ruttenberg has been helpful through the years, and he also has his own views that vary somewhat from mine. I have an indebtedness to my other brother, Milton, which is personal.

Ordway Tead, my publisher, has been a great taskmaster, making me rewrite and rewrite until the bulky manuscript was distilled into this final brief version, always giving me valuable editorial guidance. His persistent criticisms were all the more painful because they validated most of the laborious work that Kató had put into our collaborative efforts on the manuscript that developed from a mere compulsion to over a half million words and finally to the final book, less than one-fifth as wordy but, we hope, more than five times as meaty.

Charles and James, our two oldest sons at M.I.T., have rendered valuable help in recent years, and Edward and Ellen have been my faithful messengers between our home and the Carnegie Library to whose staff I am indebted, especially Rose Demarest who has made such a living institution out of the Pennsylvania Room.

I am grateful to Douglas McGregor, Professor of Industrial Management, Massachusetts Institute of Technology, for his excellent critique.

To all those others to whom I am indebted, the only way that I can acknowledge their intellectual and spiritual invoice is through my purity of purpose, courage of conception, and integrity of thought.

My secretaries during the 1950's, Ethyl Joynt and Leona Scrivo, have contributed their excellent typing services, and I am also indebted to Eleanore Engelmore for her great proficiency in typing the last two drafts and delivering the final one a few weeks ahead of her first-born.

For the freedom to develop my faculties and a position of relative independence enabling me to speak my mind and express my spirit without having to cater to any economic or sectarian group, I am indebted to the United States of America.

I am indebted to the coalminers' children in Nemacolin, Pennsylvania, with whom I went to grade school and grew up as a child; to their parents—coalminers, steelworkers—to these naturally warm—kind and mean—individuals whose lives in the coal patches and steeltowns I was able to share during my formative years; and with whom I fought side by side, on occasion eating tear gas and dodging bullets, to translate into reality the sentiments expressed in the Declaration of Independence and the Constitution, and to achieve "an equal chance" as incarnated in the person of Abraham Lincoln. The depth and intensity of my feeling for the individuals who make up humanity everywhere, which stems from my Hebraic heritage, was intensified by twenty-two years of intimate association with the men, women, and children whose lives are devoted to the mining of coal and the making of steel. They have made me the man that I am in the process of becoming.

That all the peoples of the earth may know
The embattled destination of the free—
Not peace, not rest, not pleasure—but to dare
To face the axiom of democracy:
Freedom is not to limit, but to share
And freedom here is freedom everywhere.

Russell W. Davenport
"MY COUNTRY" 1944

Two roads diverged in a wood, and I—
I took the one less traveled by,
And that has made all the difference.

Robert Frost
THE ROAD NOT TAKEN

SELF-DEVELOPING AMERICA

CHAPTER ONE

THE TOTALITY OF AMERICA

What is America?

America is a work of human art, fashioned by the peoples of many lands. For centuries they have pursued our dream as they wandered from Palestine, to Greece, to Rome, to Europe, to the British Isles, and finally to these shores. America is not the private possession of Americans. It is a universal achievement in the process of becoming the common property of everybody, everywhere. Within our borders, for the first time in human history, it has been demonstrated that a more equal and better life can be achieved on earth—in this life, if not within the lifetime of this generation. With all the undried and smeary paint still on our canvas, America is yet an inspiring work of art that belongs to the world just as do the great works of music, architecture, writing, sculpture, or painting.

The United States of America, where everybody is free to strive for everything, cannot be kept as a purely national treasure. We are the proud possession of all mankind. The peoples of the world see us as an unfinished work of human striving, with

3

liberty to achieve a freedom and an excellence that we are still in the formative stages of fulfilling. With defiance in their voices, envy in their eyes, jealousy in their hearts, everybody loves America. They impatiently await our awakening to the realization that our continued growth and development are inseparably dependent upon their own self-development; their development, in turn, is dependent upon ours. We are all neighbors who have to live-and-help-live not just live-and-let-live. This is our America whose promise of human betterment and freedom we can help fulfill by facilitating the release of the dignity of man that lies within the bosom of every person, young or old, alive or yet unborn, in all countries.

Americans are not a static people living in either a finished society on the way to the grave or an affluent society being overtaken by Marxist societies. We are a dynamic people in a self-developing society on the way to an Age of Excellence; the Marxist societies are still struggling to achieve a form of materialism that we are in the process of outgrowing.

THE THREE E'S IDEA

The one great idea produced by America did not come out of any one person's mind. No single writer conceived it. No philosopher has claimed it as his thinking. It simply developed as the United States developed, and it is the most potent, revolutionary idea abroad in the world today.

Poverty can be conquered. Knowledge and freedom can be shared. Everybody can have all of the necessities in life, and more and more of the better things—everything. The conquering of poverty and winning of freedom are no longer a dreamer's idle dream. They are a reality in the United States and can become a reality everywhere. This is the American idea that is stirring the hearts and passions of all peoples. It is the most potent idea in the Soviet Union. It did not originate there. It came from America, the land of the free and the home of the brave. It is infecting our primary fatherland countries in Western Europe, as well as our secondary European fatherland countries that are ruled by

Russian armored tanks. It is sweeping the ground out from under the Marxist socialist dogmas in Western Europe and the Marxist Communist doctrinaires in Soviet Europe. It has long since swept the ground out from under the capitalist dogmas in the United States. It has India in ferment; it has awakened that long-slumbering giant, China.

Your country and mine is not a meaningless mass of materialism populated by carefree, thoughtless people. There is a reason for America's existence, derived from its origin, written in its history, and projected into its future. The future greatness of the United States of America is synthesized in the concept of the three E's (see below) that sums up the processes in development that migrated to our shores, beginning with the living processes of religious worship, leading to the processes of the three R's—readin', 'ritin', and 'rithmetic—and growing into the three E's that are spreading with the three R's to all lands.

These processes of learning (three R's) and of doing and living together (three E's) reached their highest stages, with the greatest freedom for the individual and the widest respect for his dignity, first in the U.S.A. In our vanity, we have mistakenly called them the American Way of Life. But as the more equal and better life develops elsewhere, in forms appropriate to the condition of each country, it becomes a Universal Way of Life.

Our continuing development is inextricably intertwined with the worldwide processes of fighting illiteracy (spreading the three R's) and poverty (developing the three E's) in the remotest corners of the world. America is the organizing force, the *primus motor,* of the world-wide processes of eliminating illiteracy, poverty, and the denial of individual dignity everywhere.

We are merely a link—albeit a vital link in the twentieth century—in the world-wide processes of applying scientific management to the organizing of brainpower, manpower, machinery, and raw materials so that everybody shall be well fed, well clothed, well housed, and well educated; and they can win the freedom, and learn to use it, for individual self-development.

America is founded on the dignity of the individual. By providing its individuals with a continuously fuller expression of their inherent dignity, we generate a forward thrust that makes the United States of America the world's greatest power. The dignity of the individual is a natural process in life, and any national grouping of people that suppresses this process thwarts its own self-development.

THE NEXT DEVELOPMENT IN OUR CULTURE

The fourth E—excellence—is now in the formative stages of development. We are in the process of becoming a culture of individuals, by individuals, for individuals. America's achievement of the three E's in the twentieth century is leading to America's achieving an excellence in everything in the twenty-first century.

America's example is the most powerful force-idea in the modern world. It is forcing all peoples to accelerate the proceses in development in their own self-developing nations to bring the three R's and the three E's to fruition. We Americans, as individuals and as a nation, have to facilitate the three R's and the three E's everywhere as part of the process of our own continuing development of providing ourselves with everything and of going on to achieving excellence in everything—a culture to which the rest of the world can aspire in future centuries since all people are now aspiring to America's richer and fuller life in this century.

Abraham Lincoln led northern white Americans to extend an equal chance to colored Americans. A century later the purpose of America is to extend an equal chance to peoples everywhere. The time has come for America to fulfill the promise for which Lincoln gave his full measure of devotion—to facilitate the development of a world-wide welfare society and to extend the Kingdom of God on earth to all peoples everywhere—not as a religious gospel, but as a conscious, dedicated national purpose and international foreign policy. As Lincoln argued, we have a moral obligation to extend the sentiments and principles contained in the Declaration of Independence to everybody, everywhere.

The totality of America is synthesized into a single concept: The living processes of development and transformation have created in America the three R's—readin', 'ritin', and 'rithmetic —that have developed into the three E's—Everything for and with Everybody Everywhere. These are in the process of developing into the fourth E of Excellence by Everybody in Everything through Enterprising and Education. America's developing structure of materialism is the product of these creative processes—spiritual forces—that are developing into an Age of Excellence. Abraham Lincoln is the embodiment of this synthesis of America: "an equal chance" and the better life for "all men, in all lands everywhere."

THE CENTRAL PURPOSE OF AMERICA FOR AMERICANS

A single all-embracing motif runs throughout American cultural, economic, social, scientific, religious, and individual life. America's central purpose is to create opportunities for a constantly rising population to earn all of life's necessities, and more and more of the better things in life, and to develop the capacity to enjoy the finer values in life, for a steadily expanding lifetime. Almost every private and public institution must shape its activities to serve this central purpose; when it wanders from this path it is eventually forced to return to promoting the three E's.

AMERICA'S NATIONAL PURPOSE IN THE WORLD

The one postulate advanced by this book, which is an analysis of America and an interpretation of its role in the world through the use of living process thinking, is this:

We are developing a moral equivalent of war in the process of finding America's national purpose in the world: to extend "to all people of all colors everywhere" America's central purpose, because we can no longer do this for ourselves alone. The national purpose of America is to bring the Kingdom of God on earth to Mr. and Mrs.

Everybody, everywhere by using our democratic strength to act toward three definite objectives:

1. Freedom for self-development of all national groupings of people.
2. An equal chance for all self-developing nations in international trade.
3. Personal freedom built upon "life-giving" social-economic-political conditions.

The continued growth, development, and freedom of America, and the future of democracy in the world, are dependent upon the pursuit of an American national purpose to facilitate the self-development of the third-party nations through a conscious foreign policy of codevelopment, as distinct from coexistence with the Union of Soviet Socialist Republics. The time has come, as William Ernest Hocking has suggested in his *Strength of Men and Nations*, to define "an act of justified creative, affirmative risk" that our country unilaterally can take to "break through vicious circles" of stalemate, distrust, fear, and frustration that are impeding our own growth and self-development as well as that of the other self-developing peoples. "An act of deliberate risk, refusing any longer to shelter one's national purpose behind the continued threat of mass annihilation," is the answer to the H-bomb missile.

My adulthood passion has been to comprehend the essence of the United States of America. I am happy to share my vision of the future of America as part of the process of forging an integrated purpose for our country. This book is not a travelogue through the corridors of industry and finance. It is a journey through the heart, mind, soul, and guts of America by a soldier in the war aganist poverty and illiteracy. I have been in quest of a growth in human feelings and mental capacity to enable me to comprehend America and reinterpret this 342-year experiment in peoplehood to my fellow citizens. For the greater part of my adulthood I have lived this book, which is essentially a report on the meaning of my life.

I am fighting time that wins all wars. This temporary consciousness is a tremendous experience. Two big ideas will keep me busy the rest of my days:

1. Releasing the creativeness of industrial man as an individual revolting against the status quo of his person and the organizations through which he must develop.

2. Making world citizens out of Americans by facilitating their growth into world developers.

Neither idea is original with me; each has found better expression elsewhere. But the understanding of how to facilitate the processes in development to translate these ideas into living forms—to evoke from exploiters their own inner humanity—is mine. I have learned the hard way. I am dedicated to labor at these tasks until the day I die. And while I shall leave more for my children and their children to accomplish than I achieve, the thrilling thing in my life—what gives my existence a genuine meaning—is how much I have been able to accomplish; and how much more I should be able to accomplish before I turn these labors over to the life that follows mine.

There is a limit to what you can do in a day and in one lifetime. Therefore there is a limit to what man can do. But there is no limit to his spirit of striving to do more than he can. Only by overstriving himself can he accomplish as much human betterment and personal freedom as he does.

Striving is painful and yields an occasional joy. You have to suffer many hurtful experiences to enjoy an infrequent satisfaction. My own life derives a meaning from alternating frequent pain and anguish and infrequent pleasure and satisfaction. While you can never fulfill your strivings, the act of striving for more than you can achieve gives your life a greater meaning and provides an inspiration to the individuals—for the life—that follows you.

The knowledge that man can annihilate himself by surrendering his humanity to his national state intensifies our war against time. "If you knew at sunrise that you would die at sunset," the Chinese philosopher asked the Chinese peasant, "what would you do with your last day on earth?" The peasant replied, "I would keep on hoeing my garden until the sun set." It is important to take our work seriously, but not ourselves. None of us counts for much; it is what we do with our lives that counts.

Horace Mann, the father of the three R's in America, put it this way, a few weeks before he died, in his final address to his 1859 graduating class at Antioch, "I beseech you to treasure up in your hearts these my parting words: Be ashamed to die until you have won some victory for humanity."

CHAPTER TWO

PHILOSOPHY OF SELF-DEVELOPMENT
AND CODEVELOPMENT

Self-development[1] is reaching the age of forty-five with twenty-five years of adult experience instead of only one year's experience repeated twenty-five times. Freedom for self-development is the finest value in life. The self-development of the individual is the ultimate purpose in life on earth. The pursuit of freedom to develop one's inner faculties, and to be of service to one's fellow man, is the only way that the individual can contribute to the betterment and liberties of mankind and at the same time give a greater meaning to his own life. Individual freedom has no meaning except in terms of developing one's intuitive capacity of inner perception. Yet the individual has to express his freedom through other people. The rare person can do it through a painting, a musical score, a work of literature or sculpture, or other individual expression; most individuals like myself can express their freedom only through organization.

"All the qualities of a man acquire dignity when he knows

[1] I am indebted to Elton Mayo for the concept of self-development.

that the service of the collectivity that owns him needs him," William James found. This finding is the key to unlocking the spiritual—the creative—energies of people. The devoted collectivity of a people is not the exclusive power of a totalitarian system of government. It can be developed by any organization with a cause for which people are willing to fight. Any American who believes that the collectivity of the American people cannot be organized within the framework of civil liberties and personal freedoms is a licked American. As leaders of a free people we must organize the collectivity of Americans to serve democracy without compromising our freedoms for self-development as dignified human beings who are ends in ourselves.

The object of self-development, except for the rare person in the creative arts, is personal fulfillment as a functioning participant in organizations that know where they are going and have a pretty good idea of how to get there. A positive philosophy for a democracy is essential for developing a national purpose around which the creative energies of the nation's people can be organized, and through which they can be fulfilled. Americans have found such self-fulfillment in the past by dedication to wars of destruction, a war against depression in 1933-1937, and a war of rehabilitation in the Marshall Plan years of 1949-1953; and they are in the process of finding it for the future by dedicating themselves to a world-wide war of construction that William James a half-century ago visualized as the moral equivalent of a shooting war.

America worships freedom as an ideal, rather than as merely a working tool to facilitate the self-development of human beings in all walks of life at every level of responsibility. The self-developers create their own greater inner strength to stand more solidly and morally on their own to greet the world confidently, in contrast to the self-adjusters huddling together on each other's feet in fear and distrust. We equate freedom with individualism and with the right of private organizations to exploit the individuals who must function through them to achieve their own fulfillment. We compound this error when we treat self-development as an end in itself, as it is self-defeating until it is coupled with codevelopment.

CODEVELOPMENT

Codevelopment is reaching the age of forty-five with as great a feeling for humanity as for yourself, your loved ones, and the organizations through which you must function. Codevelopment is the basic tactic of democracy: the development of organizations designed to evoke the inner humanity of people.

There is an inner humanity in every person that can be evoked for the practice of man's humanity to man. There is an inherent creativeness in every person that can be developed to serve society and to make the individual's life more meaningful. There is an inborn self-reproducing spirit of equality in every person seeking meaningful social-economic-political forms of expression. Codevelopment is the interpenetration of the individual's inner growth and development with the functions and purposes of the organizations through which he must find fulfillment. But when the organization for its own limited purposes denies the individual his personality, liberty, or dignity when he gives himself up to the collectivity, he must organize a counter-group to evoke the inner humanity of the leaders of the original organization. In the unfolding of this process, freedom for self-development is rewon for everybody in the codeveloping organizations.

I have seen exploited steelworkers and coal miners revolt. I have seen and helped them cancel their exploitation through unionization that has reminded their exploiters of their own humanity. This has created a solidarity in the basic steel industry, for example, that has restored the normal freedom of both the steel managements and the steelworkers. This development of human freedom and betterment is the work of the inborn dignity of the individual to create. This urge, this duty, to create is a natural process in life that, for example, will transform the "organization man" into a freer, more self-respecting individual. He will revolt. He must revolt. When a man in a democratic society allows himself to be repressed in an essential way to hold on to his job or to maintain his position, he is committing a form of suicide. The more he conforms, the more he will hate himself. This is no less true in the labor movement, whose staff and line individuals below the level of the top official or executive board are as cowed as any "organization man" in any corporation. One has to espouse the Democratic cause; for the other subservience to the G.O.P. is a condition of continued employment. I could not write this kind of lay-it-on-the-line book if I were an organization man in either a large corporation or a large labor union.

Individual freedom is a quite limited reality in America in those high places where power is exercised and basic policy decisions are made. I explored this question with a couple of dozen Sloan Fellows at the Massachusetts Institute of Technology (October, 1957) when I was the evening's guest lecturer. These were all middle management men, getting a year's schooling after ten to fifteen years of experience. They are the elite being groomed for tomorrow's openings on the ladder to the top executive suite. This group laughed down the one man who challenged my observation that the expression of individual freedom—especially on noncorporate matters such as the G.O.P., balanced budget, taxation of incentives, etc.—was limited. "You accept and preach the prevailing economic and political dogma of the top executive suite," I said, "pretty much as rigidly as your counterparts in the Soviet Union accept and preach the Kremlin's latest interpretation of Marxism." This group agreed.

The answer to the problem of reconciling our individual liberties with the process of giving ourselves up to a collectivity lies in organization.[2] Abraham Lincoln certainly abridged some individual liberties in organizing the northern collectivity to fight and win the Civil War. William James's finding that "all the qualities of a man acquire dignity when he knows that the service of the collectivity that owns him needs him" describes the situation inside the Soviet Union as well as the situation inside

---

[2] I am indebted to Philip Murray for an insight into how the individual can find freedom through organization.

American corporations and labor unions. I know that when I take a position in an organization I must submit to its group disciplines to function. I also know that to get things done you have to function through an organization. When I disagreed with the basic policies of the United Steelworkers of America, I had to submit or quit as I did in 1946 after a dozen years. When I had to face up to the inherent double morality of the steel corporation that I then joined as vice-president, I was again confronted with submitting or quitting, which I did within thirty months. I then pursued my own self-development by creating my own corporate organization in which I found my fulfillment until I sold it in 1959 to complete this book.

The fallacy of the concept of individualism is the attempt to reconcile the conflict between the individual and organization in terms of the individual. The resolution of it by individual action only demonstrates how impotent the individual is in fighting by himself. John Brown proved this a century and a year ago at Harpers Ferry. Abraham Lincoln demonstrated how the liberties of the individual, which are always under pressure from organized society, can best be preserved through organization.

The basic steel industry is a current illustration. The individual steelworker's liberties were constricted by his organized employer from 1859 to 1937. The idea that he could give meaning to these denied liberties as an individual, however, was preached by such people as Judge Elbert Gary when he headed U.S. Steel. But only through organization—yes, a counter-organization—could the individual steelworker do anything about his employer's constricting practices. Through a counter-organization the steelworkers solved many of their individual problems and bettered their lot. But their basic problem of individual liberties continues. The steelworkers now have a new set of masters, their union leaders. This is a real step toward industrial democracy, because their union leaders have to stand for re-election, and union members do have the legal freedom to vote for new leaders. The current domination of their union leaders is a step forward from the tyranny of either an oppressive or benevolent paternalistic employer. The individual steelworker has found freedom from the organization of his employer by trading it for security to the leaders of his own labor union, his own organization.

The answer does not lie in freeing the steelworker from the domination of his union leaders. The answer lies in creating a functional meaning of freedom—as, for example, in humanation, through which the steel union serves the inner needs of its members as well as their bread-and-butter requirements. The 1959 116-day steel strike accomplished two practical steps toward humanation. The suffering caused among steelworkers acted as a cement to strengthen the union organization. The steelworkers acquired a new dignity in surrendering to the collectivity of their organization. Their victory over management was sweet despite its economic senselessness. "It will take them five years to regain their losses during the strike," the union critic avers. The solidarity that they rewon in their own organization ranks was more than worth the idle time and loss of wages. David J. McDonald now heads a revitalized labor union in which, incidentally, the members do have a modicum of freedom in electing their leaders. But his continued leadership is dependent upon serving the whole steelworker, and not just his economic side, or else the union members will revolt against their leaders.

On the management side the 1959 steel strike was also a morale builder and will become more so as the steel-industry leaders realize that while they lost the battle in the 1959 strike, they won the war for increased productivity. U.S. Steel, for example, did not lay off or curtail the pay of the organization during the strike. Intensified training sessions were held. U.S. Steel's organization men are now nearly equal to the union's, due to the human relations training they have received during the last two decades. The two counterorganizations by 1962 should be equally skilled in social psychology, group action, and personal leadership.

What of the future? These two organizations are not out to annihilate each other, although they preach this threat to themselves as a tactic for keeping up their respective fighting spirits.

This reflects the lack of a well-defined positive philosophy in each organization. They are developing organizations whose affairs interpenetrate. Their future growth lies in codevelopment. As I shall discuss later, humanation, the annual wage, wage-productivity, collective bargaining will be their next instruments of codevelopment. These next developments in our culture are not the last; they are merely part of the process of ever-developing, ever-becoming.

Where does the individual fit in? Obviously, it is as a functioning participant in his respective organization. What about individual liberties, both in the corporate and the union organization? The labor leaders have made news in recent years resisting the unionization of their staff. Will management's organization men also try to revolt? They are not likely to join the A.F.L.-C.I.O. because the leaders of the historic labor movement just do not comprehend the developing revolt. Yet as their individuality, personality, and dignity are violated in the limited interests of the corporation, the organization men in the $7,500 to $25,000 salary range will revolt. They will demand the return of their soul that, step by step, they have been surrendering to the collectivity to which they have given themselves. They will form counter-groups to evoke the inner humanity of the individuals in the top executive suite. In the process each group will regain their lost freedom for self-development which they will pursue through the codevelopment of their respective organizations. America is in the process of developing from self-adjusting individuals in an acquisitive society to self-developing individuals in a functional society.

This process of codevelopment, as I shall discuss later, is at work in Russia and in the world vis-à-vis the U.S.A. and U.S.S.R. and vis-à-vis these two powers and the third-party nations between them. Each is evoking the inner humanity of the other.

SELF-DEVELOPING PEOPLE

A people pass from underdevelopment to self-development either when they quit sitting around waiting for somebody to do something for them or when they cease permitting somebody to exploit them, stand up on their own two feet, and, in the words of Lancelot Law Whyte, say, "We are going to raise our standards of life; help us if you will, but obstruct us or exploit us at your peril." To call the emerging people of the world under-developed is to fail to comprehend the social revolution in process.

Self-development is revolt against the status quo. The three R's are its foundation. Thinking through your situation to break through to higher planes of living and greater expressions of freedom is the first step. Then come the tactics. But underlying it all there is a feeling for growth, a compulsion to emerge, a demand for a place in the sun. "I demand a right to earn a living and the freedom to participate in decisions that affect my destiny, and I mean to gain them come what may." If the Chinese were still slumbering as they did in Napoleon's time, the People's Republic of China would not be the giant that she is becoming. If the emerging people of Africa, Asia, and Latin America were still content to be exploited and enslaved, America and Russia could sit at the Summit and divide the world up between them. Did not our European fatherland countries divide up the world among themselves in the fifteenth to nineteenth centuries when the people of Asia, Africa, and Latin America were content to wallow in chronic underdevelopment? The difference in the last half of this century is that these underdeveloped people are emerging into national independence and are demanding a place in the sun. That is self-development.

To give meaning to their self-development, these emerging people have to achieve a life-giving codevelopment with the former, present, and would-be exploiting nations. The facilitating of this process is the role of America on the world scene. This role at the current stage of world development is peculiarly ours because, as we shall discuss later, Russia—despite her loud bragging and effective missiles—is still one of the emerging countries. Not until a country recognizes the individual dignity of its people can it develop, as the United States of America has, into a nation in the process of becoming a free, democratic society.

CHAPTER THREE

NEW WAY OF THINKING

No matter how much we learn, we never really know very much. The crucial factor is *how* we think. Both theory and practice are necessary conditions of understanding. Generality is essential to give meaning and perspective to the specific, but the specific makes the generality understandable. A new way of thinking[1]—living processes of thought—is in the formative stages of growth and development in the United States of America. The reader is invited to cross the bridge with me from the doctrinaire world of dogmas and static concepts to the natural world of living processes. To enter the age of excellence we have to turn our backs on the doctrinaires in politics, philosophy, theology, economics, and the other disciplines and open the door to living process thinking to see the vistas of the future. Thus, in the course of our fleeting years we can more effectively pass on to our children and their children's children the great unfolding living processes that we, as individuals, facilitate for so short a lifespan.

[1] I am indebted to Lancelot Law Whyte for a greater facility in living-process thinking.

The natural processes of life develop changes and experiments. They, in turn, produce results such as the three R's which in turn produce the three E's. They do not create doctrines of lasting quality. This is why even doctrinaires are always revising their dogmas. Individuals are born to live and die, and so are the thoughts and societies with which they grow and develop. The only thing that is permanent is change. Doctrines or concepts are merely tools—to be used with genuine realization of their impermanence—to organize diverse facts into meaningful theory that can serve to facilitate processes in development. The three E's are such a concept; they are a shorthand expression to describe processes in development.

The grand sweep of the concept of the three E's is one of motion, movement out of the kerosene-burning kitchen stove to the electric range, out of the train to the plane, away from the yellow press to the periodical of solid information, out of the turgid slums to the plastic suburbs, away from self-indulgence as a way of life to self-development as a goal in life, away from mass annihilators to world developers—out of the dead past, away from the static present, into the living processes of ever-changing life. This is a whole new way of thinking about yourself, your society, your country, and your world. You are throwing forward passes and catching them on the run, not standing still waiting for someone to run into you. You are moving with changing life. You are not standing still with your feet trapped in the unmoving concepts of ideals and perfections. You are not either a liberal or a conservative, a progressive or a reactionary, a doer or a thinker; you are both a creator and a conservator, performing in both roles simultaneously and alternately as you develop from one stage in thought and life to the next. You are freed from the frustration of dualistic dogmas and the despair of static doctrines. This freedom, which I have enjoyed for the greater part of my adulthood, is the source of my confidence and the basis of my optimism.

The age for doctrines is past. Our job is to define what we

do, how we do it, and why; to identify the processes of living, of working, of thinking in America; and to extract from them ideas that can be useful in facilitating our own self-development, and the world-wide processes in development of which the United States is an integral part. We are not short of food, cars, radios, etc., but of ideas and a working philosophy to give meaning to the dynamics of our lives. For the better part of twenty years I have been trying to define America and judiciously to construct, in the words of Elton Mayo, a theory of America, "not a philosophical theory, nor a grand effort of the imagination, nor a quasi-religious dogma, but a modest, pedestrian affair, a useful walking stick to help on the way." I feel that the concept of the three E's developing into excellence meets this specification.

In October 1959 when I discussed my basic views with Dr. Fritz J. Roethlisberger, student of Elton Mayo and Donham Professor of Human Relations at the Harvard Graduate School of Business Administration, he was doing a foreword for a new edition of Elton Mayo's *The Human Problems of an Industrial Civilization* in which he wrote what he got out of what I had to say:

When, with some trepidation, I explored with him the contents of his proposed book, I found that the gist of his message was something like this. I hope I do it justice when I put it in my own words. He told me that what America stood for was *self-development for everybody, everywhere*. It was on this premise that he had been successful as a union and management leader. It was on this premise that in relation to his foreign customers his business grew. He was very careful to tell me that his doctrine was not pro- or anti-union, pro- or anti-management, pro or anti any particular nation. It envisaged growth for the union as well as for management; growth for everybody everywhere. This, as he saw it, was (is), (could be)—I did not press—America.

This is how he stated what he felt was important in his more than twenty years of experience in three very different leadership roles. And to whom did he feel indebted for this discovery? Mayo. In a refreshing way, this man had stated Mayo's credo.

"A unitary science compels attention of the race to a way of thinking which can unite mankind," Lancelot Law Whyte wrote in *The Next Development in Man* in 1943. His analysis of historical processes in development in the world and the U.S.A. has proved remarkably accurate and has a validity today that was not as apparent when he wrote while the Luftwaffe carried death over his head in London. Whyte is a more advanced historical-process thinker than Karl Marx. When I was at American University in the nation's capital (where I completed my first two college years), I had the good fortune to find a three-volume (Charles H. Kerr, 1908) edition of *Capital* in the library cellar. I read them from cover to cover, and was saved all the headaches and heartaches that befell so many of my generation who fell for Marxism during the thirties. Marx and Friedrich Engels pioneered in process thought, which they distorted with static concepts into doctrinaire dogma. In the winter of 1931-1932 when I read them, I knew in my boyish intuition that they were not writing about the working people with whom I was raised in Nemacolin, a coal-mining town in southwestern Pennsylvania. I sure was lucky that I knew that the proletariat is an abstract concept and that the working people are real, live, human individuals.

But their use of process thought must have stayed with me. I am indebted to Whyte for improving my facility in living-process thinking, and for giving me a clearer understanding of Marx. In his *The Next Development in Man*, Whyte properly acknowledges the use of process thought by Marx, who "recognizing process in nature and man . . . [distorted it into] his tremendous gospel of conflict . . . in which the end justifies the means" and the human individual is neglected. But Marx saw that the processes of production could produce bountifully. All that was needed was a central purpose around which to organize them, and he projected onto the world his distortion of (quoting his own words) "the natural laws of capitalist production . . . working with iron necessity towards inevitable results." He and Engels could not foresee that the natural processes of production were separable from capitalism and that private capitalism would be transformed into welfare enterprise in America. Nor could they foresee that this development would lead to E^3, a war of construction to conquer poverty everywhere, as a central purpose around which America could organize, as I believe it *is* organizing, its political economy—and will be doing so increasingly as the twentieth century fades into time consumed.

While Marx distorted the natural laws of life into the materialistic interpretation of history, he was a process thinker. I am not a Marxist; I, too, am a process thinker, but one who has not subscribed to the distorted package of Marx's inevitable-conflict process thinking. I am indebted in this respect to Stephen Raushenbush, whose fatherly counsel on how to function effectively without losing my moral integrity kept me from the pitfalls of Marxism and from becoming entangled in the spiderwebs of Communist organizations and of the moneychangers. But the materialistic interpretation of history and dualistic concepts have had widespread acceptance in the U.S.A., and American examples of these sources of some of the dogmas that tend to confine us are self-evident.

Karl Marx and Friedrich Engels failed to recognize the dignity of the individual as a natural process in life and the spiritual freedom that flows from it, whenever it can break through the repressive practices of governments and organizations. If they had, of course, their entire gospel of inevitable, violent, social conflict could not have been projected. Spiritual freedom is the unifying force in America. It is compounded of moral forces and scientific discoveries. My field of specialty is the worker and manager in industry in which I have perceived these natural unities. Specialists in all fields can verify the unifying forces in nature from their own experiences, studies, and investigations. Only the unobservant is ignorant of the unnatural division, the unhealthy separation of body and mind, thought and spirit, matter and soul, physical and spiritual, and inner self and outer world.

The ignorance that binds us is this dualistic concept of man, which misled Karl Marx into imputing all the evil facets of man to capitalists and all the good ones to rulers in a classless society. It's the same man, no matter what the form of his society, or the tenets of his religion, or whether he shoots down ten workers in Chicago on 1937's Memorial Day or a thousand workers in Budapest on a cold, November morning in 1956; starves a million people to death in his own land or kills 170,000 with A-bombs in an enemy land. He is both good and bad, but above all he is a whole man. When I hear doctrinaire leaders preach that we are in a moral crisis, I feel that we are in a crisis of moralists. They will adjust themselves to self-developing whole man, or they will be left by the wayside while man struggles against himself to achieve that unity in life with which he was originally endowed and without which a workable unity in the world cannot be achieved.

The individual is a whole human being. He must not be split apart to dominate his thinking and control his actions. As developing man regains his natural wholeness, the restraining influences of the dualists will decline. The more you develop, the more of your own thinking you do. It is the thinker who plays havoc with the prevailing dogmas that rule men's lives. This applies alike to both religious and Marxist dogmas. Karl Marx has had a much greater influence on the course of the world over the last hundred years than any individual can hope to have in the next hundred years. Whyte observes that he was the last of the great doctrinaires to produce a dynamic dogma that promises much. Karl Marx and his interpreters are on the wane; they have had their big day. The next piece of the future belongs to whole men who are free of restricting dogmas that violate the natural process of the dignity of man.

We should learn to think in terms of processes. While Americans live and work with processes all the time, we get tongue-tied when it comes to thinking and speaking in terms of them. Nikita Khrushchev, when he visited us in the fall of 1959, twitted us with his process thinking: "Capitalism developed out of feudalism in America and is in the process of developing into socialism, as socialism developed out of capitalism in Russia and is in the process of developing into communism." We all sensed the error of his judgment, but at the same time were uneasy because we could see the appeal of his method of thinking. We knew that he was wrong, but we felt that he was right in viewing society as ever-changing, ever-developing; our experience in America is an experience of becoming. We are not standing still. We are on the move. We know it. We feel it. But, when it comes to expressing it, the cat has a hold on our tongues. We have to outgrow our Marxist psychosis.

Whyte says "processes are to be interpreted as forms in the course of development . . . [and] the process of development . . . runs unmistakenly through the history of man." These processes are acts of man. Whyte continues:

The human process consists in the continued development of process forms. The individual may seek, or believe that he seeks, independence, permanence, or perfection, but that is only through his failure to recognize and accept his actual situation. As an organic system man can never achieve more than a continuing development in response to his environment. The factor which stabilizes and harmonizes all the component processes in the individual and in society is not permanence but development. . . .

The need to formulate ideals, and in so doing split man asunder, is itself an expression of the very human but futile desire to escape the uncertainty of process and to find spiritual security in the aim at least of a permanent harmony. Unitary man can achieve this realization, and see himself as a whole, because he is ready to accept his personal life for what it is, a transient development through changes which cannot be foreseen. . . .

The processes of the three E's are producing results that are moving the peoples of the world to great actions. It is the influence of America's processes in development—not the thinking of any one man—that will have a greater effect on the world during the next hundred years than Marx has had over the last century. Whyte's view of "the unitary world trend" commands attention in the 1960's because of its remarkable accuracy about the 1950's. As world developments coincide with the unitary world trend in the decades ahead, Whyte's historical-process thinking will command still further attention. We can forget Karl Marx and quit living with the ghost of his thinking. Great Britain, which sheltered Marx, has given us Whyte, a native son, who has produced for us a purer system of historical-process thinking in which the dignity of the individual plays his natural role.

The processes of the three E's are a synthesis of America in the sixties and reflect the thinking and direction of our country, which are "the process of ever-becoming, ever-developing" in the words of George Madison Priest, the American translator of Goethe, who says that this is how the great German poet "saw all things." It is the way that Whyte sees the developing world society and the way I see the developing United States of America.

America can be the most powerful facilitator of the processes in development toward a world-welfare society of whole people who, realizing and comprehending the impermanence of life, will be making life on earth more meaningful for themselves and those yet to be born. This is our country's role in the world.

Impermanence has always been a fact of life known to thinking men for centuries. It has now become widespread knowledge among Americans in whose country, for a decade and a half, almost every newspaper and magazine contains some reference to the possibility of man ending what we know as conscious, human existence. No one can write a serious book in America without mention of the common knowledge that life for all can end. This knowledge is a shock to Americans because it upsets their traditional optimism about moral progress. A majority of us now know and feel that the ideal of permanence is an illusion. We panicked during the 1950's because our discovery of nuclear power pierced the illusion of eternal life, and we lacked a widespread, working philosophy—a way of thinking, viewing, and feeling—to go with our disturbing knowledge that the mass annihilators can terminate humanity.

While this development has caused despair among my

Toynbeeized and Orwellized friends, produced a crisis among the moralists in our pulpits, and given birth to the beatniks, it has strengthened my confidence in the future. This widespread, common knowledge about the impermanence of life is a formative process. It gives birth to the need for universal principles that can unite mankind into a world-welfare society that preserves the diverse characteristics of everybody everywhere. No longer can we evade the fundamental questions about life. They must be faced in the here and now. No longer can we evade our proper role in the world. The threat of massive retaliation has become a two-way street and must be replaced with national policies— growing out of a rediscovered, basic, national purpose—that defuse the fission-fusion-fission superbombs.

We are now confronted with the knowledge that the human race itself may terminate its own existence prematurely—before the astronomical clock sounds the final chime. With this knowledge we cannot live, because life becomes meaningless if we are not building for a better tomorrow. The few thinkers down through the ages have always known that the astronomical clock ticks for Homo sapiens as it has for all of the races that preceded him. But people generally have been able to ignore or disbelieve the writings of these thinkers. However, the American people cannot ignore (and few of them disbelieve) the ability of modern man to destroy his race by his own hand using nuclear power of his own discovery and making. The idea of all-out nuclear war being the end of humanity is the *primus motor* of the formative process leading to the development of unifying, universal principles in the world. Americans and Russians generally accept the idea that nuclear war would terminate humanity and are compelled, therefore, to pursue a working arrangement for peace on earth and good will toward all men.

America is neither going to hell (just because Rome fell) nor is it going to be enslaved by technology and science as George Orwell predicted. Two uniting, universal principles are capable of transforming our disunited planet into a world-welfare society. These are:

1. The self-development of the individual is the ultimate purpose in life on earth.
2. The dignity of man is a natural process.

These basic principles are in the process of development in America and throughout the world. The more consciously (and therefore effectively) America facilitates their development everywhere, the sooner we shall succeed in unfusing the fission-fusion-fission superbombs. The development of both of these principles—on a broader scale and in a deeper way—at home is a first essential to Americans becoming effective facilitators of these principles in the world.

"IT IS PROCESS ALL"

Men of God begin with God. Men of science—with just enough exceptions to prove the rule—end up with God.

Lancelot Law Whyte asks, What is Man? He says, "We feel and perceive much that we cannot say in words," and quotes Goethe, "I should like to give up entirely the habit of speaking. There is something about it that is useless, idle, foppish . . . I should like to speak like Nature, altogether in drawings." But we who can paint only with words, must speak. My mother told me not to shed a tear when her time came to die. "Just think of our joys together," she advised. "Lead your children from my final resting place to one of those big after-funeral meals, and look to the future." When I look into my daughter's eyes, I see eternity. I feel my mother's presence in my every act and thought. Whyte in his discussion of unitary man observes that we cannot escape the "knowledge that the personal life is finite (and) must find eternity in the passing moment, for it can be found nowhere else."

My mother's death facilitated my self-development. Each time someone dies another person grows up some more. I have been better able to live through the disasters and misfortunes that I have encountered since my mother died in 1953. I thought this peculiar to myself. But death is a function of life, and how we die is vitally important for the life that follows ours. "The dead do not die once, but endlessly: one never reaches quite the end of that finality," Lewis Mumford wrote in *Green Memories*, the great story of his nineteen-year-old soldier son killed in Italy. Four years later he wrote. "More than one page in *The Conduct of Life* owes a debt to my son—sometimes to his words, sometimes to his example." Death is merely a function of life, last function that it be.

My Judaism has always been a source of strength to me. I find in the process of nature the unifying forces at work in the universe that theologians call God and scientists identify as process. There is a unity in process. Julian Huxley finds that "the different branches of science combine to demonstrate that the universe in its entirety must be recognized as one gigantic process, a process of becoming, of attaining new levels of existence and organization."[2] As Benjamin Paul Blood said, "It is process all. The most sublime result, if it appeared as the ultimatum, would go stale in an hour; it could not be endured." William James writing in his last months quotes Blood further with this observation,

The result is that, whether it be taken generally or specifically, all that which *either is or is not* is or is not by *distinction* or *opposition*. "And observe the life, the process, through which this slippery doubleness endures. Let us suppose the present tense, that gods and men and angels and devils march all abreast in this present instant, and the only real time and date in the universe is now. And what *is* that instant now? Whatever else, it is *process*—becoming and departing; with what between? Simply division, difference; the present has no breadth for if it had, that which we seek would be the middle of that breadth. There is no precipitate, as on a stationary platform, of the process of becoming, no residuum of the process of departing, but between the two is a curtain, the *apparition of difference*, which is all the world."[3]

[2] Sir Julian Huxley, Introduction to *The Phenomenon of Man*, by Pierre Teilhard De Chardin, New York, Harper & Brothers, 1959, p. 13.

[3] William James, "A Pluralistic Mystic," an essay on Benjamin Paul Blood in *Memories and Studies*, New York, Longmans, Green, and Company, 1934, p. 406.

CHAPTER FOUR

THE DIGNITY OF MAN: ABRAHAM LINCOLN

All roads of American thought, all paths of inquiry into the nature of our country, and this search for the national purpose of America, lead to one American: Abraham Lincoln. Lincoln had a spiritual quality to him. America has a spiritual quality to it. This is the key to the meaning of our country and its purpose in the world. It is the source of the American idea of mission.

"It is a still largely unresolved sociological problem why and how it happened that this shining idealistic vision of the dignity of the human being and of his basic right to equality of opportunity originated and maintained its strength through untold centuries of blatant inequality and oppression," Gunnar Myrdal observes in *Rich Lands and Poor.*

The answer lies in spiritual freedom being a natural process in life. Spiritual freedom is the individual recognizing himself as something in his own right and therefore equal to all others and expressing his personal dignity as a whole man in the totality of his being. It is as natural a process for the individual to express himself thusly as it is for him to reproduce himself. The fact that he has been denied equality and been kept from expressing himself has not killed his self-recognition any more than it has killed his powers of procreation. Each conscious human being carries his inherent dignity in his bosom, whether it is suppressed or released. Myrdal expresses surprise that despite so much inequality "through the ages people have kept a sanctuary in their minds for such a high-pitched ideal as is expressed by the equality doctrine." It is as natural a process in life for the individuals of each generation to discover this as to discover their ability to reproduce themselves, because it gives a meaning to life no matter what the circumstances in which they have to live their lives.

Whether any given generation achieves this meaning fully, partially, or not at all, the next generation discovers it by itself. Hope springs eternally, because hope is life. It grows in the mind of man just as naturally as the "fertilized ovum, by a continuous but structured process, becomes an adult, fulfills itself, and is dispersed." In the process the individual reproduces himself by the exercise of his "forming power" which Lancelot Law Whyte calls the "supreme beauty" in *Accent on Form*. This same forming power, operating in other parts of the human body, creates in each individual the supreme beauty of the idea of equality from generation to generation in all human societies. This finds expression in the form of individual worship of idols—the sun, stars, trees, animals, man-made images—in the concept of One God, and the great religions with their own concepts of the role of the individual in this life and in eternity, and next in practical social expressions of human dignity that are now developing in all lands.

The idea of equality, with its inherent dignity, suppressed from finding social expression for dozens of successive generations, persists until it breaks out. It is not rediscovered after each Dark Age. It is always there. It is refertilized by developments in all fields of human activity. This is what my wife and I witnessed in many forms as we visited the Far East, the Middle East, and Latin-America.

The more than one billion people who are stirring in the

twentieth century have not discovered the idea of equality all of a sudden. It has existed since the first self-conscious man. Western man did not teach it to the present strivers for equality. He just showed them how to do something about it practically. It is America that has most dramatically demonstrated that poverty can be conquered and equality can be achieved in this lifetime or in this life. That's what all the shouting is about.

Spiritual freedom is a natural process from which Americans derive their forward thrust. Its development on these shores since the landings at Jamestown and Plymouth Rock has been the unifying force in American life. Moral concepts, ideals, and the idea of progress have been its tools of facilitation, the means toward equality, human betterment, personal freedom, individual dignity, and a rich life that are not ultimate ends. Spiritual freedom in the United States of America has never been—except for brief periods—the tool of property, privilege, or political power. It has not been unnaturally restrained to serve the rich, the powerful, or the status quo. Spiritual freedom has been able to function freely as a natural process. It has not been distorted into a god of repression and ignorance, as it has been in parts of Europe and elsewhere. Spiritual freedom has been, and continues to be, the liberator from poverty, ignorance, and a fruitless life. By being able to function as the natural process in life that it is, spiritual freedom has catapulted Americans into a position of world leadership in this stage of the development of man.

A natural process reproduces itself. Spiritual freedom in America is not national, but universal, and reproduces itself everywhere in the world. The historical process of spiritual freedom, which emigrated to these shores from Europe, knows no national boundaries, recognizes no unresolvable disunities, and is the universal unifying force in the world. America is in the process of becoming conscious of its role in the world as an agent of facilitation for spreading the natural processes of spiritual freedom to all lands. The form of spiritual freedom varies from individual to individual, group to group, country to country. In this discussion we are not concerned with the religious form of spiritual freedom, but with its social, economic, and political forms—particularly how it shapes the national purpose of America. Russell W. Davenport was on the right road in his *The Dignity of Man* when he perceived, "Only if we can give the word 'spiritual' a real and self-evident content, can we hope, in turn, to give meaning to the political principles on which our system is based."

We have no choice but to use the word spiritual in discussing nonmaterialistic realities. I hasten to disassociate its use from theological dogma. It is not synonymous with religion. It is something that I have in my bosom, just as every other individual does in America, Russia, and everywhere else. To be able to communicate with the words that are available, I have to speak of spiritual freedom in its social forms and emphasize that it is essentially an individual expression that gets robed in social forms.

The process of creating, the exercise of the supreme beauty of the forming power by an individual, is the spiritual reality of this life on earth. The Kingdom of God on earth is one theological way of expressing this same concept. It is the creation of a more equal and better life on earth by the individual, for the individual, and gives a meaning and purpose to existence. This is the concept around which our government and society are organized. It is the light that chases out the darkness in our lives.

America's political institutions have been built around the dignity of the individual. Here is the self-evident spiritual content of the United States of America that Davenport disclosed so sensitively. The dignity of man is a universal process. The world-wide, revolutionary power of the American example, symbolized in the person of Abraham Lincoln, derives its propulsive force from the dignity of man which was written into the Declaration of Independence, incorporated into our form of government, and embodied into our way of life.

The supreme beauty of the processes of equality and of the dignity of man have made America the country to which all mankind looks. It is the first land-mass country in the world where enough freedom prevailed to create the Kingdom of God on Earth in which each individual is recognized as having an inherent dignity that must not be violated. When Mark Twain's character went to Europe saying, "I am a free-born sovereign, sir, an American, sir, and I want everybody to know it," he was talking to our fatherland countries where "in the great majority of cases official Christianity was utilized by the ruling classes against the proletariat movement for greater liberty . . . [and] monarchy and capitalism [were] defended as divine institutions." Each American has become a sovereign in his own right, because on these shores Christianity, the dominant organized religion, has been utilized to make the state and economy serve the human being. When a would-be coal baron in the anthracite region at the turn of the century said that God was on his side, America laughed at him and he has since been ridiculed in history books. His coal miners revolted to evoke his inner humanity; they unionized with the help of leaders of the churches. The European practice of ordaining exploitation never had long success in America.

Since the time of the first self-conscious man, the supreme beauty of the twin ideas of equality and individual dignity have reproduced themselves in each succeeding generation of individuals. Since the landings at Jamestown and Plymouth Rock, Americans have been in the process of translating this natural, self-reproducing process into social, economic, and political reality. This is the historical development of spiritual freedom, which has migrated from country to country for several millennia in search of an environment where it could bloom and flower. It has found it in America. And it is marching on to other environments, everywhere on our planet, to continue to bloom and flower, to reproduce itself. All governments and all societies are in the process of transformation into systems of politics and economics where the dignity of each human being is recognized through the practical creation of devices for establishing an equal chance for all. Man as an end-in-himself is the revolutionary idea that is stirring all people.

You either believe in the dignity of man or you don't. If

you are not willing to place your future, and that of your children, into the civilizing power of this natural process in life—which is also a basic tenet of western religious belief and democratic thought—then you are a distrusting cynic with no faith in the inherent humanity of your fellow man. This is the spiritual unifying force at work in the world reconstructing the atomized individual into a whole man. The lives of the great thinkers of days gone by and of the moderns all[1] add up to this central fact or idea—depending upon whether their thinking is influenced by religious or scientific studies—that the individual is the center of the universe of mankind. Each person has a spark in him. Get the fuel to him and he will light up. You can attribute it to your concept of God or to your idea of nature, but it is the most powerful force at work in the universe of conscious man.

The dignity of man has made the great monotheistic religions, and not the other way around. This natural fact about man asserts itself without religious auspices. It is the *primus motor* in the U.S.A. for our self-developing society of individual excellence. It is the generator propelling the Soviet Union too. The churches in America are a developing part of our society because they have facilitated the processes of human betterment and freedom on earth in this life. But they are being left out of developing Russia, as they took the other course there. "The human problems of industrial organization remain identical for Moscow, London, Rome, Paris, and New York," Elton Mayo observed in 1933. The theologians are claiming too much for their dogmas by their pattern of thought, making spiritual freedom, dignity of the individual, and religious gospel seem synonymous. The identification of man's self-asserting dignity with theological sponsorship has tied America down, and this dead

---

[1] Except those who reject life, but defame their own thinking by living out their own natural lifespan. Or those who can find no meaning in human existence, but persist in existing as long as their lifespan allows. All of these thinkers benefit in their lifespans from the hard work, sacrifice, suffering, and dedicated purpose of those who came before them. How they can enjoy, or endure, all to which they are born without developing a sense of moral obligation to contribute to the betterment and freedom of the life that follows theirs is the difference that separates them from my thinking and feeling.

weight, unfortunately, is still tied around our necks. We have to untie it, because as each fertilized ovum develops into a human being, a natural dignity is born simultaneously with the natural capacity to reproduce itself.

Spiritual freedom—expressed through the better and more equal life—is the faith of America. It has not been lost during the past generation. It has just been unbalanced on the side of economic forms (bigger cars, better houses, and other "things") at home and military forms (Mutual Security Pacts) abroad. As we discover our national purpose, and we shall do so increasingly during the 1960's, balance will return to the development of spiritual freedom in the U.S.A. It will find expression in accelerating the processes of the better things in life at home and in facilitating the processes of the necessities of life for the self-developing people of the world, including those of our own people who are still struggling with illiteracy and poverty. It is up to each self-developing people to accelerate the processes of the finer values in life for themselves, as these vary from home to home, city to city, and country to country.

How many centuries it will take for the natural processes of spiritual freedom to take root in the social, economic, and political life of each national grouping of individuals on our planet only time will tell. The development of the H-bomb, which spreads out among the people the knowledge about the impermanence of life, is accelerating the natural process of spiritual freedom to reproduce itself among the self-developing peoples of the world, including us self-developing Americans. Some idea as to the length of time and the social-economic-political forms of spiritual freedom involved in the functioning of this natural process elsewhere can be had by tracing the development of the functioning of this process and by comprehending its partial fulfillment in America. The dignity of the individual is the most powerful force at work in all societies as it is a natural process in life. The task of free men is the practical work of discovering ways for individuals to express their inherent dignity and of devising workable means in organized society for facilitating such expressions.

PHENOMENON OF THE DIGNITY OF MAN IN RUSSIA

While the Kremlin rejects the concept of the dignity of man, it is busily engaged with the phenomenon of the dignity of man. This self-asserting natural fact of life is playing havoc with the concept of dialectical man. It can take the hunchback out of communism in Russia. It made the Kremlin in 1956 renounce the more barbaric forms of its tyrannical rule. After the first big purge following Stalin's demise the dignity of the deposed Kremlin leaders was recognized at least to the extent of not being sent to the gallows. The need to provide some equilibrium to the inner life of individual Russians is being met with more eggs, butter, houses, and "things" and decentralization. The spirited responses of Russian students in 1956 indicated that the needs of the inner life call out for means of expression, but the Kremlin had to deny them. *Doctor Zhivago* gave expression to "the freedom of the soul" and, though suppressed at first, will be read by millions of Russians in the sixties. The late Boris Pasternak buried dialectical man in his definition of man (*This Week Magazine*, February 22, 1959) that could become accepted by the Kremlin in the near future.

In this era of world wars, in this atomic age, values have changed. We have learned that we are the guests of existence, travelers between two stations. We must discover security within ourselves. During our short span of life we must find our own insights into our relationship with the existence in which we participate so briefly. Otherwise, we cannot live! This means, as I see it, a departure from the materialistic view of the nineteenth century. It means a reawakening of the spiritual world of our inner life, of religion. I don't mean religion as a dogma or as a church, but as a vital feeling.

When I observed the reactions of Russians after the Kremlin buried Stalin in 1956, saw how students and Russians of my age who had been reared completely under communism reacted, I became more confident that the dignity of man, spiritual freedom—the individual recognizing himself as something in his own right and therefore equal to all other individuals—is a natural process in life. It is transforming the Kremlin's view of man as indicated by Pasternak. Khrushchev returned to Moscow after witnessing the "mass strike of steelworkers" in Pittsburgh and declared, "Ever since private ownership of the means of production and classes appeared, a constant struggle has been going on between labor and capital, and it will go on until it ends in victory for those who created all the material values of life." It is becoming obvious that Khrushchev's successors will be transformed by the phenomenon of the dignity of the individual, instead of Americans shedding any blood over the meaningless title to the means of production. We have developed a much more effective social expression of spiritual freedom. Abraham Lincoln expressed it in his March 21, 1864, reply to the New York Workingmen's Democratic Republican Association, "Let not him who is homeless pull down the house of another; but let him labor diligently and build one for himself, thus by example assuring that his own shall be safe from violence when built." This is the moral basis of American society, and when the power of the government has been needed to facilitate a man's efforts to build his own home in America, it has been used.

The Eisenhower administrations are the first Republican ones since Abraham Lincoln to accept as national policy Lincoln's definition of the role of the Federal government, "The legitimate object of government is to do for a community of people whatever they need to have done, but cannot do at all, or cannot so well do, for themselves, in their separate and individual capacities." This is the policy for which Franklin Delano Roosevelt was called a "Communist" a quarter of a century ago. Roger Blough, board chairman of U.S. Steel, favorably cites this Lincoln formula in his *Free Man and the Corporation*. Americans are now united on this moral concept for facilitating human betterment and freedom at home. Our task in the 1960's is to achieve a commanding majority agreement among Americans on this concept in world-wide terms, while not compromising it at home.

Davenport acknowledged, and rightly so, what the United States and Russia have in common:

The doctrine of philosophical optimism, in one case absolutist and brash, in the other, relativistic and hesitant; an optimism in both cases, however, which sees man as a creature of earth, whose salvation must be expressed in terms of social goals, and can be achieved only by means of a high degree of industrial production, economic plenty, and a cooperative attitude of mind.

The individual performs best, as Elton Mayo found, when he achieves "an inner equilibrium." We have discovered this through our religious concept of man and have reaffirmed it through scientific disclosures. Fundamental to the outer world, which gets expressed materially, is the inner world, the spiritual nature of man. The individual in Russia is the same whole man that inhabits the land of the free and the home of the brave. His inherent dignity cries out for expression, and step by step the Kremlin is yielding, pulling back, yielding again to the spiritual needs—inner equilibrium—of the Russian people. Exploitation of the individual for the state is ordained by the Kremlin religion, but as the revolt of the inner man—as expressed by Pasternak—gains momentum in Russia and gets expressed in homes with private bedrooms, roads and garages with private cars, and the other meaningful material expressions of inner man, the tenets of the Kremlin religion will get revised at Party congresses. A man is a man, whether he is a citizen of the United States, Japan, Russia, China, or any other country.

America is founded on these spiritual facts of life, which are built into our way of life. Russia has to acknowledge explicitly and consciously develop these inner expressions of the human individual to begin to generate the forward thrust that we already have. These human developments take decades and as a self-developing, functioning society we are well ahead of Russia. Individual dignity as a working part of American life is in its teens. In Russia it is just being born. As this natural process finds freedom of expression—in civil rights, individual worship, unrestricted movement of body and mind, and other means of individual self-development—in Russia, these two technocracies will have arrived on the same path toward the more equal and better life on earth. There is a single thread of development running through the human journey. In the words of Abraham Lincoln, spoken on September 30, 1859, before the Wisconsin State Agricultural Society,

Let us hope . . . that by the best cultivation of the physical world beneath and around us, and the best intellectual and moral world within us, we shall secure an individual, social and political prosperity and happiness, whose course shall be onward and upward, and which, while the earth endures, shall not pass away.

No threat of nuclear annihilation hung over Lincoln's head when he qualified his hopes for the future with "while the earth endures." Philip Van Doren Stern noted that Lincoln had "the sense of impermanence and the implicit death-longing in the phrase 'And this, too, shall pass away.'" Lincoln knew about the impermanence of life. This knowledge provokes thinking, which is the protein of self-development. I enjoy living today. I can find no prior time in history in which I would rather have been born. I do not envy my children who are destined to outlive me in the coming age of excellence. This is a time when we are most conscious of the clicking of the astronomical clock. It ticks each hour of our waking day, and we fall asleep at night to its rhythmic chimes. We wake each morning aware of the impermanence of things and the temporal nature of man. A reawakening has been born. My generation is the midwife for the embryonic world-welfare society that is now being born amidst great labor pains.

All birth carries the risk of death or distortion. Such are the natural processes of life. The mass annihilators may kill the world-welfare society a-borning. The Kremlin or Chinese Communists may come to dominate it. And the American world developers can thwart both, by facilitating the self-development and dignity of the emerging people and an equal chance for all nations to participate in international trade. No man can foretell history in advance. Which of these three processes in development will win out, only time will tell. It is for each man to identify the processes in development in his time and to facilitate the best of them.

The processes of the dignity and self-development of the individual have made America the country that she is in the process of becoming. America does not belong to Americans alone. It belongs to everybody, everywhere, because of the universality of human dignity and self-development that are its spiritual essence. These two unifying, universal principles are natural processes in life that, consciously facilitated by America, can transform Russia and China and their satellites into self-developing societies that bury their own mass annihilators simultaneously while we bury our own. This great task of transformation is not a work of years; it is a work of decades and centuries. By undertaking it as our dedicated national purpose we release freedoms everywhere, while giving a greater meaning to freedom in our own country.

Americans should shed their H-bomb psychosis and quit worrying about being snuffed out by the blinding flash of a fission-fusion-fission superbomb. Of course, it can happen. But look at all of the tremendous possibilities in development that can defuse the superbombs and work for the fruition of these developments. Every time that I get into a plane and soar into the sky the threat of death can be heard in the roar of the engines. When you are afraid of death, you are afraid of life, since they are the two sides of the human equation of life on earth. As we soar into the skies of our planet as world developers the threat of the superbombs can be heard in the whine of the jet engines. It has always been so. And so be it.

We now examine the central purpose of America for Americans before we board the jets to America's national purpose in the world.

CHAPTER FIVE

E—TO THE FIRST POWER IS TOWARD THE KINGDOM OF GOD ON EARTH

The theory of American political-economic development is expressed in the formula of the three E's. E is the symbol for conquering poverty. The multiplier is the organizing force of a central purpose.

E—to the first power is conquering poverty in the U.S.A.

E^2—E to the second power is conquering poverty in Europe.

E^3—E to the third power is conquering poverty everywhere.

The multiplier for E is America's central purpose plus feedbacks; for E^2, feedbacks to Europe; for E^3, feedbacks to everywhere. E—to the first power developed out of E^2, and its continuing development is dependent upon E^3. The three E's are the foundation processes for the development of the fourth E of excellence, the enjoyment of the finer values in life through self-development and personal growth through codevelopment.

Legal freedom for Negroes opened up the development of economic freedom for all American workers and farmers culminating in the New Deal, a seventy-year (1865-1935) march of progress. In their twenty-year administration on the home front Roosevelt and Truman delivered on Hoover's premature promise to the American electorate: cars in the garages and chickens in the pots. During these three score and ten years the social gospel humanized industry and facilitated E to the first power—victory over poverty in America. Feedbacks to Europe, the 1914-1918 and 1939-1945 wars and the 1948-1952 Marshall Plan, provided the necessary supplemental central organizing force around which the United States of America successfully organized its economy to achieve the E to the first power breakthrough, which became obvious to all during the 1950's. Just producing for ourselves was not enough to achieve this breakthrough against poverty, and its enlargement and extension to our own 36 million underdeveloped people can only be achieved by a national purpose of facilitating the war against poverty and illiteracy in all lands.

White Europeans founded the United States of America, killed off or penned up the red Indians, imported black and brown Negro slaves to help clear the virgin land, and denied access to the yellow peoples of the Orient for this purpose: to provide themselves with a better life, both physically and spiritually. And they have. This has been the organizing force of the central purpose around which our economy has been built and which I identify as the Unifying Force Law of the United States. It is the foundation idea for the concept of the three E's.

The central purpose of America for Americans is expressed in its common objectives: to create opportunities for a constantly rising population to earn all of the necessities in life and more and more of the better things, and to develop the capacity to enjoy the finer values in life for a steadily expanding lifetime.

E—to the first power in America is self-evident. The United States of America is living proof that poverty and illiteracy are conquerable and that freedom from want and freedom from fear are an achievable reality. Since 1945, when I first undertook these labors, I have written upwards of 300,000 words on the economics of the United States in which I became bogged down, and only the passage of time has freed my thinking and released me to treat with the totality of our country. I travel up and down and across America, mostly by air, as if it were one big city. There is hardly a large metropolitan area in whose downtown I am not at home. The airports of this country are as familiar to me as subway stations are to a New Yorker. When I hop out of a plane into a rented car I seldom need to consult a map. The whole of our basic 48 states are my home. Pittsburgh is just my base.

The United States of America is not becoming a Utopia, where there would be no steel strikes and everybody would be free just to pursue happiness. Utopia is in conflict with the natural processes of life, because when you run out of problems you are dead. The concept of perfection is a static doctrine, and the men who are ruled by it are men of dogmas. Twenty miles from Pittsburgh the Great House of Economie stands as a museum of one of the Utopian societies that flourished and died in America. Father George Rapp was the dogmatist who led Economie and Harmonie. He decreed celibacy for his people, who joined him, one by one, in the grave. When you try to stop the natural processes of life, you are playing with death. That's why all the experiments with Utopian societies in the United States of America have floundered.

KINGDOM OF GOD ON EARTH

The Kingdom of God on earth—the more equal and better life, as Abraham Lincoln defined this concept in nontheological terms—is the meaning of America. More people die in the U.S.A. from overeating than from not having enough to eat. Spiritual freedom is enjoyed by all Americans, including our Negroes and Jews and the few Orientals who have made it to American shores. America is demonstrating that there is no ceiling on human welfare and well-being; and that the ceiling on the number of years that the individual can enjoy everything can be ever lengthened and prolonged. And everything includes worshiping the God of your choice as you please.

How have we done it?

Spiritual freedom is an expression of both the individual and of society. "Our inherited Christian faith dealt with individuals," Walter Rauschenbusch wrote in 1907. "Our present task deals with society."[1] The pioneer founding people of America left their many lands where spiritual freedom was an individual matter to found a new country where spiritual freedom could be translated into social action. Rauschenbusch precipitated into words what Abe Lincoln taught and achieved, and these two Americans, who combined learning and doing, each in his own way, facilitated the processes of spiritual freedom that transformed our private capitalism into welfare enterprise and saved America from the fate of Russia or the Union of South Africa. Both men helped mold the Kingdom of God on earth that America is in the process of becoming.

Lincoln freed the Negroes from political slavery and extended an equal chance to the colored people of America, who are still in the process of converting it into reality.

Rauschenbusch and his counterparts in the other faiths followed up Lincoln by freeing all Americans, of all races, colors, and creeds, from the bondage of restrictive theology and religious orthodoxy and extended to them an equal chance for economic, social, educational, and political opportunity, which they are still in the process of converting into reality. The process of converting spiritual freedom into reality is continuous, never-ending; it is life on earth. The tall buildings, giant factories, huge sweeping farms, shiny cars, and other monuments of materialism are the end products of America's spiritual energies—creative forces

---

[1] Reinhold Niebuhr says that Walter Rauschenbusch, 1861-1918, professor in the Rochester Theological Seminary, Baptist, author of *Christianity and the Social Crisis* (1907) was "the real founder of Social Christianity in this country," and Henry Pitney Van Dusen says that he was "the greatest single personal influence on the life and thought of the American church in the last fifty years." Coming from among the majority Protestant faith, Rauschenbusch had an influence that was not possible for spokesmen of the social gospel from the minority faiths of Catholicism or Judaism, each of which produced their own spokesmen for social action. The social gospel of Christianity and practical Judaism, as I comprehend them, are one.

—which are part of a continuous process developing inner as well as these outer expressions of the spiritual vitality that throbs in the bosoms of people. If the process ended with self-indulgent materialism I would not be writing this book.

Lincoln killed human slavery, and Rauschenbusch killed the idea that the poor must always be with us. The story of Lincoln is known to all, though comprehended by few. The story of Rauschenbusch is known by few, though comprehended by all. He gave the word spiritual a real and self-evident content, for which Abe Lincoln paved the way. Before Lincoln, equality and the dignity and freedom that go with the supreme beauty of the phenomenon of man, were merely a prayer and a hope and so many fine words.

The suffering of four years of the Civil War made us one people. The dead and maimed cast the human metal of America that had been in the process of development into a distinctive American character, so strong that all the post-Civil-War immigrants, and especially their descendants, have been molded in its likeness.

Right up to the final draft of this book I was subscribing to the dichotomy of Old Stock and New Americans. The late Pittsburgh congressman, Edward O. Tabor, of Czech origin, developed the New American concept in his 1932 speech at the one hundred and forty-fifth anniversary of the University of Pittsburgh in his talk, "The University and the New American." I had experienced this distinction sharply through school, the labor movement, government service, and industry. Louis Adamic adopted Tabor's New American concept: and I accepted it uncritically until recently. It is, however, patently obsolete for our children. We are all becoming Americans. The melting pot is being melted down to scrap, and being recast into a developing, mature, American character—aware of his responsibilities in the world and preparing to assume them. My personal story shows how the division between Old Stock and New Americans is being broken down. The nomination of Senator John F. Kennedy for the presidency in 1960 is further evidence. For Charlie, Jim, Eddie, and Ellen it will be merely something to talk about in their adulthoods. They will not experience it in any seriously restricting way.

Abraham Lincoln is the true father of America, as he saved the work of our founding fathers from going down the drain of history. The four years of the Civil War made America one country, validated the principles contained in the Declaration of Independence, forced the amendments to our Constitution without which it was a partial document, and accelerated the processes that are making us 180 million individuals into one people. These processes cannot be stopped. They began to come to fruition when mass immigration was cut off a third of a century ago—beginning a process of the making of America for Americans only, which is a formative process in the world leading to two unifying, worldwide developments: the forging of a more distinctive American character with a dedicated purpose in the world; and the forging of self-developing societies in all countries, whose most restive and creative people have to stay at home and work out their problems among their own countrymen, and where the dignity of the individual is emerging in the social, economic, and political institutions now in the process of development.

To define the nature of America, to trace the history of the essential American ideas, it is not necessary to go back before Lincoln. All that came before "Mr. Everybody" arrived on the American scene is prelude. Those who go back to the founding fathers primarily to discover the meaning of America get lost in the romantic concept of individualism. Tom Jefferson was my first American hero in learning, and Andy Jackson my first American hero in doing. And all of Jackson that properly belongs in this discussion is the mere mention that he facilitated the processes of economic freedom that laid the foundation for the social gospel to achieve equal economic rights for poor and rich alike in the United States of America after Lincoln put the Declaration of Independence into our Constitution. Without Lincoln's work our Constitution would be an instrument of exploitation instead of an instrument of liberation that is being used to give economic, social, and political opportunity to our colored people whom Lincoln freed from legal slavery.

Jefferson wrote a few days before he died in 1826:

All eyes are opened, or opening, to the rights of man. The general spread of the light of science has already laid open to every view the palpable truth, that the mass of mankind has not been born with saddles on their backs, nor a favored few, booted and spurred, ready to ride them legitimately for the Grace of God. These are grounds of hope for others.

This idea of self-development to the fullness of individual capacity in the here and now by everybody, of course, was not original with Jefferson. What he did to translate it into social action was his unique work. The founding fathers created the spiritual quality of our country. Jefferson spoke for his contemporaries when he said that the social practice of religion, and the function of government, are to unbind man from his earthly bondage, and not to deliver him to heaven or hell all bound up in illiteracy and poverty for the benefit of a favored few. Jackson gave these words economic meaning when he stopped the favored few from using the Federal government for special privilege and liquidated the remnants of colonial America. But it was Lincoln who gave them human meaning when he abolished legal, human slavery.

The professional scholars who have their entire lives invested in American history, I realize, will point out that the three E's are an oversimplification of America. But they distill the essence of America into a single concept that reveals the basic structure of the U.S.A. as the three R's reveal the basic structure of education. To be sure, there is more to both concepts, and I suggest that something more is revealed in the concept of the fourth E, excellence in everything through enterprise and education, that is in the process of developing America into a culture of excellence of, by, and for individuals.

THE AGE OF EXCELLENCE

In a society like the American, where the individual enjoys so many social, cultural, economic, and political expressions, materialism is not likely to be an end in itself leading to degeneration. It is a formative process, fertilized by the inherent creativeness of individuals leading to an unprecedented cultural achievement in the history of man. My vision of our future is an act of faith in everybody, everywhere—the fourth E of excellence.

The burden of this book is to make explicit the three E's. The fourth E of excellence is a projection into the future based on the unity of the three E's. I shall pinpoint embryonic processes of excellence in America. In a quarter of a century evidences of excellence should begin to overtake the mediocrity, self-indulgence, double morality, and status seeking that are the dominant characteristics of America today.

Excellence can neither be ordered from an employment agency, produced in a Sabbath school, nor graduated from a university. It is something that one develops into. It is the work of generations. Excellence is the fusion of learning and doing, the combination of feeling with intellect, the product of education enriched by experience—as in Thomas Jefferson's case— or experience enriched by education—as in Abraham Lincoln's case.

The personal growth of Abraham Lincoln is an outstanding example of the working of experience and education. In writing Jesse W. Fell on December 20, 1859 "a little sketch" of his autobiography, Lincoln advised, "When I came of age I did not know much. Still, however, I could read, write and cipher to the Rule of Three; but that was all. I have not been to school since. The little advance I now have upon the store of education, I have picked up from time to time under the pressure of necessity." Abraham Lincoln never got a Ph. D. and no Ph. D-er has ever equalled his example of the self-developing individual whose growth is the result of feeling as well as thinking.

This process of self-development now evolving into an age of excellence is the next development in our culture. Americans are being forced to do more of their own thinking, and the world situation finally is compelling us to display more fully our natural Judaeo-Christian compassion for all people in every land.

To deny this development in America is as absurd as to say, as too many of our critics proclaim, that the distortion of the three R's[2] into mass mediocrity and the distortion of life's necessities and more and more of the better things in life—the three E's—into fleshpots of self-indulgence inevitably lead to America going to hell because Rome fell. This idea is based on the view of history as the rise and fall of civilizations. All of mankind's struggles are a continuous process developing into a worldwide civilization. America is a continuing key link in the emerging civilization for everybody everywhere. America forged the three R's and the three E's as instruments of self-development for the use of all peoples in the twentieth century. We are in the process of forging the fourth E of excellence to further our own self-development and to serve as an instrument of continuing self-development for everybody everywhere in the twenty-first century.

THE FUNCTION OF FREEDOM

The great tool of facilitation of the three R's, the three E's, and the fourth E is freedom, which Lincoln synthesized into one brief statement when he spoke at Lewistown, Illinois, on August 17, 1858, on the Declaration of Independence, a mere thirty-two years after Jefferson died:

[2] The phrase, the three R's, originated with Sir William Curtis (1752-1829) when he used it as a toast while Lord Mayor of London. Horace Mann (1796-1859) was our father of the three R's, which originally were Reading, 'Riting, and Religion, but became Reading, 'Riting, and 'Rithmetic in secular America. The first teachers of the three R's in our country were the clergy and lay leaders of our churches who founded most of our colleges. We are indebted to Horace Mann for the public development of the three R's that freed them from the bonds of organized religion. But we should not overlook the two basic processes that gave birth to the process of public education: 1. The protestant revolt in Europe where the real battles for freedom of religious worship (which migrated to and flourished in America) were fought. 2. The development of religious freedom in America that nurtured learning, knowledge, and the free inquiry of the human mind.

Wise statesmen that they were, they knew the tendency of posterity to breed tyrants, and so they established these great self-evident truths that when in the distant future some man, some faction, some interest, should set up the doctrine that none but rich men, or none but white men, were entitled to life, liberty, and the pursuit of happiness, their posterity might look up again to the Declaration of Independence and take courage to renew the battle which the fathers began—so that truth, and justice, and mercy, and all the humane and Christian virtues might not be extinguished from the land; so that no man would hereafter dare to limit and circumscribe the great principles on which the temple of liberty was being built.

No more need be said about freedom, except to spell out its functional character and ferret out its abuses by the corrupters of moral standards and ethical values without which there can be no meaning for freedom. Freedom for freedom's sake is as banal as knowledge for the sake of knowledge. Whether you vegetate in learning or ignorance, you are vegetating.

Lincoln spoke a universal language. On February 22, 1861, on his way to take office he said that he "would rather be assassinated on this spot" (Independence Hall) than to give up "that sentiment in the Declaration of Independence which gave liberty not alone to the people of this country, but hope to all the world, for all future time." When Lincoln was assassinated, Leo Tolstoy said that he had become a world folk legend through "peculiar moral powers and greatness of character." Lincoln must be shared with all people. He is more than a national figure. Lincoln is a universal character, the greatest product of America. An empathy exists between the image of Abraham Lincoln and everybody everywhere. As we travel from country to country we find him translated into every tongue. He symbolizes what America is becoming, what all peoples want their countries to become: a Kingdom of God on earth.

The moral powers of Lincoln, expressed in the Declaration of Independence and the Gettysburg Address, continued in America after his assassination. But the forces of growth and development expressed in the exploitation of natural resources for the immediate benefit of the favored few, and the virulent forms of private capitalism, became dominant in the closing decades of the nineteenth century. Capitalism, private and unregimented, was a vital process in the conquering of the large land area that makes up the basic 48 states. We are deeply indebted to it for opening up this continent, although we have to hold our heads in shame for the price that it charged in wanton wastefulness, merciless killings, inhuman exploitation of colored people, white man's inhumanity to other white men, the denial of civil liberties to industrial workers, the moneylending robbing of farmers of their hard-earned lands, and all of the other shameful parts of our political-economic history.

By the time that the twentieth century opened up, these forces had developed to a boil, which was lanced by another great American of deep "moral powers and greatness of character."

What Walter Rauschenbusch wrote in *Christianity and the Social Crisis* in 1907 has become the core of the unifying forces in our developing American society, "To live a great life a man needs a great cause to which he can surrender, something divinely large and engrossing for which he can live and, if need be, die." In Rauschenbusch's time the great issue was domestic. He wrote:

Our business is to make over an antiquated and immoral economic system; to get rid of laws, customs, maxims, and philosophies inherited from an evil and despotic past, to create just and brotherly relations between great groups and classes of society; and thus to lay a social foundation on which modern men individually can live and work in a fashion that will not outrage all the better elements in them. . . . The Christian Church in the past has taught us to do our work with our eyes fixed on another world and a life to come. But the business before us is concerned with refashioning this present world, making this earth clean and sweet and habitable.

To accomplish these objectives, Rauschenbusch participated in the tough, salty, unhospitable field of practical social reform and politics. He and his fellow reformers helped organize people so that through their organized strength they could evoke the

inner humanity of their exploiters. The spokesmen for our large
financial and industrial institutions take credit for America's
great victories over man's inhumanity to man. But every one
of the social, economic, and political gains since the Civil War
had to be evoked. Exploiters will not cease to exploit until the
exploited remind them of their humanity.

A country that could sacrifice the flower of her youth in a
four-year Civil War to evoke the white man's humanity for the
Negro, it is obvious, was able to sacrifice the blood, sweat, and
tears of its social reformers to abolish economic slavery as well.
Neither task is finished, as all we can ever win is the continuing
freedom to facilitate the processes of self-development and codevelopment on earth. Walter Rauschenbusch was their moral
spokesman in his time as Abraham Lincoln was in his. The immortality of Lincoln lies in his being cast in the role of President
as an instrument of the people. In the case of Rauschenbusch
and his whole group of reformers, immortality lies in their moral
concepts being cast into the Unifying Force Law of the United
States which is an instrument of the American people. The
central purpose of America is to provide a constantly rising
population with all of life's necessities, and more and more of
the better things, for a steadily expanding lifetime.

This unites all Americans in all walks of life whose political
parties differ in emphasis, not in fundamentals. Khrushchev
said in Pittsburgh that he could see no essential difference between the two 'capitalistic parties of Republicans and Democrats." He was not upset about all the "things" he had seen in
America; he knew that we had achieved a great expression of
materialism, and seeing such widespread evidences of it was not
upsetting. He had set a comparable achievement as a goal for his
country. But he was upset. Did his observation of a developing
classless society in America—where essential differences can
arise primarily because of varying capacities and desires for self-
development—upset him? Was the phenomenon of the dignity
of the individual that he saw expressed all over America upsetting him? I suggest it did because he had not set a comparable

goal for his country to achieve this very phenomenon. Nor could he within the framework of his inherited dogma. The dignity of man will have to transform that dogma to see daylight in the Kremlin.

The great issue in the 1960's is world-wide. The scene has shifted from the United States to the planet since Rauschenbusch helped recast the basic moral concepts for twentieth-century industrial man. But the great issue is still the same. "We are actors in a great historical drama. It rests upon us," Rauschenbusch wrote early in the century, "to decide if a new era is to dawn in the transformation of the world into the Kingdom of God, or if Western civilization is to descend to the graveyard of dead civilizations, and God will have to try once more." Like Lincoln, he was not talking about the Kingdom of God just for Americans. Rauschenbusch was talking about all of God's children everywhere.

OUR EVER-DEVELOPING SYSTEM OF WELFARE ENTERPRISE

We began as an acquisitive society and are in the process of becoming a functional one. But the slogan-ideas of private capitalism outlive their practice, and we have to replace these obsolescent concepts with the functional ideas that are an essential part of the society that we are in the process of becoming. I am an enterpriser. My passport identifies me as an industrialist. I am a money-maker. I work for profits. I understand the function of profits and know the life-or-death nature of producing profits to facilitate the processes of the three E's. It is simply "No profits, no three E's." Corporate profits are development funds for corporate enterprisers. This vital organ of capitalism has been transplanted to enterprise. But it is not the whole body of enterprise. The making of profits is only a part, albeit a vital part, of our developing system of welfare enterprise. The spiritual forces in America that evoke man's humanity to man are forcing profit-making institutions to give up greedy, selfish, me-first-and-the-hell-with-the-common-good exploitation of human beings and natural resources. The leaders of industry are in the process of shedding their old straitjacket concepts of free enterprise for the developing concepts of welfare enterprise.

The process of renaming our economic system started some years ago. Frederick Lewis Allen in *The Big Change* (1952) noted "that we've got something here . . . that defies all the old labels." To facilitate the renaming of our political-economic system I have constructed a name tree.

Here is the name tree that I have constructed:

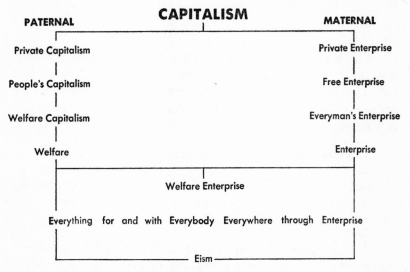

The bare use of the name capitalism has been out of vogue for several decades. *Fortune* observed that "capitalism [is] a term that, by the way, came into general usage with Karl Marx." It was bad enough that the name for European socialism and Russian communism came from Marx, let alone the name for the economic system of the United States. On the paternal side we gave Capitalism a first name, Private; but on the maternal side we changed the last name to Enterprise. But our enemies abroad kept calling us capitalists while we rightly insisted upon calling ourselves enterprisers.

Next we changed our maternal first name to Free and equated our new first name with political freedom. But the accelerating processes of the three R's and production in Soviet Russia demonstrate that we cannot equate enterprise with freedom. The Russians are as enterprising as beavers, but not as free as beavers.

To talk about free enterprise is nonsense. This is demonstrated by our huge corporate enterprises administering prices and having their losses in any one year averaged out with profits earned during the preceding three years and/or the ensuing five years, by governmental umbrella-subsidies over the farmers' heads, and by our large union enterprises administering wages and muzzling the freedom of their members to criticize their own leaders.

Our enemies unjustly still called us capitalists. So we wrongly bowed to their insistence, but changed our first name on the paternal side to People's. The use of the name People's Capitalism grew out of Russell Davenport's declaration of war on capitalism in Europe:

It is high time the American businessman realized that it is not European socialism but European capitalism that is the chief block to "free enterprise." "The problem of Europe," as one observer puts it, "comes down to who is to liquidate the capitalists of Europe: the Russians—or the Americans."

People's Capitalism has not taken hold despite the money poured into this attempted renaming of our economic system through the advertising council. It did not use the word enterprise, which over the years has been developing into the dominant factor in our economy. Many of America's leaders are still too much under the influence of Karl Marx to bury the name capitalism. A decade ago Davenport, who saw straight through the concept of capitalism, understood the process of enterprise in America. He also understood that the demand for welfare had to be met by the enterprisers who run our economy or the state would have to do the total welfare job. In his "The Greatest Opportunity on Earth" Davenport asked, "1. Is the demand of the American people for 'welfare' a justifiable demand . . . ? 2. If it is . . . is there any way to satisfy it without recourse to the authoritarian state?"

His answer was "yes" to both questions, and just how the

U.S.A. has been promoting everybody's welfare at the corporate, or enterpriser's, level is the big story of America. Davenport defined "American industrial enterprise" as "that vast combination of capital and labor . . . the people actually engaged in the economic process, namely, the owners, managers, and workers." In "Enterprise for Everyman" he said that, "if it is to survive at all, the enterprise system must survive as a whole. It cannot survive as the special possession of those who own it or run it, with those who work for it excluded. Those who work for the enterprise system must join the enterprise system, must become enterprisers." This is the concept of enterprise that Clinton Golden and I advocated in *The Dynamics of Industrial Democracy*, and which I further develop in Humanation, which will be discussed later.

Referring back to the name chart, we observe the changing first name of capitalism on the paternal side from Private to People's to Welfare. Capitalism can be dropped in America as it is being transformed into its descendant, Enterprise. This leaves the first name Welfare. Over on the maternal side the changing first name from Private to Free to Everyman's washes itself out in favor of the last name, Enterprise, because Everyman's is included under Welfare. Marrying the two into Welfare Enterprise gives us a new name for our economy that has grown out of the developments of the natural processes of life in America.

In several private meetings with some of the younger leaders of American management and industry during the last half of the fifties I developed the concept of Welfare Capitalism. In fact, at such a meeting while under cross-examination for my views the idea of the Welfare State—another dogma that is dying a hard death—was thrown at me. In this discussion with the controllers of most of the big coporations in Pittsburgh, held in the Duquesne Club in 1957, I first hit on the formulation of the concept of Welfare Capitalism. This formulation says that the primary purpose of industry is to promote the welfare of everybody, and the better you do this, the more profits your enterprise will make.

Davenport, as much as any other individual, was responsible

for the development in industry of private pensions and private supplementary unemployment benefits during the fifties. He was responsible at least to the extent that the individual generating ideas can influence the decision-making managers of society's practical affairs. The burden of his thinking was that "the chief hope of escaping the illusory promises of the Welfare State" lies in private enterprise facilitating the processes of welfare (human betterment) consciously as an accepted central purpose. During the next ten to twenty years the newer and younger leaders of industry increasingly will be preaching and practicing this basic concept of welfare enterprise, which term was first employed by Davenport.

The end result is the rooting out of poverty in all corners of the United States and the elimination of the ill-fed, ill-housed, ill-clothed, ill-healthed, and ill-educated. In his January 20, 1937, Second Inaugural Address, Franklin Delano Roosevelt said, "I see one-third of a nation ill-housed, ill-clad, ill-nourished."[3] A short nineteen-and-one-half years later his widow, Eleanor Roosevelt was able to tell the 1956 Democratic Convention in Chicago that "one-fifth of our people are ill-housed, ill-clad, and ill-nourished."[3] And she deplored it. Both parties agreed—America agrees—that one of our purposes is to enable all Americans one day to be able to say, "In America everybody is well-housed, well-clad, and well-nourished." There is unanimity in all parts of the U.S.A., by people of different persuasions, that our central purpose is to provide all Americans with all of life's necessities and more and more of the better things in life. The whole of America's corporations and productive facilities are organized toward this single purpose. Americans differ over how, and how fast, not over either the desirability or practicality of providing everybody with everything.

Charles E. "Engine Charlie" Wilson was right when he said, "For years I thought what was good for our country was good

[3] This is 43 million Americans in 1937, 33 million in 1956, and 36 million in 1960. An impressive statistical case can be made that there are 50 million people in America still living in poverty.

for General Motors, and vice versa." My Roosevelt New Deal friends and brothers have a hard time swallowing this, but it is as true as its manner of expression was inept. The leaders of the auto and steel industries and of the other segments of industry have long since been unable to earn profits by exploiting workers. The only way that they can earn a sustaining profit, except for brief periods of time, is by operating their mines, mills, and factories at near capacity, and to accomplish this they have to promote the welfare of all people all of the time. This is the motivating force that is forging an integrated social philosophy for mangement in which welfare enterprise is accepted as the central purpose for corporate activities.

To make a profit in the United States you have to promote the welfare of the great consuming public. You cannot make profits by exploiting people. For General Motors or General Electric to operate at a sustaining profit, they have to run their plants at or near full capacity. This is even truer for smaller companies, and a life-or-death condition for the small and marginal firms. To do this they have to help promote the economic well-being of their customers. My employees are your customers, and vice versa. That is welfare enterprise, which is our economy, and it is much more than the welfare state.

The general consensus is pretty well formulated that the promotion of the general welfare of all Americans is the central purpose of enterprisers operating on a profit and loss statement. It has long since been the central purpose of the enterprisers in government, organized labor, and America's other institutions that operate on cash flow budgets instead of profit and loss statements and balance sheets. We need not labor this general consensus that has developed out of the acrimonious debates that in my time began with the enterprisers in industry calling Roosevelt a Socialist-Communist, while F.D.R. in turn called them economic royalists. This debate extends back to our earliest days as a country. The current form of the debate among American enterprisers—in which this book as a whole joins in the affirmative —is, "Resolved: that the United States of America has to promote

the welfare of everybody everywhere as an essential condition
to successfully promoting the welfare of its own citizens and
completely abolishing poverty in America."

EISM

Many of us have a good chance of living to see a 100 per
cent American-grown name for America's enterprising economy
gaining general acceptance. Referring once more to our name
chart we observe the persistence of Enterprise on the maternal
side and the three E's evolving out of Welfare on the paternal
side. Marrying these together gives us Everything for and with
Everybody Everywhere through Enterprise, or simply the three
E's or Eism, which in the twenty-first century would also stand
for Excellence in Everything through Enterprising and Education by Everybody.

This next stage of development of your country and mine
can be defined as follows: America's purpose is to promote the
welfare of everybody everywhere; to enrich the dignity of
man; to increase the leisure time of everybody and to enlarge
human capacities to drink up and contribute to the developing
American and world cultures; to enjoy freedom from poverty
of the body, the soul, and the mind, and freedom from fear by
facilitating the self-development of everybody to achieve a well-
rounded excellence to the limit of their individual capabilities,
and to give their own lives a greater meaning by using them in
the service of mankind in all lands.

American Eism is not a static dogma of finished achievement; it is the concept of the American political economy being
a system of ever-developing and ever-becoming.

THE ELEMENT OF STABILITY

Where change becomes the norm, as it does in Eism, the
stabilizing forces are vital. In the view of Lancelot Law Whyte
they are to be found in processes of continuous development in
contrast to permanent ideals.

The well-fed American, living under a roof that does not

leak, with a well-clothed body and a mind that can read, write, and cypher to the rule of three is an unprecedented achievement in world history. But he is not a finished product. He is merely the raw, human meat from which a culture-building man worth saving from mass annihilation can develop. I see him in the process of development, battling the forces of greed and ignorance that could keep him from emerging. The creative forces at work in America, effectively facilitated by dedicated men who know their business, can evoke the inner humanity of American leaders whose creative urges are dominated by their conservative natures. I am betting on these creative forces to win as they derive their forward thrust from the natural processes of the dignity and the self-development of the individual, which enjoy a freedom of action in America that is also unprecedented in world history.

Lewis Mumford observes, "the de-building principle is at work, along with the creative, at every moment of man's existence." He is unfair to Lancelot Law Whyte, though, in describing his unitary process thought as "using a one-directional formula of process and organization" and claiming that Whyte fails "to give an adequate account of these downward tendencies." Whyte recognizes the two-way character of process, as I certainly do in this book. As I view the countervailing processes of up-building and de-building, our human task is to achieve a higher pinnacle on each upswing, when creative forces are dominant, and not to fall back so low on each downswing. Ralph E. Turner, Durfee Professor of History, Yale University, defined process as "the creative functioning of forces," fully recognizing that death results when "forces lose their power."

The debuilding forces are countervailing to the upbuilding or creative forces and are an essential condition to stability; they are not "downward tendencies." "Worshippers of progress sometimes suggest that all creative activity is intrinsically good, but that would surely imply that the old ways which it seeks to destroy are necessarily evil," Whyte outlines in *Accent on Form*. "They are balanced by those conservatives who worship the past and regard all novelty as harmful." Whyte concludes:

Development arises from a tension which is experienced as a painful conflict of two principles, stability and change. . . . Some persons and groups are vital, developing, and creative others cautious and conservative. . . . The creative must create, and the conservatives must provide the indispensable element of stability. Without his creative élan man could never have become man, but with too much he cannot survive.

We Americans are all creators and conservators and are tied together by our common concern for people. Unemployment is a unifying force in America, because, except for brief periods, we will not tolerate large blocks of idle workers. To provide jobs for everybody we have to operate a growing and expanding economy fully. The conservative elements of American society play a vital role of keeping people like me from accelerating the processes of growth and development too fast or too much. My role is to evoke the inner humanity from our conservative leaders who otherwise would surrender their better instincts to their dominant fears of change. One of America's great strengths is the way its organized politics combines the creative individuals with the stabilizing individuals in each party.

A quarter of a century of adult experience in American industry, divided almost evenly between the labor movement and welfare enterprise with a couple of years in the War Production Board, has made me a welfare enterpriser. Welfare enterprise is an ever-developing way of doing business—converting raw materials and talent into finished goods and services and distributing them for cash or credit. It gives the individual the greatest opportunity to use his creativeness in relative freedom and pays the largest rewards for such creative effort. This system first produced the greatest economic results in history, but only when it has been able to run at full capacity. Feedbacks to Europe and now Everywhere have been an essential condition —the necessary supplemental organizing force to our central purpose—for running our economy fully. We turn now to the meaning of these feedbacks.

CHAPTER SIX

E^2—E RAISED TO THE SECOND POWER IS AMERICA'S FEEDBACKS TO EUROPE

Economic feedbacks are a regenerative process that make our economic system tick. They recharge our industrial and agricultural activities. They provide jobs for our growing population, outlets for our farm surpluses, and markets for our surplus industrial capacity. America cannot self-develop in isolation. We have to codevelop with our fatherland countries in Europe where the United States of America was conceived and of whom we are an extension in time and space. We have to codevelop with the emerging power of the Soviet Union which is helping to evoke our inner humanity toward the emerging people of Africa, Asia, and Latin America. And we have to codevelop with the emerging countries instead of exploiting them as our fatherland nations in Europe and the United States, each in its own way, has done for several centuries. Their revolt against their exploitation is evoking Western man to practice his humanity toward them. Cuba is the most recent, painful, and nearest example.

A pernicious sickness in America is our false pride thinking that the rate of American economic growth has been the result of "that great system of free enterprise." Actually our accelerated rate of growth in the twentieth century has been the result of feedbacks to fight wars that laid great waste to large parts of our fatherland countries. Europe's tough luck has been our good fortune. The Japanese and Korean wars further served to accelerate the development of the three E's. With the ever-changing pulsations of the human processes of growth and development the three E's broke through the egg's shell in the fifties where everybody could see them. Are these living processes of human betterment and freedom irreversible? While such a conclusion can be inferred from this discussion, I make no such assertion. A case might be made for irreversibility on a long term historical and worldwide basis. For example, human betterment and personal freedom were advanced in America during Hitler's efforts to turn the clock back. I question the irreversibility case on a short-term national basis. But I would not want to be the man who tried to preside over the liquidation of the three E's in your country and mine, or over the strangulation of their emergence in the world.

E^2—E raised to the second power is the root of my thesis. America's fatherland countries provided the United States of America with a supplemental central purpose around which to organize its political economy. It has been the extra organizing force of this central purpose that has enabled America's politicians and enterprisers (labor leaders fall into both functional groups) to wage a successful war against poverty in the United States. While private remittances to relatives in the old country and commercial trade have been important components of America's feedbacks to Europe, the dominant component up to the Marshall Plan has been wars of destruction. These feedbacks enabled America to conquer poverty at home and opened the way for Europe to do likewise. The media of E^2 were largely wars of destruction. The media of E^3 are wars of construction, using weapons of construction—the three R's, ideas, plows, water-well drills, bulldozers, shovels, tractors, moral concepts, and all the other weapons employed in releasing the spiritual or creative energies of people to defeat poverty and illiteracy. These we shall discuss in later chapters after we demonstrate how the 151 million individual Americans in 1950 turned the corner in their war against poverty in the U.S.A. E² is my interpretation of the political-economic history of America in the first six decades of the twentieth century. The largest single factor of influence on the growth and development of America in the twentieth century is the organizing force of USA's feedbacks to Europe, feedbacks to fight her wars, and feedbacks to rebuild the devastation of these wars. Deficit financing and higher taxes have been a key to these feedbacks. This is E², America's productive capacity multiplied by a central purpose around which to organize it effectively.

I will illustrate America's economic history during the past quarter century by assuming that this is the year 1936, and that I am predicting what will happen by 1960.

The next twenty-five years will be fantastic. Steelworkers, who are averaging 87 cents an hour now, will be making almost $4.00 an hour in 1960. Workers for U.S. Steel who are struggling on $29.16 a week will be deeper in debt when they earn over $150 a week in 1960. From an annual income of $1,516 they will rise to over $6,000; and while their cost of living will double, their real income by 1960 will also be double what they are earning now in 1936. And U.S. Steel will fare even better. Its 1936 profits after taxes of $50-½ million will rise to over $350 million in 1960. It will pay more than eight times $50 million in taxes it is paying in 1936, and be able to charge off over $250 million for depreciation as against only $59 million in 1936. This will be made possible by increased productive efficiency, but primarily by the fuller utilization of its capacity (now running at only 63 per cent of capacity), which will be increased from 30 million tons to more than 42 million tons by 1960. These enormous gains in living standards for steelworkers and earnings for U.S. Steel, in which the rest of the steel industry and America will share, will be made while our national economy swells from a gross national output of $75 billion to almost $500 billion in 1960. Herbert Hoover's cars-in-garages will have real substance in 1960 when over fifty million autos will be on the highways.

The bitter industrial and G.O.P. leaders who are vilifying Roosevelt for spending ten billion this year and pushing the national debt to $34 billion, in 1960, when they are in the White House, will be spending $78 billion in fiscal year 1960 with a national debt of $288 billion. While the Democrats are apologizing today for over ten million unemployed after four years of Roosevelt, in 1960 they will be criticizing the Republicans for having only four million unemployed in 1960. And there will be 58 million more Americans in 1960 than the 122 million of today. The steel industry that is operating 78 million tons of capacity at 63 per cent this year will be operating over 148 million tons at 75 per cent of capacity in 1960.

America grew considerably under Roosevelt, Truman, and Eisenhower. How? By practicing free enterprise under private capitalism? Because of the hard work of free people in a true democracy? By being a land of God-fearing people? These and a score more basic factors have played their part in facilitating the processes of the U.S.A.'s growth and development, but during these twenty-five years four key political-economic developments took place:

We poured $341 billion into the 1939-1945 war.

We poured $18 billion into the Marshall Plan.

We poured $50 billion into the Korean War.

We poured $25 billion into Atomic Energy.

Without these key developments and $434 billion expenditures, the indices and statistics of the 1936-1960 period would read differently, and America would not be the country that she is today. Americans who think that the great achievements of the United States, our high living standards, and our victory over poverty are the work primarily of free enterprise or private capitalism claim too much for one part of their economic system. During this last quarter of a century the federal government of our country engaged in $254 billion of deficit financing. Instead of this bankrupting us or ruining us with inflation, the United States of America is the showpiece country of our planet with the most stable currency. Facts are cruel; you cannot argue with them, only ignore them to your peril.

FEEDBACKS HELP CONQUER POVERTY

Our big breakthrough in the 1950's in conquering poverty is largely a by-product of the stimulation and organization of our economy to fight Europe's wars. The effects of the wars on the United States provide the difference between our success in conquering poverty and the failure to do so for a majority of our people. Our historic central purpose of providing all of ourselves with everything in America—by itself—does not provide enough of an organizing force to run our economy at top speed. To shift into high gear, to achieve an adequate annual rate of growth, we need the organizing force of our national purpose in the world to supplement that of our central purpose for Americans.

The 1914-1918 war was the first big feedback. The 1939-1945 war was the next. Then came the Marshall Plan feedback. All during this time the United States withdrew brainpower and manpower from Europe to make her economic system work. Without these feedbacks to and withdrawals from Europe, America would still be struggling with the elemental problems involved in conquering poverty and illiteracy, instead of being in the strong position of having proved that they can be licked. While Commissioner of Education in Massachusetts, Horace Mann went to Europe for guidance in facilitating the three R's through public education in America. I once lived in Charleroi, Pennsylvania, named after a town in Belgium from which fatherland country an entire glass plant and crew of skilled workers were imported. We pirated the tinplate know-how from Great Britain and developed our steel and tinplate enterprises behind tariff walls. These are two examples of our history that have been well documented elsewhere, amidst romantic stories about free enterprise and rugged individualists. America developed by building on the achievements of other countries, and we are now primarily on the other side of this self-development process. The facilitators as well as the facilitated develop in the working of this process of codevelopment.

The United States bought her freedom from Europe in the first World War. We were a struggling debtor nation in another depression when the war of 1914-1918 pulled us out of the hole, by providing us a central program around which to organize our economy. And then it began to work. But with precious few liberties and freedoms (outside of the privilege of going to your own church) for the working people. That war began to make our economic system work at high speed, but as soon as it was over the system fell apart. After a few years, however, the momentum picked up again, and a few new industries—auto notably —and some overseas subsidies of American production via foreign credits, gave the system a five-to-six year run before it fell apart again in 1929. During this period the farmers were held down, and from 1924 to 1931, for example, the steelworkers and coal miners never got a change in their wage rates until they were cut in 1931 and 1932. There were no counterorganizations to make the leaders of these industries practice their humanity toward workers.

The Roosevelt revolution gave our system a lift with the aid of a few more new industries, but the lift only carried for five to six years when we began to fall apart again in 1938. Then came the war of 1939-1945. America again had a supplemental central purpose around which to organize its political economy. The rest is history so close to us that, while we can feel it, we do not comprehend it.

AMERICA PROFITS FROM WAR

The 1939-1945 war pulled F.D.R.'s chestnuts out of the fire. Neither he nor Woodrow Wilson were able to deliver on George Washington's Utopian hope to stay clear of the old imperial foreign alliances; codevelopment is a natural process in life.

In 1939 my brother Stanley, who is now Research Director of the A.F.L.-C.I.O., and I did a study of New Castle, Pennsylvania. Our subject was the impact of the war on the steel towns, "War and the Steel Ghost Towns," *Harper's Magazine* (January, 1940). We recorded:

"It's started," a lean-faced, bedraggled, unemployed steelworker announced excitedly. "I mean the war. Hitler's marching into Poland. I just heard it on the radio," he explained further to a group of sullen men loafing on South Mill Street, across from the relief headquarters in New Castle, Pennsylvania. The dead silence broke. Within an hour news of the outbreak of war in Europe was all over town. Rumors of good things to come began to fly fast and furiously. This is going to be a long war. . . . There's going to be a big boom all over. . . . The mills, factories, and mines will soon be needin' men. . . . There'll be work and plenty of jobs. . . . A few days later the Mayor of New Castle solemnly told us that U.S. steel had received a large order from Japan and that the obsolete hand-mills would soon be reopened because the modern strip mills were being taxed to capacity.

As soon as the war was over, my wife and I started to spend weekends in New Castle, and in December, 1945, I published "New Castle, Pa. Has a Future" which quotes the leader of the town,

Five years ago when the appellation [ghost town] was attached to our city, many of us were in the frame of mind to do bodily harm. Fortunately the energies so aroused were directed into proper channels and we became fighting mad enough to do something about it. . . . Today because of the spark that was in us, there have arisen splendid and well-equipped buildings, employing more people earning more money than ever was earned in the city. . . .

The job for the future is not a job for one or two, it is the job of everyone, from the humble laborer to the great industrialist. "We need fear no future that faces us."

I concluded this follow-up study on New Castle: "Whether New Castle needs to fear the future, of course, remains to be seen. I'm betting on her and I hope to go back in five years to learn how my bet turns out."

The three E's have won the bet. I have been back to this

town whose future typifies that of America's. At age twenty-six in 1940 I was invited by one faction of the Greater New Castle Association to speak to them. The hall was packed and supercharged with emotion against one of the men who had blackened the name of their fair city. But I was not afraid. Four years earlier, when Philip Murray had sent me here as an organizer, I was escorted out of town with a pistol in my back. The city detective who bounced me was at the meeting. I joked about the contrasting experiences, and the crowd sobered down to a serious consideration of its problems. I acquired more faith in America's individuals, as I was able to facilitate the processes of an American town's rebuilding. There is an inner humanity in all people. In New Castle I gained another experience in how to evoke it. I also acquired one of my good friends and business associates, Thomas P. Johnson, whose family is one of the oldest in New Castle. He is a prominent attorney in Pittsburgh and is also president of the big bank in New Castle today. He reports, "Town's doing well. Has lots of problems. But who doesn't in the U.S.A.?" This is America.

New Castle illustrates how the war gave its enterprising citizens the opportunity to diversify their industries, in the same way that it gave the American economy the opportunity to show what it can do when organized around a central purpose. New Castle gained from the war, corporations and farmers profited richly, and the working people did all right by themselves, too. Philip Murray told a large staff meeting of organizers in the William Penn Hotel, Pittsburgh, at the start of the war:

Come what may we are going to organize every steelworker in this country. America's going to win this bloody war for bloody Europe. And we are going to win our war against the steel masters. We'll strike when we have to. We'll picket when necessary. We'll organize, organize, organize. Until we build a labor union, over a million strong, that will make this war worth fighting. This is our God-given job, and go out and do it, war or no war, defense production or no defense production. Organize, organize, organize.

This policy produced a crisis in my young career. I told Murray that the war, defense production, America came first. I said that I would not go along with using them to promote the selfish interests of the union. He listened, and walked away. Next morning he came into my little office, lined with shelves full of books, boxes stuffed with clippings, and room for only one visitor's chair. He kicked the floor-level latch on the door, closed it, and sat down.

"Harold, I want to educate you. Boy, you're not dry behind the ears yet. What do you think the rich bitches are doing? Sacrificing their damn property for the war? Hell, no. They are out fattening their bellies. This is life. Everybody gains in a war, except the poor luckless people who get killed or maimed. They ain't going to be any less dead or hurt if we foolishly throw away this golden opportunity to build the union. What are you going to do? Go out and muster a gun? Peel potatoes? I need you here."

Murray rose, pulled some papers from his pocket, placed them on my desk, "Harold, take care of these gripes for me. Will you please?" I was standing by now, shaking in my shoes. He put his strong left arm around my shoulder (he was as large as I physically) and said, "Boy, stick with me and I'll make a man out of you."

Murray placed me in the War Production Board (W.P.B.) after Pearl Harbor as an assistant director of the Steel Division. He was pleased with the way my service in the W.P.B. had taught me the economic facts of life. He enjoyed ribbing me about all the instances of feathering your own nest that I daily encountered in the W.P.B. That is a book in itself. In this discussion we need only cite that every corporation in America came out of the war a lot stronger than it went in, with just enough exceptions to prove the rule. Our basic concern in this book is how America benefited from the war as a nation. The biggest benefit to America was in the raising of its people's living standards. This went right on during the war since the United States never used more than 45 per cent of its capacity for war production. Philip Murray and his union played a vital role in facilitating the processes of licking poverty in the U.S.A. during the war. They also helped lay the groundwork for the push over the hill in the war against poverty that is the economic history of America during the 1950's. I cite an illustration.

COSTS MORE TO LIVE BETTER

During the middle of the war Murray pulled me out of the War Production Board to help break the "Little Steel" wage formula that was being used to control wages. Driving back to Washington from Pittsburgh one fall weekend in 1943, Murray said, "Harold, there's something wrong with the government's cost of living index. It shows a rise of only 23 per cent since the start of 1941, and I just came from eating in a worker's home where, I swear, their costs have gone up a damn sight more. You better look into it." I advised that the index was a statistical measurement based on computations that were not designed, nor could they be, to reflect the distortions of a wartime economy. "Harold, I want you to take that damnable index apart. You and I don't have to argue any more about who benefits from a war. You've been in the W.P.B. long enough to get dry behind the ears. I'll put someone else there to represent us. You go to work on that index."

While our boys were fighting and dying overseas, this is the kind of battle that Philip Murray was fighting for them on the home front so that they would not have to return to the kind of depression-ridden country they were reared in as boys during the 1930's. Murray persuaded F.D.R. to send a memorandum to the War Labor Board (October 22, 1943) requesting the appointment of the President's Cost-of-Living Committee. The labor members of the committee fired the first shot three months later with a "cost of living" report claiming that living costs had risen 43.5 per cent from January 1, 1941, to January 1, 1944, as against the U.S. Department of Labor's Index that merely recorded a 23.4 per cent rise.

When you understand the opposing concepts that accounted for this wide disparity, you understand much about America.

We lost the battles over the statistics of the cost of living, but won the war over the concept. On November 10, 1944, William H. Davis, as chairman of the President's Cost-of-Living Committee, ruled that the U.S. Labor Department's index only understated the wartime increase of prices by 3-½ to 4-½ percentage points, and not the 20 percentage points claimed by the labor members. But the professional economists and statisticians who took our statistics apart, (and the government rounded up the deans of the trade to batter us down) recommended that the index "should be given a less misleading name." This index of the Bureau of Labor Statistics (BLS) of the U.S. Labor Department is now known as the "Consumer Price Index." Will Davis clearly perceived the opposing concepts:

Change in the cost of a fixed standard of living has been confused with the cost of a changed standard, or manner, of living. But I think almost everyone understands the common-sense idea that cost of living is something everyone would like to see go down, while the standard of living is something we should all like to see go up. . . . Every head of a family knows that an increase in his total family expenditure may be a forced increase to cover a rising cost of living or it may be a voluntary increase to cover an improved standard of living or it may be a mixture of both. . . .

I would . . . go along with the Mitchell Committee's suggestion that the BLS index might well be given another name, particularly if the new name could emphasize that the BLS index measures changes in the total cost of a fixed standard of living, not changes in total family expenditures due to changed standards of living.

The Bureau of Labor Statistics got money from Congress for a new family expenditures study after the war, which detailed the new and higher American living standards the price of which the new Consumer Price Index measures. Philip Murray argued that the cost of living to working folks' families is a simple and specific concept—namely, to most people cost-of-living means the amount of money a family spends. This is the idea, the concept, that Philip Murray put over in 1944, and, after his death it got his steelworkers a seventeen-cent-an-hour wage increase between 1956 and 1959. The significance for America was explained in 1959 (July 29, *Pittsburgh Press*) by Ewan Clague, fourth-term Commissioner of the Bureau of Labor Statistics:

Do your budget and your wife keep telling you the high cost of living is zooming higher fast?

Not so, says the man who keeps tabs on such problems for Uncle Sam. It's the cost of high living, not the high cost of living, that's taking us all for an escalator ride. "Actually consumer prices have been relatively stable for more than a year and are likely to continue so," said Ewan Clague . . . "But people keep asking me how this could be so when they're spending so much more than they used to. What they forget is that they're living better, too."

Today, Mr. Clague pointed out, most Americans think they have to have such things as television sets, cars with plenty of gadgets, frozen and prepared foods, backyard barbecues and homes of their own. Until recent years, all these were either unavailable or were classed as luxuries out of the average family's reach.

When the boys came home from the war in 1945 and 1946, it was to an America that provided its veterans with large bonuses, credits to buy homes and to go into business, loans and grants to get an education, and all of the other Acts of Congress that facilitated the big inroads which the United States made during the fifties in its war against poverty at home. America went into the 1914-1918 war as an international debtor and came out a creditor nation; it went into the 1939-1945 war as a people still struggling against poverty and came out a richer nation, on the road to victory over poverty. The job, I repeat, is not done, but America has demonstrated to the world that poverty can be licked, and that's what all the shouting is about.

THE IRRATIONAL FIFTIES

As soon as we caught up with the demands that accumulated during the war, our economy went into its first postwar recession in 1949. The economic literature of that recession is replete with claims that America was on the road to pulling out of the 1949-

1950 recession months before Korea. And they are correct, but not for the right reason. Most of their claims are designed to prove that our economy was recovering before the June, 1950, Korean War shot in the arm. It was, but for reasons not unrelated to war or the fear of war. On September 23, 1949, President Harry S. Truman announced that Russia had exploded her first A-bomb in a test four weeks earlier. This public knowledge that the Russians at last had the A-bomb distorted the development of America in two directions:

We accelerated the "living-it-up-for-today" spree that increased the poverty of our community services, while we proved to the world that we could eliminate poverty for the individual.

We went on a "witch hunt" that outdid the Palmer Raids, Red Scares, vigilantism, and Ku Klux Klan agitations of the 1919-1921 years.

McCarthyism was in process before McCarthy gave this distorted American development his name. It coincided with the fall of China to the Reds in 1949. Since then, with a fervor that pulsates with the intensity of a religious crusade, America has opposed Red China. The "irrational" American no-trade, non-recognition policy toward China is the last major vestige of McCarthyism that is still alive. The "thoughtful" panic period into which we began to move after the 1954 Senate censure of McCarthy, 1955 Geneva Summit Conference, the Russians dropping an H-bomb from a plane six months before we did in 1956, and Sputnik in 1957 might be converted quickly back to "irrational" panic if, and when, we should ever begin to fear the "yellow menace" of Red China over the "Red menace" of white Russia.

The Korean War (June 24, 1950) did for our political economy what the European wars had done in 1914-1918 and 1939-1945. Free enterprise functioned magnificently again. But the extra organizing force of the Korean War is a fundamental factor that pervades all the economic activities and statistics of the 1950-1953 period. By 1954 our economy began to come apart again. The very brief 1954 recession has been recorded by the most eminent economists and scholars as a downturn that was corrected, not primarily by governmental actions, but largely by consumer confidence. Individuals dug into their savings and bought America right out of the 1954 recession. But why? Did the American consumers get their confidence to dig into their savings from the knowledge that, while the United States exploded an H-bomb in the fall of 1952, the Russians put off one of these big hydrogen busters in August, 1953? I disagree that consumer confidence pulled us out of the 1954 recession. The American people kept on buying because they had no confidence that they had a future. They are afraid that they might be A- or H-bombed out of existence any day. That's why they buy like mad, and Harlow Curtice, when head of General Motors, was able to lead them into debt for more than an additional three billion dollars to buy over seven million autos in 1955, many on thirty-six month payouts.

The most explosive part of my speeches consists of the simple statement, "Everyone of you have been eating high off the hog ever since we A-bombed the Japs in August, 1945, because none of you have the confidence that the same fatal thing won't happen to you and your children. So you're living it up good—while you can. And you're letting the devil take the hindmost." The fierce reaction that this simple statement about postwar America always evokes, confirms my intuitive judgment that the A-bomb panicked America. The national hysteria symbolized by McCarthy is the sharpest evidence. After every speech several individuals accost me to argue, "It ain't so." Those who will stay and discuss their basic, personal, postwar decisions—and some do—leave chastened by the knowledge of the insidious influence, unconscious in most individuals, of the widespread fear that the A-bombs, and now the H-bombs, can end life on this planet.

Correlations are the bones of economic statistics. Correlate the Korean War and Russia's 1949 A-bomb and 1953 H-bomb with America's indices of economic activity, and you have the economic history of the fifties, the decade of "irrational" panic.

The 1955 boom developed a momentum that carried us into the 1957-1958 decession (it was not bad enough to be called a depression but was too severe properly to be called a recession.) Did Sputnik make a decession out of the 1957 recession? Before discussing this, I cite an evidence of the basic policy of Americans living-for-today-for-there-may-be-no-tomorrow.

The conservatives were grossly unfair to President Truman during the Korean War. They criticized him bitterly for pursuing a policy of "guns and butter," as if he had any other choice. He knew then, instinctive natural politician that he was, what his opposition began to learn when they occupied the White House in 1953. To be sure, Americans would, and did, support the Korean War. But they refused flatly to do so at the expense of their own living standards. They not only insisted on maintaining their living standards in fighting the war, but demanded that these standards be raised simultaneously while prosecuting it. The conservative voices in America cried out in vain for "sacrifice" during the Korean War. The American individuals responded by producing more and more babies by the millions and demanding more and more consumer goods so that they could live it up now. And free enterprise responded with capital expenditures by the billions that expanded America's industrial capacity to produce both guns and butter. I cite this part of the history of the 1950's in support of my judgment that fear of being A- and H-bombed out of existence was a primary motivating force that propelled Americans during the decade of "irrational" panic.

How come in 1959 and 1960 while we secured a remission in the 1957-1958 decession, we are still not able to run our economy at capacity, and provide jobs for everybody in the United States, despite our pouring $47 billion a year into defense, atomic, and aid expenditures?

The Korean War, feedback aid to Europe, military and economic aid to non-European countries and people, plus an armaments program to meet the Soviet danger (I don't quarrel with it, as the danger is real enough) have helped to keep us

going since the first cracks in our economy appeared in 1949-
1950. These feedbacks to Europe and other continents have been
the make-or-break factor in providing the supplemental organizing force to operate and expand the American economy.
During the 1950's they have provided us with the needed extra
organizing force to expand and operate our productive capacity
at near full capacity until the 1957 slowup. But since Sputnik
we began to shed the "irrational" panic that pervaded our lives
during most of the 1950's. Our big binge of 1945-1957 self-
indulgence in a multiplication of physical things has begun to
subside, as we begin to discover that the pursuit of the three
E's is not the chief end of man, and that the H-bomb might not
get us after all.

PENTAGON EMPLOYMENT

We have been pouring over 8 per cent of our annual wealth
into defense, and over half our Federal budget. Yet the severity
of the 1957-1958 decession, continuing into the 1960's through
the underutilization of our productive facilities and manpower,
demonstrates that defense production for wars of destruction is
not enough "extra" to run the American economy at full capacity. The weapons of total destruction do not provide enough
"extra" jobs to underwrite full employment in the United States,
because as their dollar volume increases the number of man-hours
and amount of material do not increase in proportion.

I was in Boston when President Eisenhower in his January
9, 1959, State of the Union message told Congress, "We are
buying certain bombers that cost their weight in gold exactly."
He made the front page of the *Boston Daily Globe* the next
morning in a story reporting that the current price of gold was
$500 a pound, while the actual price of the Navy A3J bomber
was $650 a pound and the Air Force B-58 bomber carried a
$567 a pound price tag.

The Boston Naval Shipyard workers made an adjoining
front page story, reporting that 1,500 to 3,000 of them would
be permanently laid off. They are human beings. They need

jobs. They have wives and children. They need steady *annual* income. They are voters. They need help from their duly elected representatives, every last one of whom organized a hot-seat session on Capital Hill for the Navy Secretary on the same day that they learned about the declining value of gold in terms of bombers. In terms of missiles it is even greater now.

Republican Senator Leverett Saltonstall joined his Democratic colleague, Senator John Kennedy, in telling the Navy Secretary that they can't do this to their constituents. Senator Kennedy said, "New England has suffered from industrial runaway shops but this was the first time the Navy had picked up an operation to leave. He asked them to give the move serious consideration." The Secretary reported that the size of the Navy is decreasing, there just will be fewer ships in business; that the future of Boston shipyard is no different from any other yard, the trend in shipyard employment in the entire United States will be down; and that some of the modern ships being constructed are worth ten old models.

His audience included the Senators of Massachusetts, representatives of the state's governor, the mayor of Quincy, the head of the South Shores Chamber of Commerce, the leaders of the shipyard workers' unions, and all of the Massachusetts members of Congress. The latter immediately set up a committee to study the problem, and elected Congresswoman Edith Nourse Rogers (Republican) as chairwoman. She promptly announced that she would carry the protest of the Massachusetts delegation directly to the Defense Secretary, and if she received no satisfaction from him she would ask to see the President on the matter.

The Boston shipyard workers have had it. There are not enough jobs for all of them. This was their outlook for the future, while the President reported to Congress: "The outlook is this: 1960 commitments for our armed forces, the Atomic Energy Commission, and Mutual Security exceed $47,000,000,000. In the foreseeable future they are not likely to be significantly lower."

At the same time the Democratic leader, Senator Lyndon

Johnson, said that we must move "further and faster in our military preparations." He was talking national policy from Capitol Hill. But a few weeks earlier he was talking for his Texas constituents. *The Wall Street Journal* (December 22, 1958) reported:

GRAND PRAIRIE, Texas—The Navy's sudden cancellation of two multimillion dollar contracts at Chance Vought Aircraft, Inc., here has touched off a series of economic and political shock waves that may have national repercussions. Company officials ordered immediate layoffs of about 1,400 workers and cancellations of hundreds of contracts with many of its 3,450 suppliers around the country. By January 1, at least 1,500 additional employees will be without jobs. . . .

House Speaker Sam Rayburn, for example, said he didn't see how the budget entered into the Navy's decision to drop the Regulus. "We gave the Administration more money for defense than they asked for." And *Lyndon Johnson, Senate majority leader,* fired off a telegram over the weekend to Navy Secretary Thomas Gates. "I urge in the strongest possible terms," he wired, "that you consider spreading Navy contracts in such a way as to keep important industrial centers such as Dallas in a position where they can contribute to the national defense whenever they're needed." *Congressman George Mahon, Chairman of the House subcommittee on defense appropriations,* said he plans to call his committee together for "consideration of this new and unexpected change in plans." [Emphasis supplied.]

The complaints that the Navy Secretary heard from Boston on ships in January, 1959, were mild compared to the barrage that he had received during the previous month on planes and missiles from Texas from where come the Senate Majority Leader, the Speaker of the House, and the Chairman of the House subcommittee on defense appropriations. Almost every state has the same complaint. Let's face it. Defense production is an integral, built-in source of employment in our political economy. In addition to the two and one-half million in uniform and almost a million civilian Pentagon employees, millions of our people live off defense production. The Pentagon is learning, as the industry enterprisers learned the hard way from organized labor and the politicians, that you just do not throw American workers out on the street with abrupt notices of terminations. You have to provide in your defense costs for severance pay for the individuals affected, as the most important concern of America's culture is the individual.

Every American is entitled to a job, to a livelihood, and if industry cannot provide it, Congress and the government will. This is one basic policy which all the politicians on Capitol Hill preach and which is in the process of becoming national policy. It follows from the tardy acceptance by the conservative Republicans of Lincoln's definition of the function of government. The heat of unemployment and idle factories has made them practice what Lincoln taught; it has evoked their inner humanity.

As the 1950's came to a close our duly elected representatives began to realize that, despite a $47 billion defense, atomic energy, and mutual security program to keep the Russian planes, bombs, and missiles grounded, America still was unable to run her political economy at full capacity or employ all who were willing and able to work.

E^2 SUMMARY

Let's sum up.

The American consumers, scared by the H-bomb, still need jobs and steady *annual* incomes to get the personal credit to keep on buying, to display that consumer-confidence spending.

The defense-armament production has changed. It takes more dollars than man hours and materials. It takes more excellence that requires decades (not years) to develop. Hence the gap in production and employment. Only a shooting war can fill the gap, and it has to be a limited shooting war, or nobody will ever produce anything anywhere.

America needs a big feedback program to run her political economy fully. Europe alone no longer provides it. In fact, the Europeans are beginning to refeedback steel, small cars, and other things to the United States and to compete with us in our own domestic markets as well as in overseas markets. This, in turn, is a formative process leading to unifying measures between management and organized labor.

We cannot get our conservatives, Democrats no less than Republicans—who play the vital role of providing the necessary stabilizing ballast for a living, functioning, creative, self-developing U.S.A.—to appropriate the money and raise the taxes to build schools, hospitals, and other facilities needed to develop excellent individuals, as a substitute for the feedbacks to Europe or the gradual reduction in Pentagon-created employment. The conservative enterprisers and politicians will tax and spend to build roads and highways, as they are essential for the auto, oil, housing, and related industries. As President Eisenhower learned the hard way in 1959, they will also do this for housing, because it is the supporting industry for the building materials industries, construction-equipment industries, appliances, electrical wiring, home heating, ad infinitum. The accelerated increasing of our public wealth, or the stepped-up conquering of our growing (with population growth) poverty in community services, have to come as by-products of full production and full employment; they cannot and will not come as a substitute for them.

America's economy is dependent upon the organizing force of a national as well as central purpose to operate at top speed, to grow and develop, and to stop wasting idle capacity and idle or underemployed manpower. During the twentieth century feedbacks to fight Europe's wars and to rebuild her devastation, and containment of the Kremlin, have provided this essential national purpose to supplement our central purpose for Americans. E^3 is the major process in development around which America is organizing its political economy, and it can take our country and our world to the next plateau of human betterment and freedom for self-development.

E^2 is the key to America's recent economic history. E^3 is the key to America's future.

CHAPTER SEVEN

E^3—E RAISED TO THE THIRD POWER IS AMERICA'S FEEDBACKS TO EVERYWHERE

The history of America is the gathering together of diverse individuals from many lands, who have produced things in unison by accepting as the one overriding principle the more equal and better life for everybody in this life. We have performed most effectively—1914-1918, 1939-1945, 1950-1953—when our society has been disciplined by a shooting war. Developing out of this, our history as a people, is the moral equivalent of war as foreseen by William James, namely, a war of construction to facilitate the more equal and better life for all: Abraham Lincoln's war to provide "an equal chance . . . for all men, in all lands everywhere," and the war envisioned by our founding fathers when they declared "all men are created equal," the doctrine that provoked our Civil War that made America the country that it is in the process of becoming. This is the national purpose of America: to use its spiritual freedom to bring the Kingdom of God on earth to Mr. and Mrs. Everybody everywhere. Ours is insecure by itself. A nation, like a man, needs "a great cause, something divinely large and engulfing," to live "a great life."

America as a civilization is as impermanent as the civilizations out of which we have developed. As we pass on and into history it is our mission to leave the world in better condition than it was when our ancestors first began to land in Jamestown, Plymouth Rock, and Ellis Island. We do not have to become the people who checked out of the world in the flash of H-bombs. We can become, and we are becoming, the people whose great gift to the world is the idea of the more equal and better life being attainable in this life if not in this lifetime—for everybody everywhere. When this gift is combined with individual freedom for religious worship, as it has been in our country, it can become the Kingdom of God on earth.

The formula for E^3—E raised to the third power—is the productive capacity of American industry and agriculture and the creativeness of American society multiplied by the organizing force of our national purpose. Thus are our full spiritual energies released. The objectives of E^3 are victory over poverty, illiteracy, and human enslavement. This is America's unfinished job at home and number one job in the world. A war of construction to facilitate the self-development of all the emerging countries is the supplemental organizing force to America's central purpose required to organize our political economy to sustain our present living standards and to achieve an accelerated rate of national growth. Without it, we are lost. With it, we cannot be bested.

E^3—America's feedbacks to everywhere—provides us with a cause that can become a discipline to organize our political economy in the 1960's and the decades ahead. This, in turn, produces practical programs that our enterprisers can understand and effectuate, for which our politicians will tax and spend, that will create jobs for our growing working forces and run our productive facilities at capacity. E to the first power—victory over poverty at home—for continuing validity is dependent upon E^2 and E^3—victory over poverty in Europe and everywhere. E^3—E raised to the third power is based upon E^2. America took the first big step on its own in 1948 with the Marshall Plan, having started down the path of conquering poverty everywhere as a participating country in U.N.R.R.A.—United Nations Relief and Rehabilitation Administration—immediately after the war. Once on this path we have kept traveling it: with the Marshall Plan, with special aid to Greece and Turkey in 1948, Point Four in 1949, and all of the other steps that we took during the fifties to fight poverty (and her bed-partner, fear) in Europe and everywhere else on the planet.

American leaders in all walks of life are devoting themselves to developing practical measures for facilitating the exportation of the American Revolution. This process in development can be slowed down, as the Randall Report did in 1954, or it can be speeded up as President Eisenhower began to do with his worldwide travels in 1960, but it cannot be stopped. We are facilitating this process from our ICA (International Cooperation Administration) offices across from Jackson Park to our USOM (United States Operations Mission) posts in every country that we can penetrate; from our Export-Import Bank, Development Loan Fund, and other federal agencies promoting the development of other countries; from the export offices of our private corporations to every nation in the world with whom we trade; from our private banks to their overseas branches; from the A.F.L.-C.I.O. Building, also across from Jackson Park, to its international affiliations overseas; from the missions offices of our Christian churches to peoples everywhere; from the American Jewish Agency to the people of Israel; from our universities with their special country study centers and I.C.A. contracts in the self-developing countries; from our charitable foundations in study and other grants in international development; and through CARE, whose initials read *C*ooperative for *A*merican *R*emittances to *E*urope until 1952 when Europe was changed to Everywhere.[1]

[1] In 1958 Remittances was changed to Relief because the meaning of the longer word was not clearly understood in many countries.

EXPORTING AMERICAN REVOLUTION

The fulfillment of the American Revolution for Americans only is no fulfillment at all. It is only the process of becoming social, democratic revolutionaries in the world. We Americans cannot enjoy our richer and fuller life in our own oasis. The processes of the three R's and the three E's cannot be limited to ourselves. They did not begin here nor do they end in America. They are world-wide and universal.

Our postwar 1945-1960 history is the story of how America, eight score and ten years after its own Declaration of Independence, began to export its own Revolution, as symbolized by Abraham Lincoln who proclaimed:

The assertion that "all men are created equal" was of no practical use in effecting our separation from Great Britain; and it was placed in the Declaration, not for that, but for future use. Its authors . . . meant to set up a standard maxim for free society . . . constantly spreading and deepening its influence, and augmenting the happiness and value of life *to all people of all colors everywhere.*

The American economy requires the organizing force of a central purpose to achieve its optimum effectiveness. Our central purpose of providing just ourselves with the good life is not an adequate organizing force by itself. The supplementing of our central purpose with a huge defense program (one-twelfth of our annual output) still falls short of generating the required organizing force to attain optimum production and employment. The shooting wars, extending into four of the six decades of the twentieth century, have provided us with the required supplemental force to enable America's economy to break through to optimum levels of productive effectiveness, growth, and development. It took a shooting war to discipline us, to pay the war taxes to raise our national debt from $45 to $245 billion in the 1939-1945 war and to unlock the devastating power of the atom; and in the Korean War, to raise the Federal government debt from $257.3 billion in 1950 to $274.4 billion by fiscal 1955.

"So far, war has been the only force that can discipline

a whole community," William James observed in 1910. We confirmed this empirical finding in 1914-1918, 1939-1945, and 1950-1953. "Until an equivalent discipline is organized," James advised his posterity, "I believe that war must have its own way." America, failing to find a "moral equivalent," has gone through three bloodbaths since James passed on to us the living processes of life a half-century ago. He had vision: "When . . . war becomes absurd and impossible from its own monstrosity . . . constructive interests may someday seem no less imperative [than the war-function], and impose on the individual a hardly lighter burden." And, above all, James had faith: "I have no serious doubt that the ordinary prides and shames of social man, once developed to a certain intensity, are capable of organizing such a moral equivalent . . . it is but a question of time."

While the Eisenhower administration began by stuttering that America had no moral obligation to facilitate a genuine equality for the Asiatic, Latin American, and African peoples, it leaves office with the U.S.A. more firmly committed to Abraham Lincoln's injunction to spread "liberty to all men, in all lands, everywhere."

"The object of this war is to make sure that everybody in the world has the privilege of drinking a quart of milk a day," Henry A. Wallace said (May 8, 1942) when he was Vice-President. The head of the National Association of Manufacturers (N.A.M.) denounced him for advocating a "daily quart of milk for the Hottentots," and Wallace had to deny this distortion of his views before the Senate Commerce Committee (January 25, 1945). What he said was:

Modern science . . . has made it technologically possible to see that all of the people of the world get enough to eat. . . . The peace must mean a better standard of living for the common man, not merely in the United States and England, but also in India, Russia, China, and Latin America—not merely in the United Nations, but also in Germany and Italy and Japan.

The N.A.M. president in 1942 was saying that the daily quart of milk was for Americans first, if not exclusively, and the hell with the Hottentots. The N.A.M. in 1960, uneasy over the cost of exporting the American Revolution across the globe, is not denouncing the Hottentots or anybody else for asserting an equal chance to drink this healthful liquid. Our conservatives instead are raising those practical questions as to whether we can afford these expensive ideas stemming from Abe Lincoln. In the meanwhile, our welfare enterprisers are shipping machines to African and Asian countries to liquify dehydrated milk that our politicians ship to these self-developing peoples when we have it in surplus. The inner humanity of the America-firsters since Henry Wallace's term in office has been evoked.

THE RANDALL REPORT'S IMMORALITY

President Eisenhower's first move in the field of foreign economic policy was to appoint a commission under the chairmanship of Clarence B. Randall, former president of Inland Steel. This able man, devoted to America, with a genuine compassion for his fellow man, was the product of his time and of the raging McCarthyism of 1953-1954, who put his name in the Randall Report to this proposition:

. . . as the need for economic aid for postwar recovery disappears, demands are increasing for general economic aid unconnected with recovery from war or preparation for defense. Underdeveloped areas are claiming a right to economic aid from the United States, in proposals in the United Nations and the Interparliamentary Union. We recognize no such right.

If this violation of the spirit of the Declaration of Independence made Abraham Lincoln turn over in his grave, what the minority report of two Republican Congressmen espoused must have made him arise:

. . . it is the function of the United States Government to take only such action as may . . . provide our people with a high standard of living . . . international relations are not an end in, and of, themselves. They are merely a means to an end—namely, the welfare of the citizens of this country.

Wherever Americans gather someone always speaks up for old Honest Abe. In the Randall Report it was David J. McDonald, president of the steelworkers union, in his dissent, "It is to our advantage that all people throughout the free world be well off economically. . . . it is a question of economic welfare being desirable in its own right, and a necessary precondition of peace." My brother Stanley worked with McDonald on the Randall Report, and he told me at the time that Point Four was being liquidated. "They can't do it," I protested, "I'm riding with Abe Lincoln." Stanley grinned, "I'm afraid you're riding for a fall." I protested that in the long run Abe Lincoln's philosophy, which stemmed from our philosophical founding fathers, always wins out in America. "I'll buy that, Harold, but your problem is to keep from going broke in the short run."

Point Four was an effort to extend the Marshall Plan for European recovery to the non-European peoples of the world whose development was "unconnected with recovery from war or preparation for defense." The 1950 Act was called "Act For International Development." It is natural for Americans to feedback their surpluses to their fatherland countries in Europe. The Orient and Africa present a problem of a different color. But the moral question is the same. Point Four would have been an abortive program except for the stimuli of the Korean War in 1950 and Russian threats in the Middle East. To save his Point Four program President Truman had tied it to the military. Randall recognized this as a reality, since Congress had already enacted it into law by amending the 1950 Act for International Development to the Mutual Security Act. This justified Point Four aid, in the Randall Report language, with "preparation for defense." While the fiscal 1960 Mutual Security appropriations totaled $3.2 billion, only $1.2 billion was for economic aid and for technical assistance unconnected with supporting our military aid expenditures, which amount to 37 per cent of the total Mutual Security. The 63 per cent, or $2.0 billion, was for military assistance and defense support.

But by 1960 Point Four had begun to fly under several

different flags. Direct United States government-to-government aid is only one of them. In this discussion, we are concerned with the basic policy, and the underlying morality of American efforts to integrate the self-developing countries into regular channels of international trade and to facilitate their development. The techniques are merely tools of facilitation and consist of such things as Export-Import Bank loans to United States manufacturers to finance sales abroad, United States government guarantee of welfare enterprisers' investments overseas, Development Loan Fund loans, soft-currency loans, "soft" loans that cannot be granted according to standard commercial criteria nor put through Congress as outright aid, grants-in-aid, sale of surplus commodities for local currencies, and regular trade. In sum total this began to approach 2 per cent of our gross national product in 1960, or almost $10 billion including our export surplus, and should approximate 5 per cent or $30 billion to $35 billion by 1970, only a small percentage of which will be a direct part of the federal budget.

It was during the 1950's that the great transformation of America's economic foreign policy began. The development of a prohumanity purpose is in the process of replacing the anti-Communist reasons for American international economic activities. Evidences of this development have to be ferreted out of the clouds of free enterprise dogmas, ignorance of the formative processes shaping the historical trends of the twentieth century, and the sentimentalism of our passive concepts of liberty, freedom, and morality. We have to call a spade a spade to understand the transformation of America's thinking in process.

POINT FOUR IS A MARSHALL PLAN OF A DIFFERENT COLOR

One road to freedom, prosperity, and self-development is to declare war on the United States and lose it. Proud as I am of victorious America over Hitler Germany and Pearl Harbor Japan, the creative act of our country that most arouses my patriotic fervor is our rebuilding of Japan and Western Europe. Were not those deliberate acts, for which we taxed ourselves, the moral equivalent of war? Do they not represent a great step forward from our immoral refusal to extend Lincoln's plan "for compensated emancipation of the slaves" to the South? Do they not hold the key to the moral equivalent of war that I develop through this spiritual interpretation of our history as a people? Americans have seventeen score and two years invested in erecting their structure of an organized society whose objective is to remove fear as the dominant factor in individual life by facilitating the natural processes of life around the globe. Yet our 342 years of building our society can be snuffed out in a flash. This realization generates our A- and H-bomb psychosis and propels us into becoming world developers.

The degeneration of the individual and the spiritual chaos of his pre-A-bomb society are in the process of being transformed into a society of moral wholeness made up of a majority of whole individuals who will have regained their moral purpose in life. We have to provide the necessary stabilizing philosophy of life to go with the common knowledge that the world has a time clock on its heart. The H-bomb psychosis is for children. The myth about the permanence of conscious human existence has been pierced by nuclear power. Adults in America have to grow up, as well as grow old. They have to face the facts of existence that mature, wise men have comprehended for centuries: the impermanence of life. And with this knowledge they have to forge their own understanding of the meaning of individual human life. Our job in life is to make human society work for freedom to self-develop so others after us may share this rich experience that inert, unconscious life and forces are incapable of enjoying. We should do this whether it is for just another generation or another ten thousand years. The end of the days of conscious man cannot be foretold.

Even before the 1939-1945 war was over we began to pour money into the United Nations Relief and Rehabilitation Administration that by 1947 totaled $2.7 billion from America for material assistance to war-devastated regions in Europe and Asia out of a grand total of $3.7 billion. We have been participating in the United Nations' fight against poverty and illiteracy ever since. In time we may merge America's agencies with those of the United Nations in this war, but in the meantime America has to prosecute the war against poverty and illiteracy by such means as a majority of its selected representatives comprehend and vote and its welfare enterprisers risk.

In June, 1947, Secretary of State General George C. Marshall spoke for America. He said that we must return to Europe with an army of peace workers who will campaign for "the emergence of political and social conditions in which free institutions can exist." The isolationist America-firsters thwarted the Marshall Plan until the Soviet coup d'etat in Czechoslovakia put a Communist regime in power in February 1948. Within two months Congress voted the first of over $18 billion worth of appropriations for European recovery that by 1956 were largely ended, and took a major step toward making Western Europe "safe for democracy." We did no such thing after the 1914-1918 war.

These feedbacks to Europe did more for America than for her fatherland countries, and were accomplished on an existing foundation of the three R's. The first big, peaceful feedbacks to Europe by United States government action were indigenous to America. We had fedback twice to help fight Europe's wars. The Marshall Plan feedback came naturally. Each feedback, in its time, gave America a supplemental central purpose around which it was able to organize its economy, further transform private capitalism into welfare enterprise, and prove to the world that poverty can be eliminated. I repeat: these feedbacks were to our fatherland countries in Europe with whom Americans have a natural empathy.

Harry S. Truman gave expression to Point Four in 1949, the year that the Soviets exploded their first A-bomb. Point Four got under way in 1950 and gathered steam from the Korean War, which began in the same year that McCarthy started to turn our post-Hiroshima panic into hysteria. The fallacious thesis of McCarthyism was that the Russians are not only a dumb, stupid, uneducated, backward mob, but also are atheistic, barbarian Orientals. Pervading McCarthyism was the insidious effort to prepare American psychology to A-bomb the Russians. This took the form of equating them to atheistic (or at least non-Christian) Orientals, which was based on the fact that we had already A-bombed Orientals in Japan. We are now extending our natural humanity to the peoples of the Orient. We cannot afford to let "Ugly Americans" deny these fellow human beings as full-fledged members of the species Homo sapiens. We have to shed our colored glasses and see Point Four with the same feeling as we did the Marshall Plan.

The United States' Point Four began in the 1950 Act for International Development which was distorted by McCarthyism into the Mutual Security Act. As fast as we can educate our Congressmen and Senators in the 1960's, Congress should incorporate Point Four in an Act for International Economic Equality in which the United States says, "We recognize a moral obligation to facilitate the economic growth of the self-developing countries and to trade with them as equals." With a full regaining of our great moral purposes during the 1960's, we can begin to achieve a breakthrough in the world for the three R's and the three E's in the closing decades of the twentieth century as we achieved them at home in the 1950's.

PEOPLE ARE PEOPLE

The color tint in our glasses is currently revealed in the question of population growth. The "population explosion" is being fed to Americans by every media. *Time* magazine (January 11, 1960), for example, featured it with a front cover. There is the blond-tinted American young mother, in a form-fitting, easily washable synthetic fiber dress over an uplift brassiere, pushing a neatly dressed two-year-old with a big loaf of bread in his hand, in a chrome-plated supermarket food buggy prominently containing a quart of milk. She and her son and six-year-old daughter are the largest figures. They are surrounded by fifteen children and thirteen mothers, two nonwhite children with bare behinds exposed, two nonwhite mothers with bare breasts exposed, and the only figures that are unmistakenly white are the American mother and her son and daughter. The other women and children are not portrayed with compassion. And across the top right corner is the black-brown-yellow scare that pervades America in the 1960's, "THAT POPULATION EX-PLOSION." The inside story gives both sides of the question, with the emphasis on the scare through a columnar chart that shows 4 billion Asians by year 2,000 compared to 315 (sic) million people on North America.

Throughout this book I keep noting America's population in the year under discussion: 2.5 million at the time of the Declaration of Independence, 3.7 million when we adopted the Constitution that recognized slavery against which the Declaration preached, 31.5 million when Lincoln led almost a million to slaughter to put the Declaration into the Constitution, 92.4 million when William James died in 1910, and double that number sometime during 1961. Reproduction is a natural process that is greatly influenced by upbuilding and debuilding processes constantly and simultaneously at work. Social customs and religious doctrine will change with self-development, as they are doing, for example, in Japan where the birth rate has dropped from 34.8 per 1,000 in 1947 to 17.2 per 1,000 in 1957—a 50 per cent drop. It is a social custom to practice birth control in America among people of all religious beliefs. This process of limiting the results of union will work in its own way and in its own times in all self-developing societies, as it does in our own self-development.

The idea that it is all right for people in the United States to go on breeding more American citizens every year—as many as the entire population of Spain during the 1950's (29.6 million) —but not for other people was expressed in 1959 in the title of a book *Too Many Asians*, by John Robbins who concludes that Asians are "breeding massive difficulties for themselves." Aren't we all? The "yellow menace" scare of previous decades is now dressed up in the "population explosion" concept, and we will be having to batter it down, item by item, speech by speech, book by book, contraceptive by contraceptive as an integral part of our moral war against poverty and ignorance—at home and abroad.

I am on the side of planned parenthood.[2] For almost a decade I have been facilitating the development of fresh, uncontaminated drinking water in the emerging countries, which increases health, prolongs life, creates more child-producing men and women, and raises population. I have also facilitated the development of irrigation water which raises food output for more people. I wish that I could simultaneously be selling a pill or a contraceptive that could be marketed for one cent each. We need a scientific breakthrough on this front. Pakistan's president Mohammad Ayub Khan has said that if the United States, like his country, were faced with a population growth that threatened its economic development, there would be no controversy. *The New York Times* (June 27, 1960) reports, "he urged that instead of arguing, Americans spur their scientists to develop a cheap, simple, effective method of contraception."

In this book the population question cannot be developed. My effort is confined to placing the question in perspective as an issue between our world developers and mass annihilators. The former commit an error when they make a frontal attack on antibirth-control theological doctrines. The real obstacles are social customs in each emerging country and the absence of a healthy, foolproof, one-cent contraceptive. I am not afraid of people. I do not believe that mankind is breeding itself to death. The time and effort devoted to scaring ourselves with *Too Many Asians* should be devoted to practical measures that should be facilitated to achieve stability in population growth in each national grouping of people. People are people.

[2] Our boys were born November 7, 1939, November 13, 1941, November 22, 1946, and planning the fourth to be a girl (June-bride idea) Ellen was born on D-Day's anniversary, June 6, 1949. Note the plan of two sets of children, five years apart, with two years between the children of each set. We should have had another set.

AMERICANS ARE LIVING OFF THE REST OF THE WORLD

The richer, fuller life that, I repeat, in our vanity we call the American Way of Life, because we have achieved it first, would not be possible except for the efficient and systematic manner in which we have been exploiting the natural resources of the world. It is one thing to operate a welfare enterprise economy, as we do, under which our own natural resources are exploited for the purpose of promoting the economic, political, and social welfare of all our own people. We are confronted with quite another thing when we exploit, as we do, the natural resources of other countries and other people for these same selfish for-Americans-only purposes. This moral question goes to the heart of codevelopment. It deals with the raw materials of our technological society, and their relationship to the growth and development of the U.S.A. America's role in the world is as a developer and not an exploiter. The emerging people are in revolt today against their exploitation by our fatherland countries and, for example, have evoked Great Britain's inner humanity as this former exploiting country is emerging as a leading codeveloper of the self-developing nations.

Iron ore illustrates how America increasingly is living off the rest of the world. In 1946, the first year after the last war, iron ore imports into the U.S.A. were less than 4 million tons; they rose to 5 million the next year, to over 10 million after Korea (1951), to over 16 million by 1954, to over 25 million in 1955, to over 30 million the next year, to 37.8 million in 1957, and then dropped 18 per cent to 31 million in 1958, but rebounded to 39.9 million in 1959. In 1950 the United States produced nine out of ten tons of iron ore consumed, by 1955 only a little over eight out of ten tons, and the 1960 forecast is seven out of ten tons, which means that 30 per cent will be imported. It looks as though half of the United States' iron ore in 1975 will be imported.

We, of course, could for a number of years confine ourselves to beneficiated, low-grade, domestic iron ores to meet our growing needs. The price would be higher, as the steel companies would tax us with higher prices to pay for the higher-cost ores, as they could not absorb such higher raw material costs. The President's Materials Policy Commission in 1952 said, "The United States must reject self-sufficiency as a policy and instead adopt the policy of the lowest cost acquisition wherever secure supplies may be found: self-sufficiency, when closely viewed, amounts to a self-imposed blockade and nothing more."

The four countries in 1958 that shipped to the United States a million or more tons of basic iron ore were Canada, Venezuela, Chile, and Peru. Brazil and Liberia are being developed, while 1958 Swedish iron ore imports (a very high grade ore that is low in impurities) were about one-fifth those of 1957. But the American Iron and Steel Institute reports: "The number of foreign countries sending steel alloying elements to the United States has increased sharply in recent years. Forty-five nations sent one or more ores of alloying elements to this country in 1957, compared with thirty-three sources in 1947, and twenty-six just prior to World War II." (Is the use of II an unconscious forecast or fear of World War III?)

A listing of these countries reads like a list of United States Operations Mission offices of the International Cooperation Administration. Russia is not on the list. The American Iron and Steel Institute reports, "Russia, once the leading source of manganese ore, no longer supplies this country. Major sources include Brazil, India, Ghana, Union of South Africa and Mexico." No steel can be made without manganese (thirteen pounds per average ton), and the United States does not have enough domestic manganese to sustain a standard of living as low as that of India's. Nor is China on the list. The American Iron and Steel Institute reports, "China, the largest supplier of tungsten ore and concentrates in 1947, no longer ships to the U.S.A." American imports its tungsten-bearing ores from Burma, Thailand, Australia, Korea, Japan, Canada, Mexico, Brazil, Peru, Bolivia, Argentina, Belgian Congo, Portugal, Spain, France, and Uganda.

Many of these are countries to which Europeans have had

to go since we closed our doors to mass immigration. They need us to facilitate their growth and development, and we, no less, need their raw materials to further our own continuing self-development. The lack of understanding in America on how our living standards are intertwined with those of people everywhere, is why our tremendous steel capacity has not been fully used since the middle of 1957 (except to fight the steelworkers union), and why we have been squandering idle plant capacity and idle man hours throughout our whole economy. But they will be fully used and further expanded during the 1960's, as a husky majority of Americans come to realize that what's good for the world is good for America.

This is E^3—America's feedbacks to everywhere from where we are increasingly importing the necessary raw materials to feed, clothe, and house our own people in the standards to which they are fast becoming accustomed—standards to which the rest of the world, including Russia, aspires so desperately.

E^3 DEVELOPS AMERICA

E^3 is the anchor E of my synthesis equation of America. America's 1914-1918 war "to make the world safe for democracy" and the 1941-1945 war "for the four freedoms" are developing into a moral war to extend the three R's and the three E's to all of our own people by spreading them to everybody everywhere. The nuclear power that we unlocked to terminate the last world war compels us to channel our pugnacious instincts into a moral war of construction in which this vast power of nature—if perseverance and luck prevail—will be used to satisfy the needs of a planet of seven to eight billion people in the centuries ahead. The Kremlin is our moral competition. Its old-fashioned war of destruction to conquer the world for Communism, as we shall discuss later, similarly is being converted into a moral war for "the greater material and moral good" of all mankind. The idea of ending the cold war is a mirage, as we so painfully learned at the abortive Paris summit conference in May 1960. I embrace the idea of converting it into the kind of moral war that William James foresaw a half-century ago.

Our conservatives, who thought F.D.R.'s New Deal would bankrupt America, demand to know where the money is coming from for all this. How can we pay for it? History has proved them wrong about F.D.R.'s New Deal and Truman's Fair Deal bankrupting the U.S.A., and so they now ask, instead of proclaiming dogmatically, won't E^3 bankrupt us?

E^3—facilitating our own development by facilitating the self-developing nations—will not bankrupt America; it will make America stronger. It will employ all our facilities and people. These great feedbacks to everywhere will do for our economy in the closing decades of this century, what the feedbacks for two European wars and two Asiatic wars did in their respective times: accelerate our own self-development so that Communism is made obsolete where it does not exist and transformed where it does.

The Kremlin is fighting a ghost in America when it aims a "torpedo at the underpinnings of capitalism." Capitalism has been transformed in America by Americans into welfare enterprise, built on the foundation of the dignity of the individual. Our concept of humanity does not call for burying Russia and the Kremlin; it calls for correcting their distortions of the natural processes of life—which they call Communism—and transforming them into a form of welfare enterprise where the most important values are the dignity of the individual and freedom for self-development. America does not seek to dominate the world with dogmas. We seek to liberate all people from fear, illiteracy, and poverty. This includes Russia and China. We are doing it through the achievement of the three R's and the three E's.

I lay no claim to discovering America's national purpose. The American purpose is the work of many hands and minds, not the least being Abraham Lincoln. What I am doing is simply this:

1. Accenting that the time has come for Americans to do in the world what Abraham Lincoln did at home a century ago: to lead the more-developed peoples to free the less-developed peoples of the world from illiteracy and poverty, and to help organ-

ize a world-wide welfare society in which all self-developing nations can participate on an equal basis.

2. Suggesting that we can afford to pay the price for these expensive ideas of Abraham Lincoln.

3. Arguing that unless America embraces the national purpose defined for us by Lincoln and faces up to paying the price to be true to the Great Emancipator, that Lincoln was correct when he said in Independence Hall on February 22, 1861, that the Union, America, was not worth saving if it gave up that "sentiment in the Declaration of Independence which gave liberty not alone to the people of this country, but hope to all the world, for all future time."

4. Concluding that America not only is not worth saving, but cannot be saved, if a majority of Americans in the 1960's reject Abraham Lincoln.

In the 1960's we have to learn that our capacity to deliver on our domestic needs is inextricably tied to turning on the full power of our potential economy to deliver the people and material to wage and win the moral war that William James sketched for us before we blundered into the last three killing-and-being-killed wars. World War III is one into which we cannot afford to blunder.

CHAPTER EIGHT

THE USA IS A SELF-DEVELOPING SOCIETY NOT AN AFFLUENT ONE

America is not an affluent society where the processes of production and living can be separated from each other, as John Kenneth Galbraith suggests. What people do for a living and how they live their lives are the inseparable process of doing and learning. America is a self-developing society with at least 20 per cent, 36 million, of its people underdeveloped. Our colored people make up almost half of these underdeveloped Americans.

Of all the nonwhite peoples in the world, the American Negroes already enjoy more freedom and higher standards of living and education than do the nonwhite peoples and many white people in any other country. This is not so much to America's credit as it is to the shame of our fatherland countries in Europe who have exploited the nonwhite peoples of the world for much longer than there has been a United States of America. Albert Schweitzer's work, for example, as a medical missionary in Africa has no great significance except against the backdrop of the white man's inhumanity to the Negroes. "The Africans will remind," the Westerner, Arnold J. Toynbee records, "that they were enslaved and deported across the Atlantic in order to serve the European colonizers of the Americas as living tools to minister to their Western Masters' greed for wealth."[1] I repeat: Only in America have white men killed white men to free colored men from slavery. America's underdeveloped colored people will not become a self-developing people until they are stirred, as the abolitionists stirred Americans in the nineteenth century, to become an emerging people. To reply that the white majority holds them back is not the answer of an emerging people. It is the answer of an evolving people.

The conservative part of me applauds the evolving-people concept as it does not disrupt my routine. America's colored people, however, need to be better organized at this stage in their development. The creative side of me screams that the chronic underdevelopment of American Negroes is a dead weight around the neck of democracy in the U.S.A. and the world.

Myron Taylor, the captain of industry in charge of U.S. Steel in 1937, could see the tidal waves of the processes of human development enveloping America. He signed an historic collective bargaining contract with the steelworkers union that set us off on a wave of organizing steelworkers and metalworkers all over America, and I soon found myself in 1937 negotiating a contract to raise wages 10 cents an hour, or by more than 15 per cent, with a company in Alabama. The employer was furious. "I've been getting along with the Niggers in my employ for years, and so did my father," he fumed. "Why don't you damn Yankees leave us alone! You came down here seventy-five years ago, and left a helluva mess after you. And you'll do it again. Damn me for ever voting for Roosevelt."

He fumed on, "These Niggers will just work a day less each week if we pay them four dollars a week more. They'll lay off and get drunk. All they need is saltback and hooch. You're pro-

---

[1] Arnold J. Toynbee, "Russia and the West," *Harper's Magazine* (March, 1953), as reprinted in *Gentlemen, Scholars and Scoundrels,* Harper & Brothers, New York, 1959, p. 616.

posing that they earn five days' pay in four, and have an extra day to get drunk on my time and money."

I remember telling this overwrought employer, "These people are starved for all the things America can produce. Pay them more money. Get them in debt for new autos, stoves, ice boxes, radios, silk panties for their ladies, and new Sunday suits for themselves, and they'll work everyday. Make them work and pay, and if you don't give it to them they'll go where they can get it or hold down an extra job as soon as they can find one. And this is not the last pay raise they'll get from you."

He signed and paid the 10-cent increase. And his employees are in debt today for all the things that I mentioned and all the new products that have since come on the American market. This basic process in development in America is sweeping everything in its path, and it cannot be arrested by interfering with the production of goods, whetting of appetites, and the satisfying of needs—real, imagined, and induced.

During my last years in the union, 1941-1946, I took a special interest in advancing the cause of Negroes. My Pitt economics professor, Frank Tyson, drew me into the Urban League movement. I read the *Pittsburgh Courier* regularly. My wife and I went to Harrisburg with Judge Homer S. Brown and his wife to fight for a state fair employment practices act (FEPC). He was a leader in the state legislature then. We had breakfast at our home, and drove two hundred miles nonstop to Harrisburg. We couldn't eat together at any restaurant along the road. I talked Robert C. Enos, an old line American who was president of the Standard Steel Spring Company, into coming to Harrisburg with me to testify for a Fair Employment Practices Law. We didn't get the bill passed in 1944-1945, but it is on the statute books in Pennsylvania today. Clinton Golden, to whom I am indebted for my opportunity in the labor movement among much else, warned me, "Harold, you spend so much time on the Negro problem, and people will be suspecting you of being a Communist." "So be it," I replied, "but you know that the Communist leadership only thrives in the absence of all other leadership." Clint Golden agreed, and I kept pushing the Negro cause.

Each step forward in the three E's unwinds American Negroes and other minorities one wrap more from the bonds of restrictions in which the white men who got here first originally tied them. Those individuals in each group who exert the greatest individual initiative are the ones who get unwound the most and the fastest. Freedom for no man, no group, comes on a silver platter. You don't get freedom without fighting for it, and you don't keep it except by keeping up the fight at home and around the world.

Fletcher Williams illustrates how the individual finds freedom through organization. He was a large, likable, intense Negro steelworker earning $4.50 a day as a chipper in the Duquesne, Pennsylvania, works of U.S. Steel in 1934. His job was to cut out the bad seams from billets with a heavy, deafening, body-shaking, air-hammer chisel. This job is now done by $25.00-a-day steelworkers who push buttons that operate automatic descarfing machines for removing surface defects. This is an example of the technological foundation for the three E's. The background to Fletcher's story begins in our nation's capital on Memorial Day, 1934. I was in Washington with the rank and filers who were threatening a steel strike. We tried to see F.D.R. in person and got as far as his outer office. But we saw everyone else of importance around him, who proposed that the steel strike be held in abeyance and that elections be held in the meanwhile. I rashly dashed off a press release for the rank and filers calling F.D.R.'s election proposal "just so much bunk." The anti-Roosevelt papers put it on the front page. But the steelworkers resented it, and this was the beginning of the downfall of the rank and filers' brief control of the union in 1934.

We hung around Washington for a few more weeks, during which we issued press releases, written by some experienced old newspapermen. We called the N.R.A. (National Recovery Act) the "national run around" and tried to overcome my "so-much-bunk" blunder by saying, "We object to General Johnson (N.R.A. chief) hanging more dead cats on the President." But to no avail. By June 15 William Green, venerable head of the American Federation of Labor was speaking to a reconvened convention in Pittsburgh, the rank and filers lost control of the Amalgamated Association of Iron, Steel and Tin Workers, which reverted to the tired old men who stayed in control until 1936 when John L. Lewis and Philip Murray bought them out to form the predecessor of today's United Steelworkers of America. No strike was called, but F.D.R. did appoint a National Steel Labor Relations Board on June 28, which held hearings in the old Federal Building in Pittsburgh during a summer, which was before America was rich enough to live, as it increasingly does, in air-conditioned comfort.

This is where my friend Fletcher had his day in court. The Board was chaired by Chief Justice Walter P. Stacy of the North Carolina Supreme Court. The attorney for U.S. Steel was Raoul Desvernine, who later became president of Crucible Steel Company. The jurisdiction of the Board was restricted to cases of demonstrated unrest. Raoul, a brilliant lawyer, was in his prime, forty-three years old, and he did a masterly job of building his case, fact by fact, witness by witness, proving that no industrial unrest existed in Duquesne, Pennsylvania. Fletcher had been led into several damaging, simple, honest statements of fact by this master of legal surgery, who, confident that he had his case proved and won, turned on poor, old, trembling Fletcher and demanded, "Tell this Board where all the unrest is that your union alleges!" Fletcher looked at the presiding officer, slowly leaned his huge bulk forward, raised his right hand to his breast, stared into his questioner's face, and said, "That thar' unrest I'se speak of is rawght here in ma he-art!"

Everyone in the room laughed and applauded but Desvernine, who several years later told me that no witness had ever beaten him quite so completely as old Fletcher Williams, who spoke for workers, white and colored. Especially the latter, who during the five-year, 1933-1938, Roosevelt social revolution in America unwound one more wrap from the political-economic bonds of slavery in which the white people of America had tied them, after Abraham Lincoln had untied the legal bonds. Freedom for our colored citizens is still too limited for us to be able to call ourselves a full democracy. We are still in the process of becoming one, as freedom is not a final condition—it is merely the opening of the door to self-development, for white and colored Americans alike.

The doors of opportunity not only have to be opened, as they are being, but the American Negroes have to take full advantage of these opportunities, which they are not doing with the vigor that is required to match their impatience for personal betterment. American Jews, for example, have had restricted opportunities for engineering and scientific jobs in America until the Nazis marched into Poland twenty-one short years ago. But as the need for such trained personnel has been accelerating from A-bombs to jet engines to solid fuels to missiles to rockets to guidance systems to better alloy steels, ad infinitum, American Jewish boys have been taking advantage of these new opportunities, previously closed to them or strictly limited.

The essential difference between the American Negro and the American Indian is that the former are part of the living processes of America, while the Indians are suspended in a state of perpetual hibernation. They are both penned up, the latter in reservations and the Negroes in their own sections of town. But the colored Americans, who are at the bottom of the economic scale, are on the slow climb to the three E's. They cannot be stopped as they are a functioning part of living, growing America in development. Yet they must beware of the doctrinaires who, if they can, will pen them up into permanent colored reservations in our large cities and down on the farm.

John Galbraith, in advocating "The Affluent Society," proposes to stop the natural growth of the processes of production —as if he or anyone else could, though obviously they can delay them. He writes of the four-day work week and says it is a fact that "we do not urgently need the goods that are produced on the other two or three" days.[2] I would like to take this author

---

[2] John Kenneth Galbraith, *The Affluent Society*, Houghton Mifflin Company, Boston, 1959, p. 105.

through Harlem in New York and the Hill in Pittsburgh and show him where the goods that we are not producing, but can produce, are urgently needed; and also show him thousands of unemployed workers who would like to do the producing.

His proposed amendment to Unemployment Compensation, for example, he calls Cyclically Graduated Compensation (C.G.C.). Since colored workers are the last hired and the first laid off, his C.G.C. would put them increasingly on a permanent dole, to hibernate for time immemorial. American workers, regardless of color, living on unemployment compensation or on relief, live better than do the colored people in any other country in the world. But the American Negro is part of America, and he insists on being given the opportunity to climb the economic ladder to the same heights as his fellow Americans whose skin is generally of a different pigmentation. As an employer in Beaver Falls I tried to open the doors of opportunity for colored workers. They have to take advantage of such opportunities before they get economically lynched by such proposals as Galbraith's C.G.C.

America develops onward. I sit beside colored Americans when I ride the airplanes. I find them at Howard Johnson's restaurants when I stop for a snack along Pennsylvania's turnpike. Negroes register with me at the hotels where I stay across America. They can't go everywhere—yet. Many doors are still closed. But I, too, find many doors still closed. They will open one by one, some by themselves, some with an easy push, and some doors of Jim Crow are so sticky you have to use a crowbar to pry them open. Persuasion and education by themselves are not always strong enough to evoke the inner humanity of exploiters, whether their exploitation be by design or passive acceptance of inherited inhumanity-to-man customs and practices.

I have always taken a special pride in seeing Negroes in places where the doors were closed to them before my children were born. But now I hardly notice them. When my grandchildren begin to ride airplanes and space ships, they will not notice their fellow passengers who are colored Americans; they won't know anything different. In 1945 Louis Adamic wrote about the tactful work being done by Negroes and Whites, South and North, toward justice and cooperation, toward the time when these lines by Langston Hughes will have only historical meaning for the Negro:

> "Oh, yes,
> I may say it plain,
> America never was America to me,
> And yet I swear this oath—
> 'America will be.' "[3]

The job of the leaders of America's colored people is to agitate for emergence, to make the white majority respond to their demand for a place in the sun in a way that the emerging people elsewhere are doing. My own case illustrates the problem. I have cast my views in terms of the inner conflict of my conservative nature and creative urges. This conflict, this dilemma, pulls at the mind and heart of most white Americans. The deep widespread reverence for Dr. Albert Schweitzer evidences the compassion of white Americans to humanize their relations with Negroes. This creative urge lies smoldering in our bosoms. The leadership job of dedicated Negroes is to agitate, agitate, agitate so that our natural conservative nature does not smother the moral spark that is within us to further the work that Abraham Lincoln advanced so significantly.

The white community's treatment of our colored people is basically the test of our ability to live up to our Judaic-Christian principles. If we fail in this test we can rot talking about our place in the world. The Negro leaders who think their job will be done for them by the white man who is under pressure to prove his overseas preachments of equality by practicing them more fully at home will rot with us all. The task falls on both of our shoulders because too many of our colored people are underdeveloped. To transform a vast majority of them into self-developing people is the job at hand for which Dr. Albert Schweitzer has shown the way. But no matter how many Albert

---

[3] Louis Adamic, *A Nation of Nations,* Harper & Brothers, New York, 1944, p. 214.

Schweitzers we grow in America, we have to create an economy of full production and full employment to nurture a self-developing Negro community.

THE AFFLUENT SOCIETY IS A STATIC CONCEPT
IN CONFLICT WITH THE PROCESSES OF PRODUCTION

The author of *The Affluent Society*, John K. Galbraith, is an economic specialist interested in doctrinal development. His method of thought is to identify "the conventional wisdom"—accepted doctrine—show its speciousness, and advance a new doctrine to become accepted "conventional wisdom." This doctrinaire method of thinking is the opposite of living-process thinking that is employed throughout this book. Galbraith's is the old way of thinking. His doctrine of the affluent society is the opposite of a self-developing society.

The affluent society concept quickly became part of our conventional wisdom, as it serves the need of flattering the national ego. While intended to focus attention on the widespread poverty of public services, it spreads the false ideas that America has conquered private poverty and that funds for increasing our public services have to come out of reductions in private expenditures. It is like *The Ugly American* which pretended to focus attention on the need for more effective Point Four aid, only to fan the antiyellow prejudices to leave the Southeast Asian peoples to their own fates. The authors of these two books that appealed to national pride in one case, and, in the other, to national prejudice, should have titled their books respectively *The Poor Society* and *The Handsome American*. Whether they still would have been best sellers is another question.

Self-developing America is in the process of demonstrating that individual private poverty can be conquered in this lifetime. We have not conquered poverty for at least 20 per cent of our people, and our continuing victory over poverty for the majority of Americans is dependent upon our extending it to everybody everywhere including our own 36 million poor. Private well-being—overflowing into crass self-indulgence for many Americans and in many things for most Americans—is a formative process leading to the development of public well-being. The processes of production have to be accelerated to operate our farms and industrial potential at full capacity to employ all of our own people, to extend our victory over poverty to our people at the bottom of the economic ladder, to conquer the poverty of our public and community services, and to conquer elementary individual and community poverty in the emerging, third-party nations. This summarizes my living-process thinking that embraces the whole of our society as a leading self-developing country in the world. Now let us summarize the doctrinaire thinking of an economic specialist that restricts itself to America.

The affluent society concept is a static doctrine that makes its case by disproving itself, which concludes that since we have reduced "poverty from the problem of a majority to that of a minority . . . we can afford to give those who are unemployed the goods that enable them to sustain their accustomed standard of living. If we don't need what the unemployed do not make, we can obviously afford them what they customarily eat and wear."[4]

Upon reading *The Affluent Society* we find out how very poor we really are. We are far from a finished affluent society, and we appear privately affluent largely by the contrasting poverty of our public sector. Nowhere in his essay does Galbraith explicitly define his doctrine. His introductory chapter begins with "the assumption of affluence" and "the problems of an affluent world." The closest that he comes to a definition is in his eighteenth chapter: "The line which divides our area of wealth from our area of poverty is roughly that which divides privately produced and marketed goods and services from publicly rendered services."[5] His doctrine stands on the premise of "ever-increasing opulence in privately produced goods" competing with "public poverty," but gets defined only in the contrasting of "private opulence and public squalor."

[4] Galbraith, *op. cit.*, p. 339.
[5] *Ibid.*, p. 251.

Galbraith sets up a backboard off which he bounces his own ideas. "Conventional wisdom . . . a name for the ideas which are esteemed at any time for their acceptability." He lumps all ideas and concepts that he criticizes into the "conventional wisdom," which term he employs over a hundred times, implying that any doctrine or idea that is less wise than his is "conventional wisdom." It is a neat shorthand phrase which he employs as a forensic device. He makes it clear that he does not want to join Henry Charles Carey (1793-1879) "in the neglect reserved for American heretics," and he points out that Paul Mazur's "forthright philistinism . . . doubtless cost him scholarly attention." Finally, in defending John Maynard Keynes against his disciples, Galbraith laments, "Such is the fate of anyone who becomes a part of the conventional wisdom."

He employs "the conventional wisdom" with seemingly equal vigor against the liberals as well as the conservatives. I was taken in by his brave courage in fighting everybody else's "conventional wisdom" until I got to the last chapter.

Scholarly discourse . . . has its rules and they must be respected. In this area nothing counts so heavily against a man as to be found attacking the values of the public at large and seeking to substitute his own. Technically his crime is arrogance. Actually it is ignorance of the rules. In any case he is automatically removed from the game . . . The reader will now appreciate the care with which the defenses against such an attack have been prepared.[6]

Lo and behold! Galbraith is a candidate for "the conventional wisdom."

The foundation for his entire program—"we can afford some unemployment in the interest of stability"—he states is "a proposition, incidentally, of impeccably conservative antecedents," and he creates the neatest rationale for a bigger sales tax in every state that I have ever seen in print. He has tried to conceal his catering to or fear of the big conservatives behind this artful forensic device of "the conventional wisdom." They are not ten feet tall.

[6] *Ibid.*, p. 350.

The conventional wisdom against which he sets his affluent society doctrine is accepted on its most vital political-economic dogma—namely, the planned idleness of large numbers of people and of a husky chunk of our industrial and farm capacity. He ends up proposing to pay the unemployed to stay idle, the way we pay farmers to keep productive acreage idle. The consequences of this to Negro unemployed has already been noted. That their plight would be shared by an even greater number of poor whites is no comfort. To live is to function. An affluent society, if one ever develops on our planet, cannot deep-freeze people. Job opportunities must be provided for all people willing and able to work. Supplying the underfed needs of public services is one of the processes in development opening up such new jobs for more and more people every year. Welfare enterprisers will produce for these needs. Madison Avenue, for example, is already inducing congregational wants for U.S. Steel's prefabricated churches. Prefab, movable schools are on the market already. This is America.

Galbraith proposes to supply the public sector at the expense of the private. To propose that we reduce individual private expenditures by raising sales taxes so that the state governments can provide more public services is to propse a redistribution of the wealth of our median-income families. I agree with Galbraith that we can get nowhere trying to redistribute the wealth of the rich in America. As we shall discuss later, the American formula is that the rich get richer by facilitating the poor to become less poor. This cannot be done by running our economy at 80 per cent of capacity. That extra wealth of increased production distributed broadly in the economy is the source of the poor becoming less poor, while the rich become richer. Public poverty has to be cured out of increased production, not by lowering the private living standards of our people. When we stop producing more each year, we run out of increased wealth with which to raise living standards. Then it is a question of whose wealth gets redistributed—the rich or the poor. Galbraith has fallen into the error of proposing to redistribute the alleged affluence of the poor! He calls workers affluent just because they are earning four to five thousand dollars a year, when they can get a full year's work; and says that seven to fifteen thousand dollar-a-year families, who similarly are struggling to keep their budgets balanced, are affluent. That's not poverty, but it is not affluence either. It is an ugly castigation to hang on the heads of America's millions who are struggling from pay-day to pay-day to make both ends meet. It is just what the conservatives of the conventional wisdom love to hear.

The American people can have both an abundant private life and an opulent public life of adequate school rooms staffed by well-paid and well-trained teachers; enough hospital beds attended by well-paid and well-trained nurses, technicians, and doctors; roomy parks and picnic areas along unpolluted streams and lakes; well-kept sanitary cities; homes designed as a way of life in place of square boxes in which people and appliances are stored; and all of the other better things in life. It is not either-or, but ever-increasing well-being in both privately produced goods and public community needs and services. And the source of this increased public and private wealth is increased production and higher productivity.

Galbraith shares the conventional wisdom's fear of "inflation —the endemic problem of the affluent society."[7] He proposes a "substitute for production as a source of income" because "finding jobs for everyone" causes "persistent inflation." He concludes: "So long as we are committed by the imperatives of employment and income to operate at the capacity of plant and labor force, we shall have the threat of rising prices."[8] His answer is to "divorce production from security" by instituting Cyclically Graduated Compensation—that is, "unemployment compensation should be increased as unemployment increases and should be diminished as full employment is approached."[9] He elaborates this to pay $71.20 a week in unemployment compensation to a

[7] *Ibid.*, p. 238.
[8] *Ibid.*, p. 293.
[9] *Ibid.*, p. 298.

worker whose normal pay is $80.00 for as long as unemployment last.[10] The Federal government would do the paying above the normal state unemployment compensation of $36.00 in his example. This is a welfare-state equivalent of the welfare-enterprise annual wage that I have been advocating since 1943 and shall discuss later.

The deficiency of Galbraith's method of thought is that he subordinates the processes of life and production to the spinning and fabrication of doctrines. This is in contrast to the living-process method of thought that *Self-developing America* employs to open up new ways of viewing and feeling about the problems and issues of our times. America is a self-developing society in the process of becoming affluent—maybe, we hope. The task is to facilitate the processes of production to achieve affluence in all walks of life, and not to spin economic doctrines that become part of the accepted conventional wisdom.

NATURE OF AMERICAN ECONOMIC REVOLUTION

The distinctive nature of the American Economic Revolution is illustrated by La Hacienda De San Gabriel in San Gabriel De Las Palmas, located adjacent to the Mexico-Acapulco highway with its entrance at kilometro 116, approximately 70 miles from Mexico City.[11] Henry "Ty" Felker, an American engineer who has been restoring this old sugar plantation's buildings and grounds into a leisure-time retreat, was showing me through the stately place that had been for over four centuries a private feudal domain. Its owners have included the heirs of Hernando Cortes, and such notables as Alexander Dumas have been entertained in the great house of San Gabriel. So much for the tourist; now for the scholar.

This place had been ransacked by the revolutionaries and occupied in 1912 by the agrarian leader Emiliano Zapata after the death of Madero. Their formula for a revolution was to kill the feudal exploiters and destroy the productive enterprise. They

[10] *Ibid.*, p. 300-301.

[11] This is also a commercial; I invested in the rehabilitation of the Hacienda into a hotel.

burned the stable filled with fine, thoroughbred horses. The screams of the dying horses as they were being cremated drove the owner, safely hidden in another building, mad. Had he devoted himself to people as he did to horses, he would have been another kind of man. The people he exploited revolted. The sugar production and mill were put out of usage. The rich were destroyed, and the poor lost their wealth-producing facility. That was their revolution. Everybody lost. They are still struggling against poverty. Freedom from the exploiters and freedom for self-development are not the same thing.

As I walked through the abandoned sugar mill buildings I realized how sharply this all contrasted with my American experience. Our economic revolutionary formula has been so different! We have said to our rich and mighty, "Okay, you can keep what you have. We don't even mind your getting richer. Just so long as you facilitate, or quit denying us the freedom to facilitate, the processes of our getting all of the necessities and more and more of the better things in life. You cooperate to this extent, and we will let you keep what you have and do not even mind if you get richer in the course of developments. We will even facilitate your getting richer if in the process we become less poor." Ours is the constructive revolutionary formula, not the destructive one. The average American, our common man, is better off today than in the 1920's and was better off in the 1920's than he was at the beginning of the century, not because of enjoying a bigger share of the national income. He is better off because he has helped produce a bigger national income which he shares with the rich and mighty in about the same proportion. Every decade he has had it better. He will have it better as each new decade progresses into history. This is the American Revolution of human betterment and freedom. This is our victory over poverty for 144 million of our people, which we are in the process of extending to our 36 million who are still ill-fed, ill-housed, ill-clothed, and ill-educated. This is the revolution that we are extending to the billion people in the world, whose plane of living is below that of America's 36 million poor.

The key questions are: How did we do it? How are we continuing to do it?

The answer is: We have conquered poverty in America by producing more, not by redistributing the capital of our rich. A fellow worker in the vineyard of American thought, Herbert Croly, who attempted a synthesis of a developing America in his time and with considerable success in *The Promise of American Life* (1909), wrote in another work:

A democratic nation cannot provide the mass of the people with the needed opportunity of activity and life merely by distributing among them the wealth owned by a minority. . . . The masses need, of course, a larger share of material welfare, but they need most of all an increased opportunity of wholesome and stimulating social labor.[12]

The rich are not sharing their capital. They have been getting constantly richer. Those who had it at the beginning of the twentieth century have much more today. Andrew W. Mellon in 1900 was not as rich a man as Richard K. Mellon, his nephew, is in 1960. John D. Rockefeller was not as rich a man in 1900 as his heirs are in 1960. Henry Ford II is a richer man today than the first Henry Ford was in 1920. The DuPonts are wealthier today than they were in 1900. A comparative analysis of the balance sheets of U.S. Steel, General Motors, and General Electric, for example, for the year each was founded with those of 1960 reveals how well these companies have fared, while their employees and customers also have been climbing up the ladder of human welfare and freedom.

When you know, realize, appreciate, understand, and comprehend this fundamental about America, then you begin to perceive the essential character of the land of the free and the home of the brave. Greed has not been conquered. The lust for personal gain is as strong in the 1960's as it was a century ago when Karl Marx observed man's inhumanity to man. Self-interest still is dominant in the daily actions of Americans. "What's in it for me?" is the question on everybody's lips, everyday, everywhere

[12] Herbert Croly, *Progressive Democracy*, The Macmillan Company, New York, p. 422.

in America. "A man's gotta look out for himself first," is the operating policy of Americans. We would all be at each other's throats, as Marx reasoned, if it were not for the restraining practices of welfare enterprise in which competition is a necessary form of social control.

The other side of the coin is that the rich get richer by facilitating the poor to become less poor. The moral character of our rich and mighty and our spiritual forces are responsible for transforming the greedy practices of private capitalism into the current practices of welfare enterprise, where almost every private and public institution must, and does, serve the common good; and when it wanders from this path, it is eventually forced to return to it. Labor unions are not excluded.

The idea of the big corporations giving up some of their profits to pay higher wages is one that the big unions have not been able to enforce. It is based on sharing existing wealth. It is counter to the proposition of the poor getting more by making the rich richer. The editorial writers who annually suggest that the wage-price spiral be solved by the big corporations cutting prices by reducing their profits, I am afraid, reveal their lack of comprehension of the fundamental proposition underlying the American Revolution. My basic judgment is expressed in this fundamental proposition: Workers can only get more benefits through union-management cooperation (Humanation) that helps to feed the cow.

The entire fabric of union gains since F.D.R., who facilitated their development a quarter of a century ago, has been built upon getting more by producing more. With many smaller companies that had to absorb more of the higher wage costs than they could pass on in higher prices, the unions have been able to redistribute existing wealth. They have busted small companies by the dozens and forced them by the hundreds to combine with larger corporations or go broke. It is exploitation by big unions of small companies against which the exploited must revolt or go under. This is one of the inequities in industry that the tying of wages to each company's productivity (in contrast to what big steel or big auto did) will help correct. A counterrevolt of small industry is brewing.

During the postwar wage-price spiral every time that the big unions have upped wages, the big corporations upped prices. This is called inflation. Actually the big corporations have been using the fear of inflation as a tool to prevent the big unions from cutting their profit margins. The time has come for them to cease sheltering their purpose behind the continued threat of inflation.

We turn now to codeveloping America.

CHAPTER NINE

CODEVELOPMENT IN STEEL

This book employs the spiritual interpretation of history—processes in development—whose method is to emphasize the inner, creative nonmaterialistic forces of man, in contrast to the materialistic method of historical interpretation that places primary emphasis on the outer, physical products of these inner forces. The products are the branches of life. The inner creative —spiritual—forces are the main life-giving trunk of the tree of individual life. David J. McDonald, president of the United Steelworkers of America, and Roger Blough, Board Chairman of the United States Steel Corporation, and their associate officers in the union and the several basic steel-producing firms are lost in the branches and do not see the main trunk. This was confirmed by the record-breaking 116-day steel strike in 1959. Codevelopment in steel contains a useful analogy for our discussion of codevelopment in the world.[1]

These two sets of organizations have been codeveloping together for almost a quarter of a century. The individual steel-

[1] I am indebted to William Ernest Hocking for the concept of codevelopment.

119

workers organized to remind their exploiting employers of their humanity and to evoke it from them. This they have done. In the process the union leaders have utilized the union organization to exploit the employers and, in turn, the steelworkers whose welfare is dependent upon the success of their employers. The union members and company employees—who are one—are caught in conflicting loyalties that produce despair, distrust, and antagonism. They are split down the middle by being forced to function in the dual roles of union members and company employees, and are in the process of revolting against both their union leaders and company officials to regain their natural wholeness and moral health that goes with it.

While conflict and strife have marked the sad tale of the growth and codevelopment of the United States Steel Corporation and the United Steelworkers of America, cooperation and the interpenetration of one's affairs with the other's hold the promise of their continuing codevelopment without mutual annihilation, which would take the form of compulsory government intervention. The 1939-1945 war disciplined them to cooperate to produce Steel for Victory through union-management cooperation to raise productive efficiency. They performed in unison at optimum effectiveness, because the steelworkers were able to function as whole moral individuals with no conflict between their roles as union members and company employees. The two collectivities to which they had given themselves to seek personal fulfillment were united by one overriding principle: to win the war by producing more steel. This was war, and not its moral equivalent.

The chaos created by union agitation among steelworkers over wage inequities from 1936 to 1945 was another instance that disciplined them to cooperate in 1946 to 1952 in the most extensive program of union-management cooperation in the history of the industry. It was the moral equivalent of war: one overriding principle, the correction of wage inequities, organized them into a common effort because the force of circumstances compelled each side to practice their inner humanity, the one to the other.

During the 1959 steel strike I called to the attention of each side the overriding principle—periodic unemployment and unstable annual incomes—that circumstances are forcing them to accept as a common discipline around which to organize collaborative programs.

The deliberate "act of creative risk" that I outlined for U.S. Steel to propose—union-management cooperation (humanation) and the annual wage—could be made only vis-à-vis the steelworkers. Nothing would be gained making it vis-à-vis the union. The social conditions have to precede their legislation into a formal contract. The channeling of their codevelopment into lines where cooperation predominates over conflict can only be achieved through winning the hearts, minds, and souls of the steelworkers and enabling them to function as whole human beings. That cannot be left as the exclusive prerogative of union leaders, whose position compels them to accent the conflicts.

Where the union has failed to facilitate the processes of collaborative efforts to raise productive efficiency and achieve the annual wage by preaching "capitalists who are only interested in profits" to the steelworkers, the steel company leaders have to respond, "We are welfare enterprisers interested in people." By so doing, the union will have to respond in kind, "Show us." By showing the steelworkers the path to a more harmonious process of codevelopment, the steel companies will have broken the vicious circle of mutual distrust and fear that characterized the 1959 steel strike. Its resolution was appeased through political intervention by Vice-President Richard M. Nixon, as it has been since President Harry S. Truman first intervened to settle the 1946 steel strike. The way to break through this vicious circle is discussed in Chapter Thirteen. This domestic development in process is hopefully analogous to the developments in process between the U.S.A. and U.S.S.R.

THE 1959 STEEL STRIKE

After twenty-two years of wage-price collective bargaining (1937-1959) in which the steel union played the predominant role of creator by introducing wage and fringe-benefit changes, the creative role shifted to management. The industry leaders forced the long strike to compel the change to wage-productivity bargaining under which the union has to help feed the corporate cow as well as milk her. And the union leaders became the conservatives. Both the labor leaders and management have concentrated on the economic man, while the inborn dignity of steelworkers has been neglected. This has tended to make automatons out of the human beings who work in the steel industry, and they are demanding—as surely as unconsciously—a more creative role in the productive processes and union function that will give expression to their personalities and inherent dignity and a greater meaning to their lives as individuals. These inner forces are compelling the United States Steel Corporation and the United Steelworkers of America into a collaborative, joint effort to advance their own separate interests by promoting the general welfare of both. This formative process has been in development since they embarked on the road of raising their respective wages and prices at the expense of the public (general welfare), which they no longer can do. Hence the shift to raising their real wages and profits (by other than just price increases) through joint efforts to raise productivity which will rebound to the general welfare of all.

During the 1959 steel strike the union leaders, employing the weapons of old, painted management as being interested primarily in profits, not people. Of course, they portrayed themselves as being interested in people first. But were they? They were just trying to get their members more money. Management was trying to open the door to everybody joining the creative phase of running the enterprise so that they could earn more money. Philip Murray had seen that this day would come, and he left his successors a general guidebook to follow. He knew that once a man had a full belly and job security, he would not be in heaven. He knew that the road to the Kingdom of God on earth was going from one struggle to another. Murray and I had a complete and full understanding on this fundamental proposition: A man is a man, and the union's job does not end with bread-and-butter collective bargaining. Each union member has an inherent dignity, and he will not be satisfied with just material gains; he wants, and needs, ways of participating in the affairs of his union and the operation of his employing company that will give a greater meaning to his life. Murray showed how in his *Organized Labor and Production* (1940) which, I suggest, the United Steelworkers of America will soon reprint and circulate to all of its members.

My efforts during the 1950's have been devoted primarily to influencing management. Selling the unions is getting the cart before the horse, because union policy in the main is merely a reaction to the basic policies of industry. Change the latter and the unions will follow although, as illustrated by the long 1959 steel strike, they sometimes have to be dragged into the future by their feet. But this is an old story of how we all—organized labor, industry, politicians, educators, and everybody else—try to preserve our vested interests. The strength of America is that we all, one by one, have to yield when our vested interests conflict with the general welfare of the country as a whole.

During the twenty-two year period of collective bargaining, 1937-1959, both the steel industry and the steel union negotiated themselves into special privileged positions in conflict with the public interest. From 1956 to 1959 steelworkers enjoyed the special privilege of having their wages insulated against the erosion of higher living costs. While every other American continued to be exposed to the ravages of rising prices, union members were able to sustain their real income. Any price rises that followed their money wage increases no longer came out of their pockets. Each time wage increases not justified by productivity were followed by price rises, the union was robbing and plundering those Americans who live on fixed incomes—exploiting them. By pursuing an unchanging collective bargaining program through rapidly changing decades, the union had converted a socially and economically constructive program of collective bargaining into a razor-sharp instrument for exploiting the retired, aged, widows and orphans, schoolteachers, scientists, and all the millions of other Americans who do not enjoy the privilege of automatic protection against increases in their cost of living.

On the other hand, the steel firms for years had insulated themselves against the debilitating effects of higher labor costs by raising factory prices—irrespective of the demand—and making them stick, that is, through administered prices. The mere elimination of the automatic cost-of-living wage increase clause is not the entire solution. There is no justice in denying union members insulation against rising prices, while their employers can continue to insulate themselves against higher labor costs by arbitrarily increasing factory prices. The steel companies and union cannot sustain their positions of insulation against the debilitating effects of higher prices and increased wage costs, while the rest of the 180 million Americans are exposed to the effects of spiraling wages and prices. Administered steel price increases, together with automatic cost-of-living wage increases and enforced wage-rate increases during depressed employment periods (administered wages), are two sides of the same coin. The whole coin has to be recast.

The Kaiser Steel, aluminum industry, and can company settlements in 1959 put a ceiling on the cost-of-living, automatic wage clause, as did the final steel settlement on January 5, 1960. This is transitional toward its complete elimination. The necessary accompanying reform is Humanation in which increased wages are tied to increased productivity as this produces wage raises without corresponding price increases. Higher wage and salary incomes that are accompanied with an increased production of goods and services are not inflationary.

During the 1930's when the unions were replacing unilateral management labor policies with bilateral collective bargaining contracts, wage inequalities were being eliminated, working conditions were being modernized, wages were being raised and hours shortened, I was asking my elders in the labor movement a simple question—namely, what do we do when these gross failings of management have been corrected? The answer was direct, simple, and continued as steel union policy to 1959. I shall paraphrase it:

We shall keep right on asking for more. Our job is to get as much for our members as we can cajole, squeeze, or force out of the companies. It is an easy job, as once we get a new and better contract, we have no further responsibility. It is entirely up to management to find the means to pay the bill. They do not want us sticking our nose into the running of their businesses anyway. So let them sweat out the ways of meeting a constantly rising wage bill every year. We are in the business of selling labor. Each year our job ends when we get the highest price that we can negotiate for the labor of our members.

I can best explain the meaning of the 1959 steel strike by reporting my terminating discussions with Philip Murray that extended over the last half of 1945 and through the first half of 1946. I insisted upon a union policy of union-management cooperation which I define later as Humanation. He conceded that a time would come when the union would have to help feed the cow in order to get more for its members. "But, Harold, that's a long time off," Murray softly argued, "there's a lot more milk in the steel industry for our members before we have to worry our heads about helping management increase efficiency."

His strongest argument against the union pushing a program of joint collaboration was that management itself was dead set against it. Murray was correct on this point, which I tried to argue away by saying, "Management has been against all of the union's program. That is no reason for not adopting collaboration. If the union fights hard enough for it, management will concede in time."

"Not in my time, Harold, you have to let nature take its course," Murray said in an almost inaudible voice, "when management no longer can carry the full load itself, they'll be around asking for the union's help on plant efficiency, but not one day sooner." This remarkable leader, who had a Lincolnian touch of greatness, looked me in the eye and smiled in a manner I shall always remember. He then rose, ending the discussion, "But,

Harold, when that day comes, I won't be around."

Thirteen years later, in 1959, the day came. As long as the steel industry could pass on increased labor costs to its customers, the union could keep on pushing up wages and fringe benefits without assuming responsibility for increased productivity. But the competition of other products (plastics and lighter metals) and of European and Japanese producers, and the limit of the efficiences that management could effect, with available capital funds and without union cooperation, put the squeeze on the steel industry. When the 1959 collective bargaining negotiations began the steel companies said "Uncle." I paraphrase their basic position, "We have had it. No longer can we go along with big wage-cost increases, because the market will not absorb the higher prices that they require. As long as the federal government permits us to negotiate voluntarily, we will not agree to any labor increases that force us to raise prices. But, if the union will co-operate to help raise productivity, we will negotiate modest wage increases within the framework of existing prices." Here is how Walter F. Mumford, the late president of U.S. Steel Corporation who died during the strike, worded it (August 7, 1959, letter to employees):

Steel management has urged upon the Union Leaders . . . to join hands, as employees, their Union, and management should do at all times, in a cooperative endeavor to lower costs, improve the operations, increase production and thus create new economic progress to be shared by the employees, the stockholders, and the customers. In other words, the parties should live within their means and derive real improvements in the standard of living for the employees that would not come out of someone else's pocket or be syphoned off by the shrinking value of the dollar. The starting point to a program of cooperation most certainly would be to dispose of contractual problems which cause friction . . .[and thus] pave the way for a program of cooperative effort to generate new economic progress to be shared by all concerned. . . .

By 1959 steel management came around to asking for the union's cooperation to help on plant efficiency. But Philip Murray was not around. And his successors refused to acknowledge what was happening until they signed their new contract with Kaiser Steel in October that took the first steps into wage-productivity collective bargaining in steel. David J. McDonald did not stop the coming of humanation, though he succeeded in postponing until 1962 the writing of wage-productivity into the U.S. Steel 1960-1962 contract. While the union won the 1959 steel strike, it lost the war; and in losing its first major effort to adopt union-management cooperation—humanation—to raise productivity, the steel companies won the war. Roger Blough was victorious in turning the corner onto the road of wage-productivity bargaining, although David McDonald kept him from getting very far along the new road in the early 1960's.

Two joint committees were created: one to work out the immediate problems of joint collaboration on local plant working rules; the other, a Human Relations Research Committee, to develop longer term ground rules for joint collaboration on the basic phases of productivity. When the next contract comes up in 1962, the parties will begin to formalize in contract language the union-management collaboration that they began to study jointly, and started to practice informally, after the "educational" 1959 steel strike. Wage-price collective bargaining died in 1959. When the contract was signed, Roger Blough did not resort to the old practice of sophistry of saying "let bygones be bygones." Instead he kept on the pressure, in a nation-wide TV-radio broadcast, for the changes to wage-productivity bargaining that have been in process for some years now.

Immediately upon settling the strike, which the papers hailed as a victory for the union—and rightly so—David McDonald flew to Buffalo, New York, and told a victory rally of steelworkers that the creation of the long-term study committee will mean there will never have to be another strike. "The committee will arrive at findings well in advance of the termination of the next agreement," McDonald said, "so that, please God, there will never have to be another steel strike." McDonald is not the first man to pray for Utopia. Roger Blough said:

The truly important thing is the cooperative spirit of all of the people who are banded together in a common effort. There is no problem in this field of production that cannot be solved through this cooperative spirit, for there is no basic conflict of interest between the needs of the company, and the needs of the steelworkers. We are all in the same boat and we need to pull on the oars together. We can do almost anything in a spirit of cooperation and accomplish almost nothing if we have a spirit of dispute and distrust.

In 1956 McDonald declared for "a mutual trusteeship" of union leaders and business executives and criticized "bread and butter unionism." "The people—workers and owners alike— have an overriding interest that will not forever tolerate the futility of unnecessary strikes caused by failure at the bargaining table when there is a better way—a way that pays off for everyone." A rank-and-file revolt in the steel union diverted McDonald from this course as he tried to out-rank-and-file his internal opposition, only to abandon purely "bread and butter" unionism in the end.

Both sides generated an inflation-fear psychosis throughout America during the 1959 strike. The people and their President knew, from a dozen previous steel wage negotiations, that the union would not forgo a wage increase, and that the steel companies would raise prices to offset the wage increase despite the claim of the union that wages could be raised while prices are frozen. This claim the union has never been able to enforce. So the President asked the steel companies to hold the line on prices and the union to temper its wage demands within the limits of productivity—so that prices would not go up.

Neither side listened to the President, although the steel companies stuck to their maximum "voluntary" offer of an annual employment cost increase of 2.7 per cent a year until the President and his Vice-President proposed an "involuntary" settlement, which was adopted, costing 3.5 per cent to 3.75 per cent a year. Whereupon steel wages and fringes (pensions and insurance, which are "private" welfare measures) went up almost 14 cents an hour yearly, with higher steel prices to follow in due course, except when increases in productivity make this unnecessary. But 1959-1960 saw an end to the postwar steel wage-price drama. In the past both sides, after having spent hundreds of thousands of dollars to induce a national fear of inflation, said that the new contract was noninflationary. Dave McDonald repeated this assertion in January, 1960, but Roger Blough said, "If there is any answer to the problem that American industry faces when it tries to reach a noninflationary labor agreement, it's pretty obvious that we, in the steel industry, haven't found it." But he noted that under the 1960-1962 contract hourly employment costs went up "a little less than twice as fast" as in the previous twenty years.

The 1959 steel strike illustrates that the economic man in the steelworkers union has been well provided for. The steel-workers' gross hourly earnings will exceed $4.00 an hour by July, 1962, under the 1960-1962 contract, or $8,320 a year of full employment. While this economic side of man will continue to need attention, just as a man has to shave daily, the union and management leaders are confronted with having to open up the doors to releasing the inherent creativeness that pulsates in steelworkers' bosoms—a process that de-emphasizes the autom-aton nature of industrial work and increases the individual stature of the men and women who produce America's iron and steel.

Philip Murray, had he still been living, would have acknowl-edged the significance of the 1959 steel strike straight away. The odds are that if he were around for 1959 there would still have been a strike. But instead of striking against going into the wage-productivity phase of collective bargaining, Murray would have struck for a price for entering this next development higher than management would have been willing to pay—voluntarily.

When I argued with Murray back in 1945-1946, I frequently referred to his book, *Organized Labor and Production*. My point was that he could not refuse to adopt union-management co-operation without at the same time repudiating his own book. He brushed this aside with the casual but prophetic observation,

"That book will become like a bible for the union someday. It will have to gather dust for some time for reasons that you cannot see today, but you should live long enough to learn that you can't rush things too fast. You have to let nature take its course. Once it comes to a boil, you can lance it. But not any sooner. Be patient, boy, keep your shirt on."

Philip Murray was a soft-spoken man, but he was also as tough as nails. Once my insistence became clear to him he said, "Harold, I'm setting policy in this man's union, and if you try to push union-management cooperation ahead of its time, I'll chop your head off."

The midyear 1946 executive-board meeting of the United Steelworkers of America was held in Thomas Wolfe's country, at the Grove Park Inn near Asheville, North Carolina. I had gone through the intellectual process of resigning, but I found the emotional process overwhelming. I was able to say, "I shall continue to work for my fellow man, because I believe that a life, especially one possessed of a little extra energy and talent, is wasted unless it is spent in the service of his fellow men."

Philip Murray gave me his blessing. Upon my resignation he wrote that I work to "build up those fine constructive labor-management relations that ought to prevail in the American industry." To this *strictum jus* I have adhered uncompromisingly, but my larger interests have been to find the answer to, "What is America?" James B. Carey, President of the I.U.E. Electrical, Radio, and Machine Workers, complains, "I see the bridges between labor and management falling away." Back in 1935 I traveled with Jim Carey to help build the bridges that have grown old and rusty during the intervening quarter of a century. New and better bridges are needed now.

It is my hope to play a continuing role in facilitating this process—the building of new bridges, releasing creativity, and raising the dignity of individuals—and to this end I shall continue to address myself directly to leaders of labor and industry.

CHAPTER TEN

HUMANATION

It is essential to understand the processes of releasing the inherent creativeness of the millions of people who work in our mines, mills, and factories, because America may celebrate the centennial of the Civil War, 1961-1965, with an economic civil war that may mistakenly be described in the materialistic terms of class warfare. When the labor strikes, management lockouts, and legislative labor reforms of the 1960's will actually have another meaning: industrial management has to facilitate the release of individual creativity to fulfill its welfare enterprise obligations. The objective toward which we are striving in developing the nonmaterialistic side of man, as defined by Ordway Tead in *Administration: Its Purpose and Performance*, is, "If I am the instrument of having you work on a job which entails only a portion of your talents and your interests, I am morally guilty in respect to the integrity of your personality at work."

During the 1936-1942 years in the steelworkers union when Clinton S. Golden and I wrote *The Dynamics of Industrial Democracy* (1942), Golden had laid the groundwork for our writing venture into the future by guiding Philip Murray into joint authorship with Morris Llewellyn Cooke to produce *Organized Labor and Production* (Harper & Brothers, 1940).

In the *Dynamics* we formulated thirty-seven "principles of union-management relations." We cautioned that these "principles are not immutable rules of union-management relations, because they are the outgrowth of changing conditions and, as a consequence, are themselves constantly subject to change." Our book served as a guide to the wage-price phase of collective bargaining that ended with the 1959 steel strike, but it also outlines the basic approach to the wage-productivity phase that is being ushered in with many birth pains during the 1960's.

The war extended the careers of Golden and myself in the steelworkers union a few extra years since we were able to mount an offensive out of the War Production Board in 1943 of joint labor-management committees to increase production, eliminate waste, and raise productivity. But as soon as the war was won and over, Philip Murray shut them off. Managements shut them off. They both agreed on shutting off this experiment —a successful one, too. I stayed on to see the union through its enormously successful strike of 1946 that launched the 1946-1959 wage-price period of collective bargaining. Golden left a few weeks after me and Joseph Scanlon with him.

Scanlon came out of the open-hearth department of Empire Steel Corporation in Mansfield, Ohio, and provided Golden and me with our first "showpiece" experiment of union-management cooperation in a basic steel company. He joined my Research Department, did significant work for the union, and went on to creating more "showpieces" for individual creativity in several manufacturing plants in New England. He taught at the Massachusetts Institute of Technology until he died in 1956. M.I.T. now offers a course in union-management cooperation. Golden went on to teach at Harvard, serve in the Federal government, and produce a series of studies on the "Causes of Industrial Peace" under the auspices of the National Planning Association of which he is vice-chairman.

I have employed the principles of humanation to outcompete

my competitors and to facilitate the processes that are leading toward the practical employment of the brains as well as the brawn of the men and women who work in America for a living. Much has been accomplished in tapping the brain power and inner resources of United States' work force during the last two decades, but the big steps in this direction are still ahead of us. One of the finest things in life is to be creatively employed. With ten years of management and business enterprise experience under my hat I reformulated the concept of union-management cooperation as originally outlined in *The Dynamics* into "humanation,"[1] and delivered a paper by this title to the National Industrial Conference Board in May, 1956. This is part of the next development in our culture.

HUMANATION

Humanation is the full release of the human creativeness of the working and managing forces, voluntarily cooperating with each other to apply their creative energies to their daily work through organized programs of joint participation in the productive processes. The purpose of humanation is to increase efficiency, reduce costs, eliminate waste, and raise quality in order to enlarge the total size of the corporate pie for the mutual benefit of workers, managers, owners, and consumers. The function of humanation is to bring everyone, irrespective of his point of authority or responsibility, into full participation in the productive process. Its organization is built around the individual and not the machine.

Humanation results not only in higher living standards and greater profits, but—more importantly—in new dimensions for the lives of the participants that give a greater meaning to their personalities as human beings and add to the dignity of the individual. To release the full creativeness of people, it is essential to eliminate their worries about holding onto their jobs. A pay-by-the-year program that assures an adequate annual income to

[1] *Humanation*, Management Record, November, 1956, National Industrial Conference Board.

everyone is the foundation for humanation. Its continuing success requires that part of the proceeds of increased productivity be used to retrain or otherwise rehabilitate those individuals adversely affected by changes wrought through this full release of the creativeness of the working and managing forces.

Far from being competitors, humanation and automation are collaborators in the limitless American quest for all of the necessities and more and more of the better things in life for everyone. Automation by itself cannot fulfill these objectives. Industry's technology experts will not be able to create mechanical and electronic ways (that can also be financed) of upping productivity fast enough in the years ahead.

At a "Productivity In Industry" discussion conducted by The National Industrial Conference Board, the Commissioner of Labor Statistics, Ewan Clague, was asked: "Is there any indication that there has been a significant gain in productivity in the postwar period, owing, perhaps, to automation?" Mr. Clague replied:

"Not that automation isn't important; it is, and perhaps will be more important in the next five years. But as far as our figures are concerned, there is nothing more spectacular occurring in manufacturing productivity now, after World War II, than there was after World War I. In fact, productivity rose faster from 1919 to 1925 than it did from 1947 to 1953. Insofar as automation may be a factor modifying previous relationships between production and manhours, our general conclusion to date is that it has no significant effect." This conclusion is confirmed by the statistics of the Bureau of Labor Statistics for the years since 1953.

The underlying philosophy of humanation is summed up in this slogan: "People Are Our Most Important Concern." While automation has essentially the same purpose as humanation, it is "a flight from labor." Its philosophy is summed up by General Electric with the slogan: "Progress Is Our Most Important Product."

Automation dehumanizes people and debases the dignity

of the individual. It tends to fragmentize the personality into meaningless parts. This makes the daily work of millions of people a bore, which forces them either into stultification or into finding outlets for their inherent creativeness away from their employment. In contrast, humanation makes daily work fun. People enjoy going to their jobs where they are free and able to apply their creative energies and where they receive recognition for their contributions. Humanation can be observed in a plant where the individuals put as much energy and vigor into punching in their cards as the automatons of automation put into punching out their cards.

While the development of machines to increase output and lighten the burdens of labor has characterized the Industrial Revolution for over two centuries, automation is a recent movement. It is barely a quarter of a century old, born out of the sitdown strikes, Roosevelt's New Deal, the C.I.O. labor unions, and collective bargaining. Automation is management's counter-offensive to union leaders' wage and fringe programs. For almost three decades now, each time the unions have raised wage costs, management has gone to its arsenal of automation to develop technological ways of offsetting these higher costs. It is very revealing that management has not developed a countercollective bargaining program to negotiate with labor unions. Such a step involves a faith in people, a belief that the capacity to think is universal and that you can sell ideas as well as soap to people. Humanation embraces these faiths and beliefs. There is an inner humanity, a natural desire to cooperate, an inborn urge to help one's fellow man in every individual and organization that can be evoked. The practical task is how to evoke it democratically; that is, by not making more problems than you solve.

Automation's philosophy sacrifices the individual to the advancement of productivity, not unlike the way he is sacrificed to the welfare of the state in the Soviet Union. The technically trained practitioners of automation no doubt love their families, but they do not like people as such, particularly in the factory; they are motivated by a strong desire to organize the processes of production to operate with a minimum of people—if they cannot be eliminated completely. Their ideal is an oil-refining plant where the valves are electronically operated by a tape recording that they dictate. The manless elevator and missile are their greatest products to date.

The practitioners of humanation are motivated by the basic desire to make life more meaningful and rewarding for the participating individuals. They are not driven by the compulsion to get rid of people that dominates the automationists. That which violates the dignity of the individual is not progress. People are the most important. The full productive potential of America will not be reached by getting rid of people to the maximum extent, but by bringing the maximum number of people into the creative side of producing goods and services. I remember Allen H. Mogenson advocating during the 1930's the idea of tapping the brain power of everyone in the plant, and how he was swimming against the tide of the automationists in management who were uttering then the sentiment that has been the basis of their practice since, "The hell with tapping their brain power; let's get rid of as many of 'em as we can with machinery."

In our quest for higher living standards and greater profits, both management and labor leaders have been placing all their chips on automation. They are both in for a rude awakening because they are worshipping an inadequate doctrine that only draws its strength from the creativeness of a relatively small group of technical experts. Automation will not bear enough fruit in the years ahead to meet America's needs; and it has to be supplemented by the practice of humanation, which draws its strength from the release and application of the creative energies of everyone engaged in the productive process.

There will be nothing automatic about America's economic progress in the next twenty years. It is not going to happen just because the 1936-1960 economic growth was so fantastic. Four million new babies every year do not automatically spell prosperity.

The automationists take too much, if not all, of the credit for the 1936-1960 production results. However, if the automationists will examine carefully the last twenty-five years, they will find that the enormous economic gains resulted not only from (1) increased productivity, but even more so from (2) the fuller capacity operation of a greatly expanded economy that (3) was greatly underutilized in the 1930's and (4) that used a great deal of its underutilized resources and industries to enlarge itself with government subsidies in 1940-1944 and 1951-1953.

By attempting to carry the full load of doubling America's gross national product in the next twenty years, the automationists will not succeed. If they can do it, of course, my thesis will be proven wrong. But I hold that during the 1960's they will be turning increasingly to humanation, because they will be needing the help—the creative energies—of everyone to enable American industry to produce the goods and services that will be demanded in the years ahead. I do not believe that the productivity rate for manufacturing and all the services is going to rise fast enough to provide higher living standards for two-and-a-half to three million more people every year and also provide the wherewithal to maintain our military establishment and win the war of construction in which we are engaged. When the leaders of industry and labor begin to realize that their chariot needs more horsepower than the automationists can put out, they will turn to the humanationists, as the steel companies began to do in 1959.

Humanation is the next major development in American industry, and it will naturally result in the current patterns of industrial relations undergoing some major alterations. The trouble with collective-bargaining contracts is that they grew out of the experiences of ten, fifteen, and mostly twenty years ago. They were authored by an economic situation that today is obsolete. As a consequence, the basic frame of reference of the large corporations' industrial relations programs, as they function today, is also out of date. The labor unions in the basic industries are still pursuing the policies, which they formulated in the 1930's, of higher wages and better working conditions that will be as obsolete in the 1960's and 1970's as the piston-engine airplane. Both still fly, of course, but jet planes dramatize the fact that just flying is not enough for the future. You have to fly faster and higher and by different means, especially in the field of industrial relations.

Automation has had the labor leaders dreaming. They observed the past supreme confidence of management that it could offset higher wage costs with new machinery and other cost-cutting automation. So the labor leaders have been assuming that industry's automation projects will cut costs, raise productivity, and increase production enough so that they can continue to negotiate adequate wage increases and other contract improvements for their members without having to exert any direct efforts themselves on the processes of production. Both groups have been doing this for over two decades and hoped that they would be able to continue along these same paths undisturbed for another twenty-five years. The challenges of the future have left them no such easy life.

Implied in the very word automation is the idea that people are being eliminated, and no longer needed, and that automatic machines are taking over the work formerly done by people. Too many of the union leaders believe this and conclude that fewer workers will be needed in the future. Therefore, to provide enough jobs for all, they believe the work week will have to be cut to thirty-six, thirty-two, and thirty hours. The union leaders are in for a surprise. They are as wrong about this as they were in error twenty years ago when they embraced the false idea that America's economy had become mature and its new horizons were limited.

The full potential of American industry cannot be achieved by just physical-engineering automation. The greatest single force for increased production lies locked up in untapped, inherent creativeness. The unions have to move ahead from their inadequate policy of higher wages and better working conditions. This policy made sense in the 1930's when wages were inadequate and riddled with inequities, and working conditions were backward. Since then, the wage inequities have largely been eliminated and working conditions, in the main, have been modernized.

In the future higher incomes for workers will be restricted by the rise in productive efficiency and the efficient and full utilization of new and existing capacity. And the degree of success in both of these areas will be largely determined by what the workers and their unions do about them. This, in turn, challenges the labor leaders to replace their traditional policy of higher wages and better working conditions—which industry describes as a policy of more pay for less work—with a dynamic policy of higher pay for more production.

The policy that I urge is humanation—the effective organization of human efforts to manage and operate physical machinery in such a way as to release the full, inherent creativeness of the managerial and operating people. This is not now being done and will not be until the current practices of industrial relations are fundamentally altered.

The idea of a guaranteed anaual wage, which the steelworkers union adopted in 1943, has been rejected in favor of a program of supplemental unemployment benefits, which is merely a fringe wage increase of five cents an hour that is deferred. It is put into a separate fund for rainy-day use when it is paid out to those eligible employees who are laid off during curtailed operations.

While it is advanced as an alternative to a pay-by-the-year program and advertised under the heading of guaranteed annual wage, the supplemental unemployment benefits provision in collective-bargaining contracts is neither and requires no basic changes. That is why the auto and steel industries accepted it and the unions have pushed it. Neither has to change his ways, adopt greater responsibilities, or make any significant alteration in the patterns of industrial relations as they have developed out of the 1930's. Under supplementary unemployment benefits, the union leaders do not have to assume any responsibilities for increasing production, and management does not have to share or dilute any of it prerogatives. The program alters nothing; it is just another nickel increase.

The unions are missing a great opportunity for greater service to their members, their industries, and their country by watering down the dynamic concept of the annual wage into just another nickel-an-hour wage increase. In 1914 Henry Ford saw the connection between mass production and mass purchasing power. And he electrified industry by inaugurating the $5.00 day. This pioneering policy of forty-six years ago is accepted dogma today by both industry and union leaders.

A pay-by-the-year program, especially one inaugurated by management, together with the pursuit by the unions of the suggested policy of higher pay for more production, would get more production out of existing facilities and new capacity, thus yielding higher annual incomes to workers than they have ever dreamed of enjoying plus record profits for industry. Such a development would be a second industrial relations revolution within twenty-five years for industry, and obviously it could not be administered in middle-age comfort. But it would assure America's victory in the world-wide war of construction.

Inherent in such new patterns of industrial relations is the need for a lot of people to change their thinking and accept new ways of doing things. But these changes are not nearly as great, nor do they appear to be as insurmountable, as the changes that were required twenty-five years ago when collective bargaining first broke through in these basic industries.

My basic contention is twofold: To meet the domestic and world demands being made on American industry, the managers have to share some of their prerogatives and bring workers into a fuller participation in the productive processes to increase production. To secure the kind of wage increases required to get the average steelworker, for example, up to $12,000 a year by 1975, the leaders of labor have to assume joint responsibilities with management for increasing production. And they must lead their members to cooperate in this great creative venture.

Any labor leader who thinks that the production job required to meet these multiple demands can be done on a thirty-hour week, or with a three-month vacation, is in for a big surprise. I am glad to see Walter Reuther, president of the auto union, join those of us who have consistently believed that we have to win the war of construction before we can enjoy the leisure of a thirty-hour week. Any leader of industry who thinks that American industry can beat the Russians on the economic and missile fronts without fully integrating their employees, and their unions, with management to increase production is in for a bigger surprise.

Humanation rests on the premise that management is now the dynamic member of the collective-bargaining relationship, and that its acts and deeds, its policies and principles, are the basic determinants of union actions and policies. After all, unions came into being as a reaction against management policies, and necessarily their whole orientation is influenced by what management does and says. By aggressive leadership, management can lead unions to the higher plateau of cooperation.

America's leaders of labor and industry have the joint job of quickly and greatly increasing the productive effectiveness of our mines, mills, and factories. The collective-bargaining contracts and industrial relations policies that they have fashioned so arduously since the 1930's are inadequate to meet the enormous demands that are now presented to American industry for fulfillment during the next twenty years.

As the unions and industry embrace humanation in the 1960's, new vistas will be opening in the closing decades of the twentieth century for all Americans. Humanation will enhance, at all levels of responsibility, the dignity of the individuals who produce America's steel and the "things" made out of iron ore, bauxite, copper, lead, zinc, and all of the other raw materials which form the materialistic foundation for the American Way of Life. Steel management led the way toward this development in 1959, and while the steelworkers union was able—with another assist from enterprising politicians—to slow it up for a

few more years, it recognized that this is the road of the future
that it will be traveling when the 1962 contract comes up for
renewal. This is the nature of our self-developing system of
welfare enterprise.

We turn now to the annual wage, the materialistic foundation for humanation.

CHAPTER ELEVEN

ANNUAL WAGE

The first step into the annual wage was taken in 1955 when the Ford Motor Company agreed to pay supplemental private unemployment benefits to its employees when laid off, in addition to their governmentally financed unemployment benefits. This was putting into practical effect the idea advanced earlier by Russell W. Davenport that industry should take private steps to promote the welfare of its employees. He advocated this as a countermeasure to the idea of the welfare state, where only the government assumed welfare obligations. The rest of the auto industry followed Ford and so have the steel and other industries. I cannot emphasize too strongly that it took the compelling power of organized labor for them to take this first step.

Returning from our trip through Latin America in April, 1955, I met David J. McDonald in the Washington airport with Pittsburgh's mayor, who is now Governor of Pennsylvania, David L. Lawrence. I told the president of the steelworkers union that the time was getting ripe for pushing the annual wage again that his union first advocated in 1943. McDonald ques-

143

tioned whether it was practical and sparked me into recasting the annual wage idea into doable form. In December, 1955, I published in *Harper's Magazine*, "Pay by the Year—Can the Unions Afford It?" which *Reader's Digest* reprinted in March, 1956. Here is how I analyze the annual wage in my discussions with the welfare enterprisers who manage the practical affairs of American industry.

America can no longer afford the inefficiency of chronic and recurrent unemployment. The annual wage, a system providing fifty-two regular, steady paychecks a year, is essential because effective consumer purchasing power can be raised faster and higher by providing assured incomes the year around, than by merely raising wage rates. Workers do not need an increase in wage rates nearly as much as they need steady jobs with fifty-two regular paychecks a year on which they can count, week in and week out. The wage increases for which the steel union struck in 1959 in no way removed the steelworkers' heads from the guillotine of unemployment. They did not dull the sharp edges from layoff notices or cutbacks to three-and-four-day-week announcements. What the steelworkers need more than higher wages is full-time work and steady pay the year around. They need, and want, freedom from the fear of unemployment. Then they can resume the fight to raise their annual incomes.

The leaders of the steel industry, and all other industries, are under growing pressure to abolish chronic unemployment for three basic reasons:

1. The big steel-using industries, such as the automobile, housing, and appliances industries, are compelled to sell a large portion of their finished products on time—regular weekly or monthly installments, payable week in and month out, the whole year long. This commercial practice of buy-now-and-pay-later is one of the irresistible forces that will compel industry leaders to advance an annual wage system, and labor leaders to accept it.

2. The welfare-enterprise-system leaders have to solve the problem of chronic unemployment to win the confidence of

the uncommitted people of the world who are striving for freedom from want and freedom from fear. For example, an Indonesian leader after visiting the U.S.A. and U.S.S.R. found awesome poverty in Russia, but he reported on our failure to solve the problem of unemployment.

3. For the United States of America to win the world-wide war of construction, its welfare enterprise leaders have to eliminate the waste of unemployment and partially utilized or idle industrial and agricultural capacity, because the Soviets use all of their productive capacity all of the time, except, of course, as they too develop surpluses.

I propose that all of the economic provisions of the collective-bargaining wage contract be rolled into one ball of wax and out of them a pay-by-the-year program be fashioned that, at the end of five years, would guarantee all employees with one or more years of seniority fifty-two, full forty-hour weekly paychecks each year. In 1962, or 1965 at the latest, management will have to advance such a proposal that will tie all of the dollars-and-cents provisions of its wage contracts together. This will require the union leaders to accept greater responsibilities which they—like all defenders of a status quo—can be expected to resist with a prolonged strike, because they have a vested interest in trying to perpetuate the obsolete, irrational, hodgepodge of collective-bargaining economic clauses that have been negotiated during the last quarter of a century. But more importantly, they will be having to assume joint responsibility for raising productive efficiency—the key issue in the 1959 steel strike in which the union won the battle but, as the 1960's will reveal, management won the war. Humanation is the next development in collective bargaining.

When I formulated the idea that "workers who live by the year should be paid by the year," I was a twenty-nine-year-old economist for the C.I.O. Steelworkers Union. That was December 1, 1943. The idea came to me in 1938 when I met a fellow alumnus of Pitt who worked his way through college with a family. "Just as we were getting on our feet again," he complained to me during F.D.R.'s recession, "the mill goes down to three days a week and our industrial engineering department is working week about." I talked to Philip Murray about this being the union's basic long-range problem. He agreed, but not until the war did he advance it. He was a practical man and feared that the idea would be ridiculed if advanced too far ahead of its time.

In my forty-sixth year I believe, as firmly as I did in my twenty-ninth, that employers cannot indefinitely expect the working folks, who must feed, clothe, and shelter their families by the year, to be satisfied with an inflexible pay-by-the-hour method of earning a living. The annual wage truly presents management with the opportunity to reassume leadership in setting the pattern and pace of employee relations. While the labor leaders started the annual-wage idea, they have been side-stepping it because, as we have seen, the annual wage takes labor leaders into the area of assuming responsibilities for productive efficiency. Over the next decade the number of people in the United States who are paid on an annual salary will grow and exceed the number of wage earners. And I predict that by 1970 most wage earners, who are now paid by the hour and buy by the year, will be working under pay-by-the-year collective bargaining contracts.

Philip Murray knew, as his successors are learning, that with the inauguration of the pay-by-the-year collective-bargaining contract the union leaders have to go back to work. No longer can they force employers to increase paychecks and then retire until the next contract time in pleasant comfort, assured that only the employers have to find the means to meet the higher paychecks. The men who lead labor unions are going to have to share in this task and help create the means to pay their constituents on an annual basis. It won't be fun. It won't be easy. But it can be done.

A pay-by-the-year collective bargaining contract would be along the following terms:

The Guarantee: We will enter into a five-year contract.

For the year 1961 we will contract to hire all of our employees with five or more years of seniority for 2,080 hours, or fifty-two weeks of forty hours each; for the year 1962, all four-year-or-more employees; for 1963, all three-year-or-more employees; for 1964, all two-year-or-more employees; and for 1965, all employees with one or more years of continuous service. Commencing in 1961, each year the probationary period for new employees shall be extended by one month until it reaches a six-month period.

Annual Pay: Each five-year-plus employee will receive at least 2,080 hours of pay in 1961 at his straight-time average gross hourly rate during the year preceding the effective date of the contract. The guarantee, for example, to a $2-an-hour employee is for $4,160 for the year. All income that he receives as a consequence of his employment shall be credited against his $4,160 annual pay. (By "credited against" I mean deducted from both the hours he owes the company per year and from the total sum owed him by the company).

The pay-by-the-year program takes away some of labor's cherished gains, but this is inherent in the annual-wage concept. Overtime pay, reporting pay, shift differentials, paid holidays, for example, are based on the fact that the method of pay is by the hour. The idea of the annual wage is pay-by-the-year, which negates the entire foundation of many of the specific provisions, most of which are essentially restrictive, of collective-bargaining contracts. For example, take overtime premium pay, designed to offset weeks when the employee gets less than forty hour's work and pay. Under an annual wage contract the eligible employee is guaranteed 2,080 hours of pay. In any day or week in which he receives overtime pay he is getting extra money. Since he will not face any week of less than forty hours' pay in the year under the yearly pay contract, the basic reason for this premium overtime money vanishes. Hence, it shall be credited against his 2,080-hour yearly guarantee.

Of course, those labor leaders who have been spoiled by twenty-five years of collective bargaining, during which they have not had to assume responsibilities commensurate with their power and authority, will want to hold on to the overtime premium pay in addition to the 2,080-hour guarantee. But this is not in the cards. They will have to recognize the logic of the annual wage and forfeit those restrictive provisions that have their entire rationale in the hourly pay concept.

The annual-wage employment contract makes business partners out of the employees. Their yearly pay is guaranteed only to the extent that their employer remains solvent and can compete profitably. The employees and their union leaders cannot retire to the ball park and golf course between collective-bargaining contracts. When they inaugurate an annual-wage contract, they take on the responsibility for the continued success of the contracting employer. The program of humanation to increase efficiency, eliminate waste, lower production costs, and raise quality becomes feasible under annual-wage contracts. The labor leaders have to face up to the fact that they become business partners in each firm that pays by the year.

Inherent in the pay-by-the-year contract is the reality that the only way that employees can increase their annual income is to help raise the output of their employer. Labor leaders will have to roll up their sleeves and go back to work. They will have to go out and teach their union members that the employer is not a cow to be milked dry, but a humble goose who has to be fed with hard, steady, and better labor to be able to produce eatable eggs. And the better the goose is fed, the more eggs everyone will have to eat. The employer has to feed the goose with better management.

There are tremendous problems to be solved by the auto, steel, and other industries as they start employing their workers on a yearly basis. But, as an old mentor of mine used to say, for every problem that the Lord created, He also created a solution; all you have to do is find it; that is, before you go broke.

"That's all very fine," the oldsters tell me, "but what are you going to do when a depression overtakes you?"

We will pay all eligible employees 2,080 hours in such a

depression year. I am not too much concerned about the next depression, but if it should appear, you can be sure that it will do so after some profitable years. And Uncle Sam has already laid the foundation for the annual wage. For example, if in 1961 our company earns a million dollars before taxes, Uncle Sam will get $520,000 of it. If, in 1962 the depression comes, and we lose $500,000, Uncle Sam will refund to us $260,000 of our 1961 taxes. And if we, and many others, pay our employees 2,080 hours pay in 1961, the dreaded depression will not be very severe. Since, as Henry Ford, Jr., observed, the government "uses its enormous tax and credit powers to counterbalance business cycles," the much-dreaded depression is not likely to wipe out annual-wage companies that otherwise would not go by the board.

The economists trained in the statistics of the business cycle, I am afraid, are being technologically displaced by the Congressmen who are legislating the business cycle out of existence. I propose that welfare enterprise legislate the annual wage into collective bargaining.

I predict that in the 1970's the hourly wage rate will not even be part of the contract. Instead, each job will be evaluated and paid an annual salary. And employees—and their labor leaders along with them—will be more company-minded than they would dare concede in the early sixties.

America needs a pay-by-the-year system of hiring industrial workers which will insure against the greatest single loss in national production: seasonal idleness. If the Ford Motor Company, for example, were to pioneer the annual wage in the full measure that I propose, it would have as an electrifying effect on our country as the five-dollar day had in 1914. Obviously Henry Ford II cannot guarantee an annual wage if he can only employ his workers for nine months of the year. The make-or-break question in terms of the annual wage is the make-or-break question for America in its codevelopment struggle in the world. Obviously we cannot outperform Russia over the years ahead if we can only employ our productive capacities and people part of the time. The answer to the practical problems inherent in the annual wage is the same as the answer to the make-or-break question for America: How do we operate the American economy fully all of the time and continually expand it as our population grows? We did in our feedbacks to Europe in 1914-1918 and 1939-1945, in our Marshall Plan feedbacks of 1949-1956, and in the Korean War feedbacks of 1950-1953. The argument of this book is that we can do it by waging James's moral war of construction, which I see as the overriding next development in our culture. The major source of income to pay for this war is increased productivity to which we now turn our attention.

CHAPTER TWELVE

PRODUCTIVITY, INNER EQUILIBRIUM, AND ORGANIZATION MAN

Once the big step into the annual wage is taken, and only then, can we fully move into wage-productivity collective bargaining to replace the wage-price bargaining of the post-1945 period. The nature of this next development is analyzed through a critical appraisal of the "Growth or Inflation" (Detroit, May 25, 1959) speech of Ralph J. Cordiner, board chairman of General Electric Company.

DEFINITION OF PROBLEM

The problem is: To what do we relate pay? Cordiner says: Relate pay—wages and salaries——to the market. I say: Relate pay to productivity. What is our practice? We relate pay to the free processes of collective bargaining.

WHAT IS OUR PROBLEM?

Collective bargaining—having nothing except the sheer brute force and power of the contending parties to which to relate pay—produces wage and salary changes that are inflationary. This was tolerable as long as the affected employees suffered from inflationary price rises. But once they began to receive automatic cost-of-living wage increases, they ceased to suffer from the debilitating effects of rising prices.

Since industry cannot absorb wage and salary increases that exceed productivity gains, they must be passed on in higher prices. As a consequence, the other parties in the body politic have to absorb the inflation. This they will do for only so long. The public has begun to revolt already. Then action is mandatory. It will not come from labor. It can come from government. It should come from industry by anticipating the need for action. It will come from government if industry fails to act. We have to respond to the general welfare anyway, so we might as well do so voluntarily.

HOW TO DO IT

General agreement on the basic idea of doing something about the wage-cost-push-inflation problem has been extant for some while. At this time the need is for specifics. I do not have all of the answers, any more than any other single individual can spell out in final detail the solution. But I can formulate the basic tenets of an ultimate solution. General Electric (G.E.) has the Management Research and Development Institute to translate these basic tenets into workable plans for each of its operating units. One of the questions asked of me when I spoke at the Institute was, "What comes to your mind when you hear the term Boulwarism?"

I replied, "For the past several years I have publicly commended G.E.'s industrial relations program, and I have written Boulware accordingly. G.E. under Boulware developed a forward thrust on its own, and took the initiative of leadership. What Boulwarism lacks is substantive content. You not only have to get up your steam to get somewhere, but you also need a program, a blueprint, detailing how your propose to get there."

The response of the attending group of G.E. managers was

so affirmative that I was enthused to bring my views to the attention of G.E.'s top echelon. I have been out trying to sell them to management and to leaders of industry for several years. I shall persist until I make a sale or concede to something better that someone else puts on the market of industrial relations ideas.

MY SPECIFICS

1. Tie all future increases in economic benefits to wage and salary employees to a comprehensive measurement of productivity.

2. Such a comprehensive productivity measurement—that measures accurately the total effectiveness from year to year of the entire organization of a business—exists in the corporate balance sheet and profit and loss statement. But neither labor nor management will agree to its use.

3. Therefore, construct an equivalent measurement of productivity that takes into account all factors of labor, management, raw material costs, capital investments, etc. The basic format of such a productivity measurement would be similar to that of the Job Evaluation Manual, and the labor union representatives would participate in it along the lines that they participate in the Job Evaluation Manual.

4. The technical problems involved in constructing the productivity manual are solvable. A company or a plant that has a standard cost system already has such a manual. You put in labor, materials, capital, machinery, and management. You take out goods and services. You adjust the price of each input and output to a common base period, and you have an accurate physical measurement of your efficiency or productivity. The only criticism of the use of standard cost systems to measure productivity that I have is that I did not think of it first.

5. Labor is opposed to tying wages to profits or to profits expressed in productivity except when they are high. Each contract time the union leaders want wage increases whether productivity goes up or not. Management has to conduct a persist-

ent and effective selling campaign on wages that sells employees on the simple idea: if you want to earn more, produce more; the honeymoon of more pay for less goods produced is over.

6. Management, and particularly the leaders of industry, are also opposed to tying wages to profits or to profits expressed in productivity. Our position is that ability to pay is irrelevant, except when a company lacks adequate profits to pay higher wages. We want to hold wage increases down when productivity goes up too fast or too much. *We have to rethink through this position.* The policy involved here is crucial, and we evade facing up to its need for revision by diverting attention to how hard—if not impossible—it is to measure productivity. We can solve the technical problems of measurement once we revise our thinking on this basic policy. We have to buy this set of ideas: no wage increase is inflationary if it is accompanied by a corresponding increase in the production and availability of goods and services; we have to see that effective purchasing power is constantly raised so that we can sell the increasing capacity of our plants at home and overseas.

7. Another way that we divert attention from coming to grips with the need to revise our policy (as noted in paragraph 6 immediately preceding) is to raise the question as to whether you use a national productivity average, an industry average, a company one, a plant or even department one. This technical problem can be resolved. I would use a company average. I would pay half of the employees' share of productivity company-wide, one-fourth to the plants with the best record, and one-fourth to the departments that contributed outstandingly to increased productivity.

8. The pattern-type wage increase holdup of smaller, less efficient, and undercapitalized companies would cease. It must be ended. Each would have its own productivity program, and the unions will only be able to get for their members what they can help each company earn. True, this generally will result in lower wage-salary scales in such plants. But you already have such discrepancies. For example, few industries in the Pittsburgh

area pay the U.S. Steel scale. The best people tend to gravitate to steel, and on down the line. The doctrine about paying competitive wages is no longer true, except between companies that are competitive as to profits, productivity, etc. Union members work for less where they have to, and they have to in many plants in most industrial areas—even in times of labor shortage. In many smaller companies humanation can and will produce higher annual incomes than the huge corporations will then be paying. But generally the pay scale in the latter will continue to be the highest paid in the community.

CONCLUSION

When I discussed this productivity program with Lemuel R. Boulware, vice-president of General Electric, to whom Ralph Cordiner referred me, G.E. was burning on the front burner. The electrical workers unions will be changing their collective bargaining policies in the sixties as G.E. leads the way with basic policy changes of its own. Whether the labor leaders do so graciously, or after fighting prolonged rear-guard strikes, will depend on how well they read the processes in development. But it is unrealistic to expect them to be any more enlightened than the leaders of any other group confronted with having to give up some vested "sacred" interests. This is America.

AN EXAMPLE OF SCIENTIFIC-SPIRITUAL UNITY

Since Elton Mayo's *The Human Problems of an Industrial Civilization* (1933) the corporate soul, which the moral forces have been humanizing since Walter Rauschenbusch's time, has been developing also under the stimuli of scientific ideas. It is from this development that my confidence grows that the U.S.A. is a society of individuals in the process of developing excellence. Because both the spiritual and scientific conclusions are tied together by the basic force of the dignity of man. This is the most powerful force in the history of man, and our failure to apprehend it grows out of the fact that the theologians for centuries have tried to make it a monopoly of their organized religions.

It has taken me twenty years to comprehend this common ground between the clinical, scientific researches that Elton Mayo brain-trusted in the 1920's and the phenomenon of the dignity of the individual upon which the Western theologies are based.

The conclusions of the Western Electric Company's researches at the Hawthorne Works in Illinois had better be right, or American industry is heading for a big fall. The reorganization of management since the rebirth of unionism in the 1930's has been built around this relatively small body of clinical knowledge, which has been confirmed by later studies. I know that these conclusions are sound, because I have employed them with practical success, and I can trace my major failures to my personal violation of them.

The fact that management in too many instances has abused them to control the organization man's life and extract his soul from him is a form of nonmaterialistic exploitation. As I have noted earlier, the middle-management men and women will revolt to correct this exploitation, and already some of the abusing companies are restoring, step by step, the inner integrity of their organization people to the exploited individuals. We may have in this brewing revolt the big surprise development in industrial —human—relations of the 1960's. It is the rare man or organization that does not have to be reminded of his or its humanity forcibly.

The basic conclusion of the Western Electric researches is a simple one, as are all great ideas. A group of individuals are put in a work place, their physical conditions of work are constantly improved, and production goes up. Then these improved conditions are withdrawn, one by one, but production does not recede to the original level. It keeps going up. There was nothing freakish about this result, which was validated by the most painstaking, scientifically contrived investigations. This is a book in itself, and it covers the work of social and medical scientists in England and France as well as in the United States. I can report that the conscious knowledge of the phenomenon demonstrated by the Western Electric researches and the ability to reproduce it have been the basis of my success with humanation in the union and in running my own machinery manufacturing business.

Mayo reports that "any theory that there was 'a return to original conditions' is nonsensical." He observes that

the individual workers and the group had to re-adapt themselves to a new industrial milieu . . . in which their own self-determination and their social well-being ranked first and the work was incidental. . . . The Western Electric experiment was primarily directed not to the external condition but to the inner organization. By strengthening the "temperamental" inner equilibrium of the workers, the company enabled them to achieve a mental "steady state."

The use of the words "inner equilibrium" and what we all comprehend in our own way by the use of the word "spiritual" derive from the common phenomenon of the dignity of the individual. The dignity of man is a fact, no less than is the developing impregnated ovum. Mayo observes that "learning and skill are not capacities which are achieved once and for all time by a given individual. On the contrary," he emphasizes, "the individual's skill is reachieved each day and consequently depends in some degree upon the external conditions of that day and inner equilibrium."[1] This is the social scientist speaking. The religious man says that the individual can do better work if he can satisfy his spiritual needs on the job.

I have been saying throughout this book that the "finest thing in life" is the release of one's inherent creativeness (humanation). Of course "it" is not "things." But our human development is partial to date, and our language is necessarily limited. So we are speaking transitionally. We comprehend a physical thing. We know that many such "things" were among the "better things in life" for previous generations (linen, for exam-

---

[1] Anyone who has watched a football team—especially the pros—perform magnificently one week and like a bunch of bums the next week has witnessed this phenomenon. Do not we all have days when we produce excellently and days when we are not worth the powder to blow us to hell!

ple), but are "necessities of life" today. We sense the non-materialistic realities in life, which I call "finer things" for lack of a more understandable language about the realities of our inner lives. I employ the expression "spiritual freedom" to embrace the nonmaterialistic realities in American life. Inborn in each individual is the capacity to produce "self-recognition." Spiritual freedom exists to the extent that the individual can find expression for his self-recognition. But his self-recognition is self-reproducing whether it has found expression in individual (religious) or social forms. A woman denied a man still produces ova. A man denied any recognition of "himself as something in his own right and therefore equal to all other individuals" still produces this inner part of himself, his spiritual qualities, whenever he has access to a woman, and can reproduce through the "fertilized ovum, by a continuous but structured process" an outer likeness of himself.

The outer body and the inner self are a unity. My body and spirit, inner and outer life, are one. I am both good and bad, creative and conservative. To use Lancelot Law Whyte's expression "the supreme beauty in life is the forming power" of the individual, the budding flower, the green blade of grass, the rising and the setting sun; and this is so whether it is expressed in the blue-green of our lawn, through the white-orange beauty of our fruit trees, in the crystal blue or crimson red sky, between two white sheets, or on the blue-lined paper on which I create these words. The creative processes of action come easier, require less arduous work, and yield satisfactions that are offset less by reflective doubting than is creative thinking. It is much easier to act than it is to think out in advance the right reasons for one's actions. Some things we do and never know why; others we do and later reason why; and, others we do having reasoned in advance why. The first category includes most of the actions of which we are ashamed. The second includes those for which we usually have to apologize. And the few actions which have been done for the right reasons, thought out in advance, include our proud achievements. I naturally believe that

I went into industry for the right reasons. The fact that I also acquired some capital (money) in the process is irrelevant to my purpose. Whyte says, "Thought is born of failure." It can be born of success, too. In every success there are many failures, and every failure has its share of successes.

"In practice, the dignity of the human being is the single most important concept that stands between us and engulfment," Russell Davenport asserted as he cried out for "the church" and "science" to reconcile "in a profound and satisfying way . . . questions comprehended under the general heading of spiritual." In my field of specialty I have found a unity between the religious and scientific concepts of man. Let us listen to the religious man. I have developed an empathy with one of the steel company presidents with whom I visit at least once during each steel strike. In 1959 he was berating both the union and management leaders:

> They have lost the vision of God. Men are honest. Sure, you'll find characters among them. That's why we have rules and government to keep these bad apples from spoiling the good ones. But now you take work rules. A man is paid for a day's work. He will not steal an hour or two of your time, any more than he will rob you of your treasury. Treat him right. Respect his dignity. He will produce for you a fair day's work for a fair day's pay.

He lectured me looking out of his window where the Monongahela and Allegheny lose themselves in each other and are transformed into the Ohio River. (That's an act of creation—the beauty of the forming power—that he looks out on every day.)

> The union leaders are missing the boat in not organizing their people to cooperate on production problems. The men want to. Management has to learn how to. It's a question of understanding, and at the bottom of it all is the spiritual wisdom of the Almighty. Respect your fellow man as an equal is the first rule of life.

Now let's listen to a scientific man, Elton Mayo:

> Restricting output . . . expresses a gross simplification which is essentially untrue. Apparently it is not enough to have an enlightened

Company policy, a carefully devised (and blue-printed) plan of manufacture. To stop at this point, and merely administer such a plan, however logical, to workers with a take-it-or-leave-it attitude has much the same effect as administering medicine to a recalcitrant patient. It may be good for him, but he is not persuaded. If an individual cannot work with sufficient understanding of his work situation, then, unlike a machine, he can only work against opposition from himself. This is the essential nature of the human.[2]

Mayo says that the human needs "inner equilibrium" which he achieves on the job when, as an individual and a member of a social group, he "develops a sense of participation in the critical determinations" in which his "own self-determination" and "social well-being ranked first and the work was incidental." This is the scientific definition of the dignity of man. He has an "inner" that requires "equilibrium." He has spiritual needs that must be fulfilled; this is the religionist's definition of the dignity of man. Where the greatest productivity is achieved by the most effective recognition of the dignity of the individuals involved, we have the scientific and religious views merging together. Let us now look at a case where they conflict.

"Coffee breaks" are denounced by one type of moralist religious view as "featherbedding," as stealing time from your employer for your own selfish gain. This is false. The very first researches of Elton Mayo established the relationship between "rest pauses" and the well-being of the individual. His researches established that you can do more work in eight hours with a couple of "coffee breaks" or "rest pauses" than without them. Of course, some people will overdrink coffee, but that is a question of competent management, of administration, not basic principles. Fundamental in the "rest pause" is the inner equilibrium, "peace of soul" of the individual that is as real as the lathe he operates or the typewriter she punches or the farm tractor he drives. Creativity is a spiritual experience—"the individual's skill is reachieved each day." This is spiritual freedom—the

[2] Elton Mayo, *The Human Problems of an Industrial Civilization*, Graduate School of Business Administration, Harvard University, Boston, 1946, pp. 72 and 119-121.

dignity of the individual. This is not an idea or a concept, but a natural process in life. The moral forces in America that have been humanizing industry for a hundred years are now being reinforced by scientific phenomena in facilitating human betterment. This is America.

THE ORGANIZATION MAN DOCTRINE

Elton Mayo is most popularly known through his critic William H. Whyte, Jr., who has written a characterization of the organization man in our conventional wisdom. *The Organization Man* is about the organization man in contrast to *The Ugly American* and *The Affluent Society* that respectively make their case by proving how handsome the American really is and how poor is his society.

Let us summarize William Whyte's doctrine.[3] The organization man belongs to the Corporation; he has taken "the vows of organization life"; he belongs to a "collective"; he believes "in the group as a source of creativity . . . in 'belongingness' as the ultimate need of the individual, and . . . in the application of science to achieve the belongingness"; there is "no conflict between the individual's aspirations and the community's wishes"; and "on such matters as social welfare they give their proxy to the organization"; "he is imprisoned in brotherhood"; "in a word they accept"; "the system, they conclude, is essentially benevolent"; the Organization "wants your soul"; and finally "the peace of mind offered by organization remains a surrender, and no less so for being offered in benevolence."

"Their values," William Whyte writes, "will set the American temper," as he sets out to comment on the "collectivization so visible in the corporation [that] has affected almost every field of work." His critical study is of "the personal impact that organization life has had on the individuals within it." His forensic device[4] is "a Social ethic . . . that contemporary body

[3] William H. Whyte, Jr., *The Organization Man*, Doubleday Anchor Books, Doubleday & Company, Garden City, N. Y., first published by Simon and Schuster, Inc., New York, 1956, Chaps. 1 and 29.

[4] *Ibid.*, p. 7.

of thought which makes morally legitimate the pressures of society against the individual"; whose "ideological underpinnings have been provided not by the organization man but by intellectuals he knows little of and towards whom, indeed, he tends to be rather suspicious." The social ethic "is a utopian faith" which he argues is the opposite of "the Protestant Ethic . . . the . . . pursuit of individual salvation through hard work, thrift, and competitive struggle."[5]

Whyte defines "the central issue" as "individualism." He believes

that individualism is as possible in our times as in others. I speak of individuals *within* organization life. . . . I am going to argue that he should fight the organization. But not self-destructively. . . . Every decision he faces on the problem of the individual versus authority is something of a dilemma. . . . We do need to know how to cooperate with The Organization, but more than ever, so do we need to know how to resist it. Out of context this would be an irresponsible statement. . . . The fault is not in organization, in short, it is our worship of it. It is in our vain quest for a utopian equilibrium . . . the soft-minded denial that there is a conflict between the individual and society. . . . If he goes against the group, is he being courageous—or just stubborn? . . . It is in the resolution of a multitude of such dilemmas, I submit, that the real issue of individualism lies today.[6]

Whyte concludes, "He must fight the Organization. Not stupidly, or selfishly, for the defects of individual self-regard are no more to be venerated than the defects of cooperation. But fight he must ."[7]

How should he fight? This business of fighting is a practical business. The big evil of the Organization against which the author wages war is the personality test. It is a "constriction" "on the individual." Of course it is. It is far worse. It is a violation of his personal liberty. What a man does privately, where he lives, and what he believes is no legitimate concern of his

[5] *Ibid.*, p. 5.
[6] *Ibid.*, pp. 11, 12, 13, 14, 15.
[7] *Ibid.*, p. 448.

employer. Compulsory interviews and personality tests that invade the privacy of a man's life and home should be outlawed as a condition of employment. This violation of the civil liberties of middle-management men and women in the 1960's is the same kind of instrument that the denial of freedom of organization to wage earners was in the 1920's. That is the way that our founding fathers thought about the private liberties of Americans when, in the fourth article of the Bill of Rights, they provided "against unreasonable searches and seizures" in "their persons, houses, papers, and effects."

William Whyte denounces personality tests as "the tests of conformity" and argues that they "punish the exceptional man." But he has his own twist about how to fight them. "The moral basis of testing has been tabled in this discussion," William Whyte notes, "but it is the paramount issue." He asks, "Is the individual's innermost self any business of the organization's? He has some rights too. . . . How much more must a man testify against himself? The Bill of Rights should not stop at organization's edge."[8] He knows this issue, and understands the moral question.

"In return for the salary that The Organization gives the individual, it can ask for superlative work from him, but it should not ask for his psyche as well. If it does, he must withhold." He continues, "Sensibly—the bureaucratic way is too much with most of us that he can flatly refuse to take tests without hurt to himself." And finally, "But he can cheat. He must. Let him respect himself." The author includes an eight-page Appendix on "How to Cheat on Personality Tests." It is as if Alfred C. Kinsey had included in his *Sexual Behavior in the Human Male* an Appendix on "How to Cheat on Your Wife" and in his *Sexual Behavior in the Human Female* "How to Cheat on Your Husband." William Whyte reports that "several" have "studied my trot" and done very well on "the tests," getting "quite a promotion" and "doing very well in the new job." This proved a handsome return for the investment in the book that can now

[8] *Ibid.*, pp. 271-272.

be purchased for $1.45 in paperback.

The tactic of cheating to succeed—bribing purchasing agents, dishonest advertising, ad infinitum—is a way of business life that produces a way of thinking. "Our future as a nation," William Ernest Hocking states, "depends largely on the moral orientation of 'business.'"[9] Hocking cites the "remarkable essay by Chester Barnard entitled 'Elementary Conditions of Business Morals.'"

I know of no essay so enlightening as to the prevalence and the strain of the double morality in contemporary business. He makes clear that a modern economy cannot proceed without a complex co-ordination of responsible activities, whose ethical pressures present " a set of problems no one adequately comprehends" and yet whose solution is one of our greatest needs.[10]

[9] William E. Hocking, *Strength of Men and Nations,* Harper & Brothers, New York, 1959, p. 63.
[10] *Ibid.,* pp. 74-75.

CHAPTER THIRTEEN

HOCKING'S CREATIVE RISK ACT IN STEEL

Dr. William Ernest Hocking proposes that the U.S.A. initiate an act of "justified creative risk" vis-à-vis the U.S.S.R. Applying this idea to the 1959 steel strike, and now to the developing steel labor-management negotiations for a new contract in 1962, is my responsibility alone. I got nowhere with it in 1959, but the long strike opened the door to my views being considered seriously. Back in 1956 I wrote to Roger Blough of U.S. Steel and to top steel officials in other basic producing companies when I sent them my humanation article, "If they [union and steel companies] wait until 1959 to make amendments to their 1956 contract, whose basic concepts are already obsolete, I predict that the 1959-60 steel strike will be the longest and most devastating strike in the history of America."

In 1957 I wrote Blough, "I am conducting a one-man campaign to avoid the six-month steel strike of 1959." But in early 1959 I was in error in publicly predicting a short steel strike, as I overestimated the ability of the union leaders to sidestep the steamroller that was bearing down on them. The strike, however, proved fortunate for them as it built solidarity in union ranks that had been in a state of degeneration. The steel industry now has a strong union with which a humanation contract can be negotiated. But the groundwork for it has to be assiduously laid during the years preceding the next negotations in 1962. This essentially was my suggestion in 1956, the ignoring of which proved so costly in 1959. It simply means proposing a new creative contract that will inspire the confidence of the steelworkers and going out among them to sell it. As long as the company leaders default to the union leaders in appealing to the steelworkers, the union will dominate the results of negotiation.

The time has come for the steel company leaders to initiate "a justified creative risk." Only such an act can bridge the gap between the steel companies and the steelworkers union. The vicious circle of distrust and fear of each other can be pierced by management taking:

1. An act of deliberate risk, refusing any longer to shelter the steel companies' purpose behind the continued threat of inflation.

2. An act that will evoke from the steelworkers union an equivalent, reciprocal act on its part and on behalf of its members.

I do not hesitate to propose such "an act of creative statesmanship." I have spelled out in detail the specific content of such an act during the last five years: humanation, annual wage, and a productivity wage contract.

During the 1959 strike the steel companies terrified the men in the mills, and the steelworkers union cast a spell of gloom and despair among steel management. This long strike was unavoidable and necessary, and the steel firms are to be congratulated for seeing it through to its inevitable political compromise, because the time for a basic change was overdue.

The tremendous suffering caused by the strike should not be in vain. The union leaders are in a helpless position. I outlined the situation to them in a public letter on August 15, 1959, when the strike was only a month old. I proposed that they breathe life into Philip Murray's *Organized Labor and Production* in which he advised that "management and labor . . . together devise improved production practices that increase the social income." They found themselves incapable of taking the initiative. They are stuck in the role of defending their Maginot Line. They cannot initiate a "deliberate justified creative risk." But they can, and they must, respond to such an act initiated by management.

Everybody knows what should be done. But nobody does it. The threat of expedient action by Congress confronts the steel industry with the necessity of being the innovator. Steel management is very experienced in making technological innovations, such as the continuous strip mill and top-pressure blast furnaces. These acts are both creative and full of risks. The time has now come for them to become social innovators of the annual wage, union-management cooperation to increase productivity and of a wage-productivity method for equitably distributing the proceeds of increased productivity to workers, managers, stockholders, and customers.

MANAGEMENT PROPOSAL

To break the existing stalemate I suggest that they offer to take the following creative act of risk:

1. Negotiate a pay-by-the-year contract that will assure all employees with two or more years of seniority 2,080 hours of pay (fifty-two forty-hour weeks) by year "X."

2. Whether year "X" is 1963, 1965, or 1970 I cannot tell. But year "X" is achievable during the 1960's, and a firm proposal to set it as a goal, and to accomplish it during the 1960's, will allay the fears for job security that the strike caused and the union leaders exploited.

In the preceding three chapters I have outlined the essential ingredients of such a proposal, and they obviously can be improved upon and further perfected.

There is a mutuality of interest between the steel union leaders and the leaders of the steel companies to free the steelworkers from the guillotine of unemployment. The commercial practice of selling everything from the cradle to the grave on a "buy now and pay later" plan is one of the irresistible forces that increasingly will be compelling the replacement of the hourly wage systems with a rational annual-wage system of pay. The International Business Machines Corporation, for example, put all of its 80,000 employees on a salary basis, effective February 1, 1958; 60,000 already were being paid salaries when the 20,000 remaining hourly rated domestic employees were advanced to salaries.

UNION RESPONSE

A deliberate act on the part of management confronts the union with the absolute necessity to respond in kind. I outline such a response:

1. We, the Union, accept your proposal, and as a commensurate act of good faith propose:

    a. To create union-management committees in all plants to review all local work rules to eliminate obsolete rules and correct malpractices; and to submit to arbitration any disputes arising therefrom that cannot be settled by mutual agreement.

    b. To negotiate displacement pay for all employees adversely affected, and to create training programs for their employment in other jobs.

JOINT UNION-MANAGEMENT RESPONSE

Once management has pierced the vicious circle of distrust and fear by initiating this act of creative risk, and the union responds in kind, the door is then open to mutual agreement to:

1. Negotiate a measurement of productivity that can be the determinant factor in future economic gains for the union members and stabilize steel prices.

2. Resolve the other never-ending, always-recurring problems of worker-management and union-company relations.

THE RISK

The proposed risk is double. As best I can calculate from the outside, U.S. Steel would be risking 40 to 50 cents a share of earnings per year. This is the maximum risk, which would be significantly reduced by the anticipated response of the union. The men in the mills are not dishonest. They are not out to rob the company. They do not want to continue to benefit from any local work practice that is unsound or morally indefensible. But they are frightened about their jobs. They live under the fear of recurring unemployment. They see the degradation of displaced coal miners. They are receptive to a great creative act from management that will show them where they are headed in the 1960's.

I feel confident that their union leaders will respond to such an act with an equivalent act in kind. But, if not, the steel companies will be in a sound, defensible moral position. In time, the union will have to respond in kind. In the meanwhile, until management initiates such an act of "deliberate, justified, creative risk," the steel companies are in the indefensible position of trying to pierce the union's Maginot Line—that is, trying to get the steelworkers to increase productivity without adequate job security or assured annual incomes.

The fact that the union's Maginot Line position is also morally indefensible—perpetuation of obsolete work rules—no doubt gives solace to the aggressive, partisan, management position. But it does not offer solution. It does not evoke the necessary creative act of leadership, for which the American national purpose in the world calls. The steel companies have no alternative to abdication or temporizing, except to take the affirmative act that I outline to the best of my ability, and which obviously can be improved upon.

There is no denying that Dr. Hocking, wise philosopher that he is, has an idea that is timely and applicable to America's current labor problem. There is no doubt in my mind that before the decade of the 1960's passes into history, the annual wage, humanation, and wage-productivity, as distinct from wage-price collective bargaining will prevail in steel and the other basic industries.

When I took lunch with Roger Blough in early December, 1959, to discuss the creative-risk idea, it was too late to implement it for the 1959 controversy but it has its obvious appeal and merits for the 1960's. The ultimate compromise settlement illustrates how the solution to these immediate, practical problems lies in the resolution of the larger, continuing problems that are no less practical; that are postponable only at our peril. Obviously we have to succeed in applying Hocking's "justified creative risk" idea in the relatively simple matrix of our own basic industries, before we dare let our enthusiasm carry us away with the optimism that it can succeed in breaking the U.S.A.-U.S.S.R. stalemate. Such success is dependent upon leadership in the steel industry and the national capitol. Ideas of this nature are the foundation for such leadership. There is nothing more powerful than a dynamic, creative idea expressed when its time has arrived.

CHAPTER FOURTEEN

CREATIVE RISK ACT VIS-À-VIS RUSSIA

CODEVELOPMENT NOT COEXISTENCE

Coexistence is a dogma of the doctrinaire-type mind, like the Kremlin's, that worships a social scientist's bible that all good is on the Marxists' side, all evil is on the capitalists' side, and that victory is inevitable for its side after it has vanquished the evil side. The wide acceptance of this static concept in America only reveals how widespread the doctrinaire-type mind is among our own people.

Codevelopment is democratic man's answer to the coexistence of dialectical man. We do not coexist with our families and neighbors in the communities where we live and die. We codevelop together. For example, my wife and I do not coexist. We have been codeveloping for a quarter of a century. We are not the same people who went to college together. In 1960 we continued our codeveloping via a trip around the world through the Orient. When we travel we subordinate sightseeing to interacting with the people we meet. We have an effect on them, and they on us. Our mutual interactions are codevelopment. So it is between groups of people in a country, and between people in sovereign countries.

Codevelopment is the free world's answer to the Soviet world's static dogma of coexistence. We coexist only in the cemetery. As a free nation, America cannot look forward to coexistence. It is the static idea of live-and-let-live that Herbert Croly criticized fifty years ago. The democratic man's opposing concept, as Croly proposed, is the dynamic idea of live-and-help-live.

I have no illusions about the Russians or Communists. They are a rough, tough bunch who fight with no holds barred. But they do not scare me. I have fought them at home in the labor movement and licked them. I have fought them around the world in the sale and use of water-well drilling equipment in several countries, and the welfare enterprise organization that I led has outdesigned, outsold, outproduced, and outperformed them. We can lick them also in the political and economic arenas for three reasons:

1. The Russian Communists are slaves to their economic dogmas and political doctrines. You can tell in advance what they will do in the long run because you know how their minds work. You can overcome their short-run gains, as their no-holds-barred tactics are self-discrediting. Ask the Egyptians what they did with their cotton, or the Burmese what they did with their rice.

2. The dignity of man and self-development are on our side. These are potent natural forces. Their full economic and political horsepower can be generated by dedicated Americans who, comprehending these natural processes, know how to facilitate them among our diverse neighbors on our planet.

3. The doctrinaire Russians blindly believe that history is on their side and will make them the rulers of our planet without having to drop an H-bomb on us. They are years away from discovering that the natural processes of human dignity and self-development will bury their doctrines and transform their system before they can drop an H-bomb, after which it would serve no conceivable purpose.

Unhappily our problem is not simply that of outperforming and transforming the Russian Communists. Our problem is some Americans—fearing Red China—might be tempted to look for an easy way out with the Kremlin. There is no easy way in life. In the 1960's and the later decades of this century, America will be having to choose between two conflicting processes in development:

1. Supplying the developing market in Russia with some of our surplus production and siding with the Kremlin in the growing conflict between the two large, land-mass, Communist powers, Russia and China; or

2. Facilitating the processes of dignity and self-development in mainland China as well as in Russia to correct the distortions inherent in Communism as it is developing in both the People's Republic of China and the United Soviet Socialist Republics.

We should conquer our historical-hysterical fear of the "yellow menace." We should follow up our significant embracing of Hawaii as our fiftieth state with a step-by-step program of siding with the Oriental peoples against the Kremlin. This is the big decision confronting all Americans in the 1960's. The first steps into the Kremlin's spiderweb are hard to comprehend, and easy to take, but the last steps could be final. It would be a crime against humanity for America to join the Union of Soviet Socialist Republics in a pact or tacit understanding against China and the Oriental peoples and, if need be, blow up several hundred million of God's children in the Orient to join the victims of Hiroshima and Nagasaki. This is not the American way.

RUSSIA IS AN EMERGING COUNTRY

Russia is today an emerging country that is in the process of yielding to the natural forces of the dignity and self-development of the individual. Marxian dogma and Communist doctrines are thwarting these natural forces. America's job is to accelerate these forces, and not to pit against them orthodox theological and democratic dogmas and religious and political doctrines that are so likely to lead to a holy war of mutual annihilation or an evil war to gang up with the Kremlin against the Chinese. The passion to believe in God runs deep in the hearts of all people. Pierre van Paassen tells in his *Visions Rise and Change*[1] how the Kremlin leaders passed out icons and called on the Church and God to help them galvanize their people into defeating Hitler's armed might.

God will find His way in Russia without any assistance from American H-bombs and missiles. A war of nuclear destruction in the name of God must yield to a moral war of construction in the name of man. We need to forge a moral equivalent of war utilizing, in the words of William James, the "disciplines, the traditions of service and devotion, of physical fitness, unstinted exertion, and universal responsibility" that we have utilized three times already in this century to fight bloody wars of killing and being killed.

What the Kremlin leaders need from us is a spiritual interpretation of the history of Russia since 1917-1918; they are not the materialists that they think they are, or pretend to be. They have been evoking the creative—spiritual—energies of their people to lift themselves out of the mire of poverty, and they have a long way to go yet to achieve the three E's.

In promising the American standard of living to their constituents, the Kremlin plays right into our hands. The more productive capacity that the Kremlin has to allot to producing living-standards goods and services, the less she has for competing with our Pentagon and Point Four. Russia cannot begin to provide American living standards to her people except by abandoning more and more of the Marxian distortions of the role of the individual in society; adopting more and more of America's individual incentive and creative practices; and transforming her economic system into a form of welfare enterprise where spiritual freedom can no longer be opposed by official Kremlin

[1] Pierre van Paassen, *Visions Rise and Change*, The Dial Press, New York, 1955.

policy. The big advantage that America has over Russia in the 1960's is this: the more that we facilitate the world-wide processes of human betterment, the stronger the U.S.A. becomes internally. On the other hand, the more that the Kremlin has to bleed its own people to facilitate these world-wide processes in development, the weaker the U.S.S.R. becomes internally. This advantage is a temporary one, as the Kremlin accelerates its internal growth and development.

The essential difference in strength between Russia and America is that our revolution is farther advanced. We have solved our elementary domestic "wants, needs, and desires" for 80 per cent of our people. We cannot stand still. More advanced individual and community "wants, needs, and desires" cry out for satisfaction. We are under pressure to satisfy them and extend them to our thirty-six million poor. We can only do this by going forward, by exporting our revolution. Russia is trying to export her revolution simultaneously while she is still trying to satisfy her people's elementary domestic "wants, needs, and desires." The Kremlin knows that she cannot stand still, that she must export her revolution, and that time is running against her as America accelerates the exportation of its 1776 Revolution of which the 1917-1918 Revolution is a distortion. Hence the Kremlin's dilemma of having to bleed her own people to be able to prosecute her idea of social revolution around the world. To take the distortions out of the 1917-1918 Revolution we have to be "firstest with the mostest" with our Revolution everywhere and stimulate demands for the good life inside Russia and her satellites. When I speak of our Revolution I do not refer merely to the anti-colonial revolution of 1776, but to the American Revolution that is defined in Chapter Eight.

The Kremlin has boxed itself in to do more than it can. We must accelerate her overextension by employing every stratagem at our command to stimulate the Russians' appetites for the good life. This will compel a cut in Kremlin military manpower and lead to a negotiable position with the Kremlin leaders.

The automobile is an essential condition of freedom in a technological society. In this phenomenon we have an example of how we might increase the pressure on the Kremlin to devote more of its productive capacity to domestic needs. When we can get the Kremlin to producing five to six million cars a year for her own people, and putting in the road system, bridges, service stations, motels, and garages requiring billions of man-hours and tons of material, we will find Khrushchev and his successors staying to negotiate at Summit meetings and being malleable in everyday diplomatic and trade negotiations.

RUSSIA IS OUR MORAL COMPETITION

It is a moral contest in which America is locked with Russia as much as a materialistic and political one, and we have to recognize this and make a virtue out of recognizing it. The two basic Russian developments of a moral character leading toward human betterment are: Russia's Point Four aid to self-developing peoples, despite the Trojan-horse character of the Kremlin ideology; secondly, the moral basis of Russia's heroic efforts to provide her own people with all of the necessities of life, despite the denial of civil liberties, personal religious freedom, and the right and means (lots of autos and roads) of free, unrestricted movement for Russians within their own country. Inherent in each of these Kremlin developments is the twin idea of an equal and better life; a recognition that the Indians and Iraqis, for example, are entitled to an equal chance and that Russians are entitled to a better life.

It would be a happy development if spiritual freedom in Russia would find a form of religious expression with which America's churchmen could make peace. But the job of building bridges of understanding between the Russians and Americans must go on independently for a number of decades, because of the Kremlin's proclivity to convert churches into grain storage elevators. Nevertheless, the dignity of the individual is asserting itself in Russia without the sponsorship of religious gospel. It can be facilitated by secular means as it has been in the United States. The phenomenon of the dignity of the individual, which is the keystone of the West, is playing havoc with the Soviets' Marxian bible.

Russia, which is one of our fatherland countries, is challenging America in assuming a moral obligation to Mr. and Mrs. Everybody everywhere. Yes, there is a basic morality in Russian Communism. This is the moral dilemma of the great America as we enter the 1960's. Our theologians have not been able to resolve this moral dilemma for the obvious reason that they cannot concede that Communism can function morally. But, for reasons that I hope I have made abundantly clear, I can, because I recognize spiritual freedom as a natural process in life.

In the fall of 1955 Khrushchev went to India and inaugurated the Kremlin's Point Four to a non-Communist government. This was right after the Geneva Summit conference which was supposed to create a friendly atmosphere to promote peace. And the first thing that the Kremlin did was to go to India and declare economic war on America and the West. America's politicians, theologians, enterprisers, and majority scribes concluded and preached two things:

1. You can't trust the Russians. You can't make agreements with them. Look what they are doing in India and the Middle East right after Geneva.

2. The purpose of Russian economic aid is to subvert the government, conquer the people, and dominate the world.

The difficulty in resolving this moral dilemma, that Walter Lippmann[2] has come the closest to formulating, is that both of

---

[2] Walter Lippmann should conquer his humility with certitude, and tell America at length the decisions and sacrifices that it has to make yet in the twentieth century to be able to continue as a free self-developing people in the twenty-first century. I have been reading Lippmann since I found a used copy of his *Preface to Morals* in a Washington, D.C. secondhand book store (1933) when I was a college sophomore. His modesty in 1943 inhibited him from reporting on the growth and development of his own thinking in *U.S. Foreign Policy: Shield of the Republic,* which is just another good book, and if he had unburdened himself, would have been a truly great book. As one of his devoted readers, whose indebtedness is clear throughout these pages, and who can now forgive myself for disliking so much of what he said about F.D.R. when I worshiped that great President, I urge Lippmann to unload his innermost feelings and thoughts on the American people, and let the chips fall where they will. "The ultimate question is . . . what the teachers are to think . . . that is the preface to everything else."

these things are true: The Communists recognize no moral obligation to maintain an agreement once it no longer serves their purposes. Secondly, the Communists are committed to an ideology of world domination. But despite these two things being true, there is a moral basis to Russia's offer of Point Four aid and assistance. While the will to power in the first years of Russian Communism took precedence over the will to remove illiteracy and conquer poverty in the lands of the Czars, today the moral purpose of providing a better life for her people is crystal clear in the Kremlin. Over 90 per cent of her people have been taught the three R's, and they are in the process of achieving the three E's. Yet, before they have, they offer some of their wealth to the still poorer peoples of the world. While big, rich America, who can better afford such aid, ties it up with her Mutual Security and thereby compromises her moral integrity. When Khrushchev stood in front of the marble statue of Abraham Lincoln, it seems clear to me, he must have said to himself, "Thank God Lincoln's sitting here in 1959, and not alive in the White House."

America's moral dilemma has been simply its inability to stand on our Declaration of Independence, embrace the philosophy of Abraham Lincoln as well as his person, and practice as well as preach to the world, "All men are created equal." As Walter Lippmann in *The Communist World and Ours* says in his summing up, "What the doctor would order for our people is that they relax their fears in order to fortify and clarify their purpose . . . formidable as the Communists are, they are not ten feet tall, and the less we plunge ourselves into hysterics, the more likely we are to take good care of our affairs."[3]

America's national purpose in the world has grown out of the processes of moral development since Jamestown and Plymouth Rock when the first Americans came to these shores to be guided by one overriding principle: the creation of the more equal and better life. As we begin to see its achievement in Amer-

[3] Walter Lippmann, *The Communist World and Ours*, Little, Brown and Company, Boston, 1958, pp. 55-56.

ica, we are being forced to see that this developing Kingdom of God on earth must be shared. In the words of Russell Davenport, "Freedom is not to limit, but to share; and freedom here is freedom everywhere."

MASS ANNIHILATION IS NOT INEVITABLE

I reject the idea of inevitability that we must first go through the blood-bath of nuclear war between the U.S.A. and U.S.S.R., which would depopulate the world of a hundred million Americans and their equivalent in Russians, before we can bring ourselves to developing a moral equivalent of a killing-and-being-killed war, if then.

We have been tending in the direction of a thermonuclear war. "The intensely sharp competitive *preparation* for war by the nations is *the real war*, permanent, unceasing; and the battles are only a sort of public verification of the mastery gained during the 'peace' interval," James wrote in 1910 accurately describing "the real war" that has been going on between the U.S.A. and U.S.S.R. since 1945. Do you think that the preparation for thermonuclear war will not lead to a shooting war, when you bear in mind that in man's recorded history he has never yet been able to restrain himself from using his "mastery gained during" the preparation period once he thinks he owns such a mastery? Every American of whom I ask this vital question shrugs his shoulders and expresses a hope that the horror of nuclear weapons will restrain man this time, or expresses a faith that God won't let it happen.

I reject the idea that man will not use thermonuclear weapons because of the horror of their agonizing consequences. Because man's mind is incapable of visualizing the horror of thermonuclear war. At times I have felt that I did visualize the horror of all-out mass annihilation, but I must confess that this concept eludes me most of the time. It is like the concept of personal extinction after individual death. At times we comprehend it, but mostly we do not think about it. And when our time comes to die we leave consciousness as helplessly as we were born. There is not a thing that we can do about it. Such is the process of life.

I detect little genuine faith in America that God will save us from a thermonuclear war, as we have been indoctrinating ourselves with pictures of the horror of nuclear war. We have been using the constant threat of mass annihilation to make our people pause and think. But our difficulties are the limits of the human mind. Hitler killed six million Jews and in the process demonstrated how the killing of human beings in great big masses stuns the individual mind's comprehension. I stood inside, walked around the tomblike cellar, and circled the French memorial in Paris (at Rue Grenier sur l'Eau and Rue Geoffroy l'Asnier) to the six million Jewish victims of Hitler, trying to visualize the act of mass extermination. Try as I could the concept eluded me. I looked at Dachau, Buchenwald, and the other atrocity-center names on the outside of the circular memorial trying to picture the mass annihilation that man committed against man in my time. I was hit hard and saw the horror of it all, but for brief glimpses. Mostly the concept eluded me.

But on an individual basis or a small group basis like 50 or 125 killed in a plane wreck, the horror of death is vivid to the human mind. On our first visit to Israel (1954) I walked about in short sleeves and a tan not unlike that of Israelies. I love to walk, and I found almost everyone nodding back to me on the streets of Jerusalem and Tel Aviv. Then I noticed that they tended to look me over more carefully. At my wife's aunt's home people kept telling me how I reminded them of a brother, a friend, an uncle that had been killed in Hitler's Europe. And finally it dawned on me: hope springs eternally and dies slowly in the human bosom. I was a new person walking the streets, and I was being stared at in the hope that a man believed killed by Hitler had somehow managed to live. This experience gave meaning to me of Hitler's mass extermination such as I could not perceive when I walked around the Paris memorial of the mass murder in 1956 and again in 1958, trying to conceive it in my mind.

Who can visualize the death of one hundred million Americans? Who can visualize the horror of killing all the men, women, and children in Russia's two hundred principal cities? Hope for avoiding a mass-retaliation thermonuclear war on this basis, it seems to me, is a vain and futile hope. We must look elsewhere for our answer to stopping this killing of human beings. We must find ways to correct this killing-and-being-killed distortion of the natural processes of fighting.

If neither God nor the horror of thermonuclear weapons will restrain homo sapiens from fighting with H-bombs then what will? I have an answer to this question. Most of the answers of my contemporaries that I have read and heard are a mere hope and/or a prayer. A few that go beyond a hope and a prayer will recognize themselves in the answer that I embrace and find most eloquently expressed by William James.[4]

The premise of my answer is that fighting is a natural process in life. Empirical evidence is all around us, and the Bible contains enough such evidence to be adequate in itself. Are not certain American theologians and laymen talking about a holy war against the atheistic Kremlin? Such a war is based on the false premise of an irreconcilability between the U.S.A. and U.S.S.R. It is the shopworn dichotomy of "all good is on our side" and "all evil is on your side." This is the concept of irreconcilability, which has been the cause of religious wars, and is invalid in the twentieth-century conflict between the U.S.A., which is dominated by Judaic-Christian doctrines, and the U.S.S.R., which is dominated by Marxian doctrines. Yet it is an expression of man's inbred pugnacity for which men of God have been famous down through the centuries. One Sunday morning in January, 1776, for example, from the pulpit of his Lutheran Church in Woodstock, Virginia (where I went to prep school), John Peter Muhlenberg proclaimed, "There is a time for preaching and praying, but also a time for battle, and such a time has now arrived." Whereupon he doffed his robes and grabbed a gun. His successors, in all denominations in the 1960's, cannot run off and grab an H-bomb. I repeat: they must have faith that God will

[4] William James, "The Moral Equivalent of War," in *Memories and Studies*, Longmans, Green and Company, New York, 1934.

find his way in Russia and China without help of American thermonuclear missiles.

The idea that the American and Russian Revolutions can converge in the progress of codevelopment is fundamental to my belief that there is an alternative to a knock-em-down, drag-it-out fight with thermonuclear weapons. But there is no alternative to fighting. There is a unity at work in the emerging world civilization that enables us to fight for the dignity of man's freedom of self-development without using those great big firecrackers that Russia had been firing into the Pacific and we have been firing down the Atlantic range. This is the unity of objectives: the more equal and better life for everybody everywhere. The U.S.A. and the U.S.S.R. have these objectives in common, and by accepting the positive and deemphasizing the negative we can, in the words of Hocking, develop an "honest competition-in-human fulfillment . . . a goal and a path in which our two world missions may interpenetrate." This is codevelopment, not coexistence. It is not a peaceful undertaking, but an enterprise that disturbs the peace of age-old social customs and habits.

I do not seek agreement with the Kremlin during the 1960's. I do not think that it is either attainable or desirable at this stage of our development. I want to fight and compete against it with everything at our command except annihilation and killing-and-being-killed weapons. These we have to defuse and pigeon-hole. Self-development and the dignity of man are our weapons. Believe in man as a creature of God or as a natural process in life, and tailor your tactics and policies around him to facilitate his growth and development everywhere. Then you can transform the Kremlin's leaders as we have been transforming our capitalist leaders in the U.S.A. and as we have to do in the rest of the Western countries and in Latin America. Neither of the two dominant nations have to use their thermonuclear weapons to wage "an honest competition-in-human fulfillment." But they must fight because, in the words of William James, "Our ancestors have bred pugnacity into our bone and marrow, and thousands of years of peace won't breed it out of us."

It is this killing of human beings that we have to outgrow in our natural fighting for new creations that give a meaning to life on earth. Man killing man is not a natural process in life but is a distortion of the process of fighting. We never apologize for fighting to free the slaves, to make the world safe for democracy, to win the Four Freedoms; but we do apologize and ask God's forgiveness for killing human beings in the process of fighting for these lofty hopes of man.

The Kremlin is challenging us to a competition in peaceful coexistence. We must respond with a moral war for codevelopment. In the process of waging such a war of construction a way must be found to defuse the thermonuclear stockpiles. All the time in the meanwhile we risk a killing-and-being-killed war. The alternative static policy of building a nuclear fortress can only lead to annihilation and the kind of inflation that America fears. The dynamic policy of declaring a war for codevelopment might lead to peace on earth and good will toward all men. Under it humanity has a chance, and this is the chance we must risk. Coexistence is the Kremlin's program for world victory. Codevelopment is our program for developing a world-welfare society in which the common objective of the more equal and better life results in "human liberty under law."

America had a monopoly from 1945 to 1955 in providing the means—material and know-how—to facilitate the growth of the self-developing nations of the world. Russia could not even attempt to compete with America in spreading the three E's until after the Summit Geneva Conference of 1955, where the nuclear powers agreed that their A- and H-bombs could not be used. It is from this point on that the "irrational" panic in America began to develop into "thoughtful" panic that characterizes America going into the 1960's. The Kremlin has become our moral competition throughout the world.

Let us also understand that the $42 billion that we are spending for "defense" in fiscal year 1960 cannot be reduced very much, if any, during the years of the 1960's. This is an annual "need" that American industry has to fill each year. None of us would be here to argue about this, or any other question, if it were not for our strategic, retaliatory nuclear power. We must maintain and strengthen this power to keep the missiles and bombs of the Kremlin grounded. Any relaxation on this front would make a mockery of all our diplomacy and all of our efforts to facilitate the growth of the self-developing countries. We do not have a chance to conquer poverty anywhere unless we also have the retaliatory power to immobilize the Kremlin's nuclear power. Only so long as we can force Russia to compete economically do we have an advantage over her. We have to have the nuclear power, in deliverable form, to buy the necessary time to facilitate the development of a world welfare society with which the Kremlin will make peace. It will not make peace with just the U.S.A. as President Eisenhower learned in Paris in May 1960.

The State Department and the Pentagon, in building an iron ring of retaliatory nuclear power around the Kremlin, have purchased us fifteen years of life, fretful as they have been. But more importantly, they have kept America in business. To be sure the Russians jumped right over our iron ring in 1957 with their ICBM engines and Sputnik. They pierced our Maginot Line of bombers and A- and H-bombs. This scared hell out of us. In a few months, however, we were shooting those big firecrackers out of Florida and California at an accelerating rate, though the Republicans were too scared of inflation to appropriate the funds, and the Democrats were too scared of the people to raise taxes, to go all-out on missiles.

Our Maginot Line, and Russia's too, is a stalemate. But neither of us is secure behind it. Our only security lies elsewhere, as either power could achieve a new breakthrough that would end the stalemate and enable it—if so disposed—to blackmail the other to surrender. America's big opportunity for creative statesmanship will come during the 1960's when, I am confident, we achieve such a breakthrough.

The Kremlin's proposal for total disarmament that Khrushchev made to the United Nations in 1959 is a response to the fear of such a breakthrough. We have to respond with the moral equivalent of war to break through the vicious circle of stalemate between the U.S.S.R. and the U.S.A. There can be no lasting peace or freedom based on blackmail.

THE ACT OF DELIBERATE RISK

We come now to outlining the "act of deliberate risk, refusing any longer to shelter our national purpose behind the continued threat of mass annihilation."[5]

William Ernest Hocking brings William James up to date. My purpose is to draw the relationship between James's challenge[6] and the challenge put before us by William E. Hocking, who, like Lippmann, studied under James.

"We must find," Hocking states, "a mental equivalent of war."[7] Hocking's use of the word "mental" instead of "moral" prompted me to telephone him and ask if there was any significance in this choice of word vis-à-vis James. Professor Hocking said that there was not and sent me in January, 1960, a section of his forthcoming book *Philosophy of Law*, dealing with "Law as Alternative to Strife" in which he discusses James's "moral equivalent of war." He concludes, "Social habits build themselves into accepted customs. Customs become the groundwork of positive law." The direction of my thinking is that we have years, if not decades, of work to do around the world creating international "social habits" before the advocates of international

---

[5] Walter Lippmann in *The Country is Waiting for Another Innovator* (*Life*, June 20, 1960) says, ". . . to affirm the ultimate ends . . . is not a substitute for declaring our purpose and leading the nation. These affirmations . . . beg the question, which is not whither the nation should go but how it should get there. The remedy . . . will be found in the innovation of the political formulae, the concrete measures, the practical programs by which our ideals can be realized in the greatly changed world we now live in."

[6] William James (1842-1910) was a professor of psychology and philosophy at Harvard University, son of a philosopher and certainly one of the top five minds among the developers of American thought. He wrote the essay "The Moral Equivalent of War" in his last year, 1910, in which he forecast Japan's war against the U.S.A., the likelihood of more wars in Europe, and the probability that they could lead to the outlawing of wars of destruction by the development of wars of construction that are their moral equivalent. All quotations of James used in the text are taken from this essay.

[7] William Ernest Hocking, *Strength of Men and Nations*, Harper & Brothers, New York, 1959, pp. 171-196.

law can achieve "positive laws" to which the Kremlin and the White House will subscribe on mutually acceptable terms. In the meanwhile they may annihilate each other: the risk!

I recommend an unabridged reading of Hocking, whose essential thought, as it bears on the main argument of this discussion, is excerpted from his latest book.[8]

The State cannot renounce its involvement with the remainder of the planet. . . . It is not alone *the state* that is everywhere: it is *each state* that is everywhere. . . . Consider the empire builders of all time. Was their common dream of worldwide sovereignty all wrong? As monopoly, yes. As world State, yes. As administered world order, *no!* If we add the principle of interpenetrating sovereignties. . . .

No nation has a right to complete nationhood, to "self-determination," until it is prepared not alone to keep order at home, but to cooperate in world-obligation and to exercise world-strength.

In the case of the USA vis-à-vis USSR . . . we have not yet taken the measure of the function of leadership. . . . The Soviet dream of world-domination [is a] . . . challenge to the latent moral strength of America. . . . No other nation is similarly called to this task . . . nor . . . is any other nation so fully qualified in terms of the moral resource demanded by this formidable task. . . . What we require is nothing less than the mental as well as moral effort. . . . We have now to analyze the conditions for such a deed.

There are, I conceive, two necessary steps, of which the first . . . need be nothing more than *defining the vicious circle* in terms both sides must recognize, avowing our own part in it, and showing that it *no longer describes the actual issue.*

For the anti-Bolshevist powers, the mental stance of 1917-1922 might have been fairly expressed in the terms of the circle: Communism must be destroyed, because for Communism Capitalism must be destroyed.

The situation now emerging after forty-odd years is:

    (i) that neither Capitalism nor Communism in the sense of 1917 exists;

    (ii) that the changes involving principle taking place during this period have been not fortuitous but necessary;

[8] *Ibid.,* pp. 167-196.

(iii) that these changes, without obliterating the opposition of principle, have been convergent.

The Soviet system may (and perhaps should) co-exist, because for the Soviets the American system may (and perhaps should) co-exist; and *vice versa*.

Both are in full accord that war is excluded as a court of appeal. And each is ready, without treason to its own faith, to tolerate the existence of the other in an honest rivalry for achieving the highest "material and moral good for mankind."

The ground is thus prepared for the second step . . . to break the circle, not by thought alone, but by an act . . . expressing good faith and tending to elicit good faith. . . . We face the final issue of a justified creative risk.

It is easy to propose an act of creative statesmanship, hard to define such an act.

There can be no shadow of doubt that they who share with us an official willingness to prepare weapons for the collective extinction of populations entertain not alone a fear of retaliation but an inward revulsion to their use.

If, I say, we find it within our mission to translate this into terms of honest competition-in-human fulfillment . . . —a goal and a path in which our two world missions may interpenetrate, there arises the possibility of an act of deliberate risk, refusing any longer to shelter one's national purpose behind the continued threat of mass annihilation.

Such an act would be based on certitude. . . . It would, indeed, be futile if done from fear; equally futile if done as an attempt to purchase good will by appeasement. (It must be done from a position of strength.)

While I am encouraged by Hocking's observation that "it is only the individual, with his private perception, that can offer the releasing idea," my confidence in attempting to define a "creative act" is based on the fact that it is inherent in my analysis of the growth and development, and future direction, of our country. Full responsibility for defining the following act is mine alone.

The stereotype of communism is as dead in Russia, as the Kremlin's stereotype of capitalism is dead in America. Our moral competition emanates from a developing form of Marxism that is adaptable to positions of strength as they are encountered—both inside Russia and around the world. This is equally true of our developing welfare enterprise system; we adjust to positions of strength as we encounter them—at home and around the world. This is the premise for the act—American creative policy—that I define.

During the rest of the twentieth century, America has to checkmate Russia by nonnuclear means. This is doable. The problem is how to do it without provoking the Kremlin to strike back with its nuclear power, especially once the success of our economic-political encirclement of Russia could no longer be denied inside the Kremlin. Despair not by this dilemma, as it is the identical dilemma confronting the Kremlin today. This is the heart of the mutual fear and distrust now extant between the U.S.A. and U.S.S.R. Walter Lippmann reports, after an interview with Mr. Khrushchev in October, 1958, that the Kremlin fears "that if the United States finds that it is going to lose the Cold War, it is likely to resort to a hot war . . . that if the Soviet Union forges ahead in technology and productivity, attracting into its orbit the old colonial territories of the European empires, the West will attack rather than lose the contest for world leadership by default."[9]

This risk cannot be avoided by either party because, in Hocking's words, "an act, as a risk from strength . . . must be a break-through, and such a break-through must have its risk, as all life-giving has its risks."[10]

Our deliberate, creative risk act is as simple as it is powerful: America must consciously assume the role of "life-giving" in Asia, Africa, and Latin America. We must work to break down the historic barriers to the emergence of the dignity of man that the indigenous leaders have erected over the centuries on these continents.

[9] Walter Lippmann, *The Communist World and Ours*, Little, Brown and Company, Boston, 1958, pp. 22-23.
[10] William Ernest Hocking, *Strength of Men and Nations*, Harper & Brothers, New York, 1959, p. 166.

It shall become the policy of the United States of America to be the willful agent of social change in each country as part of the process of raising living standards and releasing human dignity, and fighting poverty and illiteracy. In India and Pakistan, for example, we must free the poor people from their bondage to the usurious money lenders, as well as social customs that deny the sanctity of every human being.

The risk is that we build up these countries to be plucked by Russia into its orbit. But Russia, in turn, runs this same risk as for instance with the Aswan Dam in Egypt and its penetration into Cuba.

America must facilitate the growth and development of every country within the Soviet orbit, except for Russia itself.

We built a military iron ring around Russia, and the Kremlin pole-vaulted over it with intercontinental ballistic missiles. That is one round. We pole-vaulted right back. And military stalemate obtains while we each feverishly work to achieve a new breakthrough. That is the military phase, which is the concern of many other books. In this discussion we can merely note its significance. Disarmament can only follow the relaxation of U.S.A.-U.S.S.R. tensions. Those who are attempting to define a "creative act" in terms of armaments and H-Bomb testing are getting their queen too far ahead of their bishops, knights, and rooks in the worldwide chesslike contest in which the U.S.A. and the U.S.S.R. are engaged.

Our concern is with the nonmilitary phase: how to checkmate Russia with ideas, the three R's, the three E's, economic aid, technical assistance, moral concepts, development fund loans, equality in international trade and all the other nonmilitary weapons in the arsenal of democracy—not the least being able to make the Kremlin really commit its productive capacity to satisfying the needs and growing desires of her own people for the something that we already have in the U.S.A.

It shall become the policy of the United States of America to build an economic showpiece ring around Russia. In Poland, Yugoslavia, and all of our other fatherland countries now prac-

ticing a form of Marxism we shall institute a program of aid and
assistance comparable in scope and duration to the Marshall Plan.

The risk is that these countries in Europe will continue to
deny civil liberties, freedom of religious worship (whose denial
is by no means absolute now), and other social-economic-political
expressions of the dignity of the individual. But if you have faith
in God, you know that He cannot be denied and will find His
way. Or if you have confidence in the natural process of life, you
know that inner human dignity will break through the repressive
practices of government and find meaningful social-economic-
political expressions. The Communist countries in Europe are
already beginning to erupt with the realization that the permanent mobilization of individuals to serve the larger social order
must give way to social progress through the self-development of
individuals. Our task is to facilitate this growing realization.

America must interpenetrate her affairs with those of China,
by fully recognizing the People's Republic of China as fast as we
can get Peiping to let us become fully reengaged in diplomatic
and economic relations.

That Red China will not let the U.S.A. recognize her now
and is thriving internally on an irrational hate-America campaign should not deter us from proposing full diplomatic relations. Peiping of course will use Taiwan as an excuse for not
accepting our proposal, but the Peoples' Republic of China will
yield to an independent country status for this island country
when international forces and its problems with the U.S.S.R.
move into position on the chessboard where full political and
economic intercourse with the U.S.A. will also serve mainland
China's national interests. In traveling through Malaya, Singa-
pore, Vietnam, Thailand, and Burma in the spring of 1960 we
found an almost unanimous desire among nationals in these
countries with whom we talked for Peiping and Washington
to begin to interpenetrate their affairs the one with the other.

Codevelopment with Russia will become more fruitful for
America as we are able to open the doors to codeveloping with
mainland China.

The risk is that we strengthen the Chinese Communist dictatorship and help build a power that might dominate the Western world in centuries to come.

But this risk is shared with Russia, as such an American act vis-à-vis mainland China could force the Kremlin to reciprocate in kind—namely, to open up its vast Asiatic lands to settlement by the Chinese. Only a positive American pro-China policy could induce the Russians to take such a deliberate, creative risk vis-à-vis Russia and China. Both such American and Russian creative risks must recognize that no one power can ever dominate the world. All of the would-be one-world conquerors of centuries past have taught us that the most we can ever hope to achieve is a world-welfare society with accepted social habits, recognizing the natural diversities on our planet, that are eventually incorporated into international law. The fear of China someday dominating the world is therefore unreal. But in any event the risk is inherent in a nuclear war of mass annihilation between the U.S.S.R. and the U.S.A. and her allies, as who then, but China, would inherit the world! A case can be made for joining the Kremlin in a program of making a slaughterhouse out of the Orient. But I believe in humanity, to use the words of William James, for the "yellow as well as the white countries." And it is this case that I make. We should facilitate the emergence of China, instead of abdicating to the mass annihilators or surrenderers in our midst who may arise and urge us to enter into a pact or tacit understanding with the Kremlin, if need be, to H-bomb a billion people out of existence in the Orient.

The Kremlin is challenging America to compete in this "life-giving" competition for the minds of the emerging peoples in Asia and Africa and the enslaved and/or emerging peoples in Eastern Europe and Latin America. If the Kremlin knew our history as I trace it in these pages, or had any idea about the magnitude of "the moral resource" latent in American bosoms (to which Hocking refers), its leaders would not be challenging us to compete in "this formidable task" of working for human betterment, personal freedoms, and international law in a developing world-welfare society. They shall learn in the years ahead what a miscalculation they are making in not seeing that America has been in the process of fomenting a world-wide democratic, social revolution for over three centuries, of which the Russian Revolution is but a temporary distortion in the process of recognizing the natural role of the individual in society with freedom for self-development.

As we accelerate and consciously engage ourselves in this "life-giving" moral war with the Kremlin, the risk of preventive or pre-emptive, nuclear war is reduced on both sides. Gradually in the course of the last four decades of this century, as the Kremlin and America facilitate the self-developing countries of the world, accommodations between the Russian and American systems will be reached, and, step by step, recognized in agreements, treaties, and other diplomatic and trade instruments. This conclusion is based on the premise, as stated, that each system adapts itself to positions of strength as they are encountered.

We are engaged in a contest with the Kremlin, to be fought by all means short of nuclear war, until the policy of the Marxian-derived systems recognizes that the individual is an end in himself. The outcome of this titanic struggle for the hearts, minds, and souls of the emerging people, it is the argument of this book, will be victory for the natural processes of the dignity and self-development of the individual. Boris Pasternak has already told his fellow Russians that "the spiritual world of our inner life" is reawakening behind the Iron Curtain.

The risk is that we will come out on the short end. Or that once we have cornered the Kremlin, it will attack us militarily just like Mr. Khrushchev fears we might do once the Kremlin, as it hopes, encircles America with unfriendly powers.

Our best, and perhaps, last hope lies in "life-giving." Communist leadership thrives in the absence of all other leadership. Provide a moral leadership, based on the dignity of the individual, and the communist leaders are licked. The creative risk act is as simple and as difficult as just that.

Democracy will come out on the long end of the eventual

accommodations with the U.S.S.R. It is not important whether a country adopts an executive-legislative-judicial system, a parliamentary system, a party-congress system, as long as the individual is recognized as an end in himself, as long as the people have an equal chance to create a social order in which the leaders, in the words of Abraham Lincoln, say, "As I would not be a slave, so I would not be a master." The White House should taunt the Kremlin with this until it is no longer true.

Prime Minister Jawaharlal Nehru of India, as Hocking states, believes that the "suppression of freedom" in the U.S.S.R. will not long be tolerated by the beneficiaries of its notable educational system. From all that I have been able to read and learn about the history of China, I would not want to be the Chinese leader who persisted in trying to keep the dignity of man bottled up indefinitely among the oldest civilized people on the planet. Walter Lippmann observes, "He would be a rash man, I think, who would say that such great masses of backward people could be persuaded by democratic methods to accept the disciplines and to make the sacrifices which are necessary to the rapid formation of capital in a primitive economy."[11] Our basic problem is to help create the social conditions out of which freedom can grow. The risk is that we lose, but we can win, too.

It follows, in conclusion, that our "life-giving" creative act in each country must be tailored to fit its conditions, and to try to impose democratic freedoms prematurely is to snuff out the "life-giving" act at birth. We had almost 250 years of history under our belts (1619-1865) before the words "freedom" and "equality" began to mean much in the United States of America, and we are still in the process of giving reality to them for millions of our own people a century after the start of our Civil War.

The Kremlin is our moral competition in this war. The outstanding impression that I got from the U.S.S.R. Pavilion at the Brussels World's Fair in 1958 is that the Russians share the Americans' fear that Mr. Fusion may end their days prematurely, and

[11] Walter Lippmann, *The Comunist World and Ours*, pp. 22-23.

they do not like it. They want to enjoy some of the luxuries of life that are so widespread in America before humankind departs from this orbiting space ship that we call our planet.

My wife and I both stood for a long minute looking at a white, ornamental, metal sign that the Soviets had effectively displayed as one mounted the last flight of stairs to the formal floral display at the base of Lenin's statue. Prominently, in large letters, through the middle of the sign was the word PAIX, and in all the languages of the world were inscribed the word PEACE. We looked at it again, and again. We came to the conclusion that it may be a superficial judgment to dismiss it as "propaganda" only.

Is this Russia's new religion? Their new faith? Is it their new icon? We are told that PEACE signs are all over Russia. Are they the new icons of the Communists?

The meaning of these signs was understood by William James. " 'Peace' in military mouths today is a synonym for 'war expected.' The word has become a pure provocative, and no government wishing peace sincerely should allow it ever to be printed in a newspaper. Every up-to-date dictionary should say that 'peace' and 'war' mean the same thing, now *in posse*, now *in actu*."

James's use of the word government is all-inclusive. Peace is war whether the word is spoken in the White House or the Kremlin. I repeat: It is the policy of your country and mine to kill all of the men, women, and children in the two hundred major Russian cities, in the words of James, "when forced upon us, only when the enemy's injustice leaves us no alternative." But war has become "absurd and impossible from its own monstrosity" when, as James further observed, "whole nations are the armies, and the science of destruction vies in intellectual refinement with the sciences of production." So we have to rethink and refeel our situation and be guided accordingly.

Hocking's idea is to evoke a reciprocal creative act from Russia by initiating—from a position of strength—one ourselves. Such an act at this time must be a vis-à-vis the third-party nations. I define the act vis-à-vis the nations surrounding Russia as a counter move to the Soviet program of encircling the United States of America with an iron curtain of Soviet-dominated countries on all continents that will bring us to our knees without fusing one bomb. Not until we win the world-wide contest for men's minds can we hope to develop with the Kremlin a modus vivendi in which the world would be safe for democracy. As our efforts create positions of strength, the Kremlin will respond with acts recognizing the kind of moral responsibility under international law that we aspire to in our better moments. In the meanwhile until our relative positions of strength vis-à-vis the other nations are solidified, we must live under the risk of annihilation. Because we are committed to the Lincolnian proposition that the world can not endure half free and half slave. That it can is the falsity of coexistence.

Let us refer again to the steel-industry analogy. As long as the company defaults to the union in appealing to the steel-workers, the union will dominate the results of negotiation. As long as the U.S.A. defaults to the Kremlin in appealing to the emerging people, the Kremlin will dominate the results of nego-tiations; always, like the union, wringing out some concessions. A creative policy, leadership from strength, can wring out of the union in the steel industry, and the Kremlin in the world, the as-sumption of moral responsibility to help feed the cow as well as milk her in steel, and to help create social conditions leading to international law instead of the exploitation of poverty for national or imperialistic gain. Such a creative policy can develop out of the American people through Congress and the White House, if the leaders in the Executive Suites with courage and foresight win out over the shortsighted who have dominated basic policy making in the past.

MAKING RUSSIA DEVELOP HERSELF

We do not help Russia by extending credits to her and shipping the capital goods that she would use to oppose us in the war of construction in the third-party countries that lie between the U.S.A. and the U.S.S.R.

America must comprehend the meaning of the words being

spoken advocating that we walk into the Kremlin's spiderweb. One such voice is that of a man well versed in the history of philosophy, who should know better. *The New York Times* (May 20, 1959) reports:

> Cyrus S. Eaton, prominent Cleveland industrialist who visited the Soviet Union last year, believes there is $3,000,000,000 worth of business waiting for the United States industries in the Soviet market. Since his return from Moscow, Mr. Eaton has conferred here with several Soviet trade officials and diplomats. . . . He was host in Cleveland to Anatas I. Mikoyan, First Deputy Premier of the Soviet Union, during Mr. Mikoyan's visit to the United States early this year. . . . Mr. Eaton said he was convinced that expanded commercial dealings would be of mutual benefit. It would provide both jobs and profits for the United States, he said, and would help the Soviet Union in its ambitious program of economic growth.

A third of a year later, in September 1959, Nikita Khrushchev came to America to sell us a smiliar package of "jobs and profits" through "trade with Russia." This package is the Kremlin's. Many other distinguished American salesmen are, and increasingly will be, trying to sell this Kremlin deal to you and me. I refuse to buy it.

Eaton's idea that we ship Russia steel pipe for gas lines, chemical plants for plastics, and other things to help the Kremlin develop Russia is as fallacious as the idea of the United States shipping to Russia uranium-235, plutonium-239, uranium-238, and other components of H-bombs to help the Kremlin blow up America. We want an arrangement with Russia to defuse the H-bombs. We want to develop two-way trade relations and bring the cold war to an end. But we have to checkmate Russia in the cold war first before we start liquidating it, or we will get liquidated in the process. Like Eaton, the conservatives on this front want to "make a buck" now and let the future take care of itself. I say, let's sell to and finance the other self-developing countries first. With success on this front we can move into profitable two-way trade with Russia, but that is some years away. It is much too early to think of changing Russia's self-sufficiency policy. No continuing markets can be developed there. We have to create markets everywhere else first.

This is how I would handle the Kremlin during the 1960's through our civilian offices:

1. Build an economic "showpiece" ring around Russia.

2. Make the Kremlin develop her own economy on her own, and stimulate the Russians to demand *now* from the Kremlin all of the necessities of life and more and more of the better things in life—before the H-bomb gets them.

3. Refuse to sell raw materials, know-how, or capital equipment to Russia until the objectives of our economic "showpiece" ring are achieved, except as this may be necessary to achieve point two above.

This kind of program calls for a great President who can coordinate the Pentagon and the civilian agencies in exporting the American Revolution. To Lincoln the great hero was the people; Carl Sandburg reminds us, "He could not say too often that he was merely their instrument." A great people make a great President provided, as in the case of Lincoln, the people have elected a man with the necessary compassion and intellect to become great. The American people are looking for ideas, for "a moral equivalent of war" to free them from the fear of "mass annihilation" and the steady diet of killing wars that they have been living and dying on during the first six decades of this century.

We do not help an opponent in such a war, as Eaton proposes. Russia must take care of herself. At the same time we have to be practical. Some trade will be expedient. For example, Khrushchev visited a cold-rolled steel mill manufacturer in the Pittsburgh area and expressed a desire to buy a cold-sheet rolling mill. Auto body and fender stock are produced on such a mill. It would be to our interest to stimulate auto production inside Russia, though the same mill could roll jacket sheets for missiles. On the other hand, we hurt ourselves in such trade because the main raw material that Russia has to sell us is manganese-bearing ore. We are now facilitating the mining of this ore in several self-developing countries, such as India, Brazil, and Ghana, and should not abandon these efforts for Russian manganese. In advocating a policy of no-trade with Russia at this stage of the war of construction, I am mindful of the multitude of reasons and practical considerations that make it unwise to be absolute in administering such a policy. But in being practical, we must not be foolish; the Kremlin leaders are a tough bunch who fight to win and fight for keeps.

George F. Kennan has proposed the disengagement of Russian and American military forces from Europe. France has already begun to kick out our military. Our armed forces in Europe are mere hostages. The problem is one of timing. We have to be fully engaged on the economic front in Europe before we can disengage militarily, as we must always act from a position of strength to evoke a reciprocal act from the Kremlin.

For over a decade we have been exporting the American Revolution. The Kremlin wants America to help her further develop Russia. In time we shall do so directly. But now we should do so only as a fellow codeveloper in the world. We have to first win the minds, hearts, and souls of the peoples of the world who are not citizens of either Russia or America. One way to such a victory is through the encirclement of Russia with developing showpieces of democracy and freedom through self-development. Once we succeed in this program, we can engage in commercial intercourse with Russia. Our purpose will then be to facilitate the transformation of the Soviet into an approximation of welfare enterprise in which the individual plays his natural role in society. That is our long-term objective. In the meanwhile we have to achieve our short-term objectives among the peoples encircling Russia. With our dynamic policy of codevelopment we can outperform Russia, because we have already demonstrated the superior satisfaction of human wants through our welfare enterprise. All the Kremlin has been able to do is proclaim that Russia is going to catch up with us. We shall see about that.

CHAPTER FIFTEEN

THE MORAL EQUIVALENT OF WAR

The time has come for believers in the dignity of man and promoters of democratic institutions to win abroad and to rewin at home the necessary freedoms for self-development, by translating into practical measures William James's moral equivalent of war. It has taken nuclear power to make James's idea (that Hocking has brought up to date) doable in this century. Nuclear war is not bloody; it is final. A case can be made for survival from a nuclear war, but humanity would not survive in any form recognizable by what we know as civilization. Survival after a nuclear war requires no great thought; it is a cesspool into which you just fall of your own incompetence and lack of courage and morality.

Examining the effects of the Civil War a half century later William James wrote, "Ask all our millions, north and south, whether they would vote now (were such a thing possible) to have our war for the Union expunged from history, and the record of a peaceful transition to the present time substituted for that of its marches and battles, and probably hardly a hand-ful of eccentrics would say yes. Those ancestors, those efforts, those memories and legends, are the most ideal part of what we now own together, a sacred spiritual possession worth more than all the blood poured out." In realistic style James then culled out three basic conclusions for his posterity: first, we would fight more wars "when forced upon us"; second, "war must have its own way" until "an equivalent discipline is or-ganized"; third, war will become "absurd and impossible from its own monstrosity."

A third of a century later the monstrosity of war was demonstrated with A-bombings in Japan. Now magnified in monstrosity more than a thousandfold, they make another world war "absurd" if not "impossible." Yet every one of us feels that war is inevitable, because, as James reminded us, "Our ancestors have bred pugnacity into our bones and marrow."

Fighting is a natural process in life. We have to fight. We do not want to fight with H-bombs and missiles, as such fighting would be suicidal. So we are now forced, a half century after James, a century after the start of our own Civil War, to or-ganize "an equivalent discipline" for a killing-and-being-killed war. We are developing a moral equivalent, a war in which ballots replace bullets in resolving disputes between nations as they have between the states of the U.S.A. Is this still the im-possible dream that all the generations before ours have dreamt? Each generation has the moral obligation to try and make that dream come true for generations yet unborn. This sense of moral obligation is the meaning of life. Reject it, and you reject life.

The Kremlin has developed a moral equivalent in its con-cept of competitive peaceful coexistence. The Russians are disciplining themselves to wage this war everywhere, fully pre-pared to use nuclear weapons when forced to, or given the opportunity by our exaggerated fear of inflation that might give them a clear mastery. Russia will use its surplus foodstuffs and industrial output, when it has any, to win the billion uncommitted peoples of the world; the Kremlin is exporting part of its current short production by denying the needs and desires of its own people. "Peaceful coexistence," says the Kremlin, "can and should develop into peaceful competition for the purpose of satisfying man's needs in the best possible way."

In mobilizing its people to forgo necessities now, to build dams in Egypt and steel mills in India, the Kremlin is ahead of America. American commentators on Russia erroneously attribute this disciplined, dedicated purpose of Russia primarily to its totalitarian regime. A more perceptive judgment might see a genuine moral fervor in the Russian people's declared war to achieve the good life for everybody. The power of the Kremlin stems from its ability to generate the spiritual, creative, inner forces of its people, more than it does from its materialistic preachments.

Israel in the Mediterranean has already become an inspiring example of what the spiritual creative energies of a free people can do with a desert and rock hills. It is the key to the Middle East that has evoked the inner humanity of the exploiting Arab shieks to begin the extension of the three R's and three E's to their own people. More importantly, Israel has begun to facilitate the emerging people of Ghana and Burma and other Asian-African people with technical assistance. Like all other natural processes, the process of self-development is self-reproducing. The stated objective of Arab leaders to push Israel into the sea, even if it takes them two hundred years, is no different from Khrushchev's stated objective to bury us. The forces of human dignity forging freedoms for self-development in the United States and Israel, on the other hand, are out to transform the enslavement of peoples to totalitarian governments and the degradation of poverty. The power of Israel stems from its having developed its own moral equivalent for war that has unleashed the energies of its people to convert the inert sands into life-giving greens.

Americans have all the equipment for greatness. It is only a question of whether and how we use it. The argument of this book is that America will employ its full equipment—mental, moral, spiritual, and material—to wage a war of construction. We have not yet developed a near unanimous public philosophy that Americans should facilitate the good life for everybody everywhere, even if the doing requires higher taxes and other sacrifices. If we had, the argument of this book would be moot.

This book, drawing on the history and thought of America, offers as national policy the concept of constructive codevelopment and proposes the mobilization of our resources and people to further our own self-development by facilitating the self-development of the third-party countries, until the U.S.A. and U.S.S.R. are forced to defuse their nuclear weapons and formally facilitate each other's self-development.

Those who fear the losing of our liberties in the process fail to comprehend the nature of democratic self-development. Abraham Lincoln waged the last civil war in America to preserve the Union that would not be "too weak to maintain its own existence." He understood that freedom requires a strong government, and he had faith that such a government would not be "too strong for the liberties of its own people."

The error of the generally accepted writers on public affairs in America during the 1950's is a lack of insight into the true character of Abraham Lincoln. His million-word record, as I read it, is the thought of the Bible translated into everyday American speech. This alone would give Lincoln's written record universality. But he was also a great disciplinarian, as is the Bible. He risked civil liberties and individual freedoms for the greater freedom of a United Union and an enslaved people. He was no visionary, but a practical social democrat. Lincoln had his conservative as well as creative side. He sought to stop the spread of human slavery in America and with a true evolutionary view of history felt that this would be a practical achievement for his generation. Such a victory, he hoped, would in time lead to the institution of slavery withering and being buried by later generations. This solution was not acceptable to the slave states, who forced the Civil War on Lincoln. He then sought merely to save the Union and freeze slavery to the states practicing it. But at the same time, as I read him, he felt that an antislavery agitation that could bring on a Civil War contained the social-economic-political horsepower to abolish the institution entirely. It was only a matter of time until the Emancipation Proclamation could be issued, within the framework of the Constitution that had ignored slavery at the inception of the United States of America. As soon as emancipation could be proclaimed as an instrument for saving the Union, Lincoln did what he never dared dream could be done by his generation. He achieved the work of several generations in one. That is social revolution.

And Abraham Lincoln, the humanist who translated the Bible into the everyday language and issues of his time which has equal validity a century later, the conservative man who believed in making social progress a step at a time, was cast in the creative role of a social revolutionist who succeeded. He won the war for the Union, which also freed the slaves. This made Lincoln a common saint for all people everywhere and for all time. Lincoln was the greatest product of America up to the Civil War, and we have never produced anything more universal since. But more importantly the person and success of Lincoln made America the country that it is in the process of becoming.

EFFECTING SOCIAL CHANGE AS NATIONAL POLICY

The continuing quarrel that people like me will have with our predominantly conservative world developers is basic. It is the difference between Abe Lincoln as an image on a penny, or a five dollar bill, and Abe Lincoln as a facilitator of social change. When we accept the idea that we are exporting the three R's and E's we have to accept the idea that we have to break with many of the ruling groups in the third-party countries. We have to accept the idea that we are supporters of great social changes that give meaning to personal freedoms. The American Revolution is not merely an idea. It is a way of self-developing life. Too many of our conservatives think that we are exporting know-how and capital. It means little in the third-party countries unless it results directly in increasing the dignity of man. Teaching the three R's is one way. Dozens of other ways are being detailed by the hundreds of perceptive Americans who are gaining practical experience, through ICA and other agencies and private firms, in the emerging countries, and by the studies being financed by the Ford, Rockefeller, and other funds.

Barely a week passes when someone or some committee does not publish a book or report dealing with the practical ways that the U.S.A. can facilitate its own development by facilitating the self-developing countries. Almost every issue of all the serious magazines carries at least one article on some phase of international economics and politics. The technical competence of America's specialists working in the field of international political economy is impressive. They are learning their stuff. But they are like a machine shop full of skilled and talented machinists. They need basic blueprints to translate into finished programs of action. America, through its managers of public affairs, has to forge a basic blueprint of purposes and goals to which they can devote their talents.

The military phases of Point Four[1] must be continued as part of the process of effecting social changes. Military assistance and defense support to the third-party countries should be raised or lowered in each country as changing conditions require. The governments of Korea, Viet Nam, and Pakistan, for example, are not democratic in the sense of 1960 America, but they are democratic in direction. They must be supported and maintained in power by military support. Alone, this support is

[1] I use the shorthand term Point Four to cover American grant and/or loans or sale of food surpluses as carried out by our several agencies, such as Marshall Plan for Europe, Technical Cooperation Administration, Foreign Operations Administration, International Cooperation Administration, Export-Import Bank, Development Loan Fund, Latin-American Development Bank, and International Development Association. My concept of E^3 embraces these and overseas development activities of private corporations which are becoming the greater part of the U.S.A.'s Point Four efforts.

bad military tactics. Simultaneously we must facilitate the development of social conditions upon which the foundations can be built for the kind of democratic government Lincoln described on July 4, 1861. We must employ human betterment as a military tactic, taking the risk that the democratic freedoms will emerge in the process.

What we have to teach is the American social revolutionary experience of the rich and powerful facilitating human betterment as a moral obligation to the maintenance and enlargement of their riches and power, with the freedom of the people to form counterorganizations to evoke their inner humanity. In the process they share the fruits of greater national production, and the economic-political decision-making power for the distribution of increased wealth. "Morality by its very nature cannot be imposed, but must be self-developed. Everyone, therefore, should share in the control of the state, which is the supreme organization for the regulation of human conduct," J. Roland Pennock[2] says in his definition of the theory of democracy. We have to learn how to translate this formula into practical measures that will work in each self-developing country. While we maintain dictatorial governments in power with military assistance, we have to simultaneously be effecting social changes among their people that build a fire under any such government that fails to share the proceeds of aid in freedom for self-development and increased national wealth with the people who help produce it.

Russell Davenport observed how the Communists have taken the word "democracy" and "transformed it into its opposite. The same is true of a long list of terms, such as 'liberal,' 'justice,' 'peace' and 'brotherhood.' These are the very terms of freedom, converted dialectically to serve the aims of the enemies of freedom. . . . That which the free world has been witnessing is a kind of philosophical rape."[3] In the crucial 1960's America has to offset the plundering of democracy's vocabulary

[2] J. Roland Pennock, "Reason, Value Theory, and the Theory of Democracy," *American Political Science Review*, October, 1944, p. 865.

[3] Russell W. Davenport, *The Dignity of Man*, Harper & Brothers, New York, 1955, pp. 52-53.

with deeds of social action. We have learned that merely exporting the words freedom, liberty, and democracy is not exporting
the American Revolution. The emerging people want the meat of
our revolution, the three R's and the three E's, as instruments of
social change through self-development. Any American program
abroad that violates this principle of social change is doomed. For
example, not all third-party nations are self-developing. Some are
underdeveloped with the people subjected to exploiting corrupt
leaders. These underdeveloped countries can be sold by corrupt
leaders to either camp; self-developing ones force their leaders
to concentrate on national needs and steer clear of going behind
the iron curtain. Free independent countries are the democratic
nations' objective; and the United States' job is to develop such
countries.

President Dwight D. Eisenhower embraced the idea of
effecting social change in other countries as American national
policy in announcing his plan for improving relations with Latin
America on July 11, 1960: "Each period in history brings its call
for supreme human effort; at times in the past it took the form of
war. Today it takes the form of social evolution or revolution."
This statement, provoked by the Cuban Revolution, did not
make a social revolutionist out of President Eisenhower, but it
gives hope that the American President who presides over the
centennial of Lincoln's presidency will be pursuing social revolutionary policies around the world, whether he is a republican or
a democrat.

Red Skelton spoke for vain, ignorant America when he
cracked, "As the Explorer orbits around the world every hour
and a half it says to each country that it passes, 'Want any dollars? Want any dollars?'" These countries in a single voice
reply, "No. We want the three R's and the three E's."

America, like Lincoln, has something that everybody wants
"to see spread everywhere over the world." In the first dozen
years of E³—economic aid and technical assistance—America
stumbled all over itself "helping" people everywhere instead of
facilitating their self-development. The A.F.L.-C.I.O., and each

of its constituent unions, have a special responsibility for facilitating the three R's everywhere. My basic criticism of the labor movement today is that its program consists of telling the President, Congress, and industry what they should do to facilitate the development of America and the world. But there is little in the A.F.L.-C.I.O.'s program that it proposes to do itself. The labor leaders are accomplished organizers, and I propose that they give leadership to the war against illiteracy everywhere, since organized labor pioneered the three R's in America. The more I see of more labor leaders, the more impressed I am with their frustrations. Just fighting for better "wages, hours, and working conditions" for the highest paid workers in the world is not very soul-satisfying. They should take the leadership to spread the three R's, getting the appropriations through Congress, and otherwise helping the missionary movement that singlehandedly is now carrying the torch to teach the three R's to the peoples to whom our politicians and enterprisers are providing military, economic, and technical assistance.

In his Inaugural Address of January 20, 1949, President Harry S. Truman defined Point Four: "We must embark on a bold new program for making the benefits of our scientific advances and industrial progress available for the improvement and growth of underdeveloped areas." With the advantages of a decade of experience we now know that he should have defined Point Four: "We must embark on a bold new program of teaching the three R's to everybody everywhere, so that they might learn from our great scientific advances and industrial progress how to facilitate the self-development of their own countries and be enabled to eradicate poverty."

America's inherent advantage over Russia in the 1960's is that we can provide more economic aid, surplus food, and technical assistance now. But we compete on an almost equal footing with Russia in facilitating literacy. We are both white men competing for the minds of the nonwhite peoples. But even here we also have an inherent advantage over the Kremlin. We have a Christian missionary movement and organization that has been fighting poverty and illiteracy for over a century everywhere, and a population of almost twenty million American Negroes of whom the ablest and most dedicated can be mobilized to go to all lands to win the minds of the nonwhite peoples for democracy, freedom, liberty, free enterprise, capitalism, moral values, the dignity of man, equality, integration, fraternity, religious freedom, welfare enterprise, free labor movement, self-development, life, liberty and the pursuit of happiness, and the three E's, or whatever words, phrases, or concepts by which you best understand America.

The missionary movement employs literacy, medical, agricultural, sanitation and other technical missionary workers. For decades they have been spreading the ideas of American democracy and freedom for others to emulate. They have learned the hard way that the biggest freedom is freedom from poverty of the mind, body and soul, freedom from want. These experienced fighters know that none of the freedoms, or democracy itself, have any meaning until the primary freedom from poverty is won. I have heard missionaries criticize themselves for not teaching God to their constituents. They call them bread-and-butter Christians. "Quit feeding them and healing their ailments, and they will quit coming to your prayer meetings," one critical missionary says to another. How can a hungry, disease-infected man pray to God, when he has to forage for his food with a swollen belly and inflamed eyes?

Obviously their sicknesses have to be healed, their elementary poverty conquered. But unless their illiteracy is also cured, when you stop healing and feeding them, they will quit America for communism, or anybody else, who will teach them the three R's, and enable them to facilitate their own self-development. To spread the three E's with lasting effects Americans also have to go out and teach the three R's. To do this America should employ its trained missionaries and its Negro citizens. Many International Cooperation Administration Missions have modest educational programs, such as those in Vietnam. These should be greatly expanded, while economic development projects that have been in their budgets should be undertaken by welfare enterprise with appropriate guarantees where local conditions require them.

The three R's work for communism as well as democracy. Kerala in India had the highest literacy and the greatest concentration of Christians. It was the first to vote the Communist party into provincial power. The three R's without the opportunity for the three E's lead the literate young people into the Communist parties, for instance, in Iraq, maybe Iran, for a while in Egypt, and certainly in Japan. A full-scale literacy drive has to be combined with the development of capital improvements, useful community work, and social changes.

NOT TOO MUCH FOOD

I draw here upon my friend Stephen Raushenbush, my senior by eighteen years who is humbled by a much greater store of knowledge than I possess. He has a charming humility that expresses a wisdom to which I aspire. He is a leading conservationist, a former senior economist for the Department of the Interior, consultant on world resources to the United Nations, author of several books, and chief agricultural economist for the Public Affairs Institute which in 1958 published his *Not Too Much Food*. Raushenbush's food ideas generate a forward thrust for the U.S.A. and the planet on which it functions. He has traveled around the world reviewing them with leaders in the self-developing countries, which is as important as the ideas themselves.

The hope that our rising population will put an end to our food surpluses is a vain one. Neither the 80 million additional Americans of 1960 to 1980, nor the 350 million Americans who will be in the year 2000, can eat enough to consume all the food that we can grow. "The chances seem to be that, if the recent rate of farm output continues," Raushenbush says, "the potential surpluses will remain, and may outrace the prospective population gains." He adds:

The prospect is apparently about as follows: If population doubles by the year 2000 and then stands at 350 million instead of 175 million, the annual rate of increase will be 1¾ percent. But farm output (on a constant acreage basis) has been increasing by two percent annually. (In 1958 the increase was about nine percent.) Over a 42-year period this difference in rates makes quite a difference in results. . . .

Clearly the prospect for the last part of the century cannot be laid out dogmatically, with any high degree of certainty. However, the chances seem to be that many of the farmers in the United States will be burdened by the prospect of surpluses throughout much of the rest of the century. Since such surpluses cause depressed prices and depressed farm incomes, the problem of handling farm surpluses is quite likely to remain a major and continuing problem for both the farmers and the nation. No quick solutions are possible. The International Wheat Surplus Utilization Conference at South Dakota State College in 1958 concluded that as long as present protective devices and technology continued "there seems unlikely to be any material change in the general surplus situation, despite the continuing increase in population."

Probably few questions have troubled some of us as much as those which involve our magnificent capacity to produce food and fiber and our apparent inability to match up our surplus with the world's desperate hunger and need. There seems to be some basic failure in our American ingenuity or in our humanity, or both. . . . There is not more food and fiber production in the United States than the world needs. There is certainly an ineffective distribution and use of it throughout the world.

Raushenbush's ideas tie up our surpluses with the building of public works in the self-developing countries that:
1. Provide work for their people.
2. Create wealth for their nation.
3. Facilitate their self-development in education.
4. Open up markets, not only for our surplus food and fiber, but for our industrial products as well.
5. Create a functioning economy which our welfare enterprisers, as well as direct government agencies, can facilitate.

The genius of his proposals lies in how they can solve our surplus agricultural production problems at home at the same time. And at no additional cost. We pay with more production, not more dollars. We finance with credits that are repayable with interest. Production underwrites the credits. The basic proposition is simple: Either we do not grow the food, or we grow it and use it to cut the cost of surpluses to our taxpayers and to facilitate the self-developing countries. We are propelled by the pressing need to find outlets and solutions to our growing surplus of foods and fibers and jobs for our expanding labor force, as well as by a compassion for Mr. and Mrs. Everybody everywhere.

During the last decade the U.S.A. shipped over twenty billion dollars worth of foodstuffs to over ninety countries on all of the continents. On a few of the first shipments local Communist agents may have attached "From Your Russian Comrades" labels. But as ton after ton arrived with Uncle Sam's emblem firmly attached, these people realized from where these foodstuffs were coming. Our ability to ship and ship has upset the Kremlin and driven it to accelerate its own agricultural production.

During the first half of 1959 Raushenbush presented his "Two-Way Food and Jobs"[4] proposal to leaders in Southeast Asia, Pakistan, India, and Iran. He stimulated their critical review, and challenged their imagination to take the bold steps into an accelerated pace of self-development. He returned home, recast his ideas in the light of his two-way exchange of knowledge, sent his sharpened proposals around the world asking interested parties for further critical suggestions.

Raushenbush says of his program, "This is a proposal and mechanism for creating new demand for surpluses by creating new employment. It is not a 'give away' or a 'dumping' program, nor one which injures normal commercial markets. It is a joint endeavor to convert surpluses into capital goods in the

---

[4] Stephen Raushenbush, *Not Too Much Food*, Public Affairs Institute, Washington, D.C., 1958, and *Surpluses for Growth and Peace*, Public Affairs Institute, 1959.

form of public works in the developing nations. An important by-product gain for America is lower prices for the ultimate consumers."

The processes in development in America that I have been analyzing will burst upon the world with dramatic sharpness during the decade of the 1960's. The United States has begun to forge the practical mechanisms for America to utilize its full agricultural capacity to encircle Russia and transform the communism of the Kremlin, and to raise farmers' incomes. We have the brains in America to do it. It is for the decision of 180 million individuals to tell our politicians and enterprisers to use them for this purpose.

The Russians have the brains to hit the moon. It is one thing for us to sit back and say, "We could have done it five years ago and will do it next year, too." It is quite another thing to sit back until the Russians hit the billion uncommitted people with surpluses and say, "We had them all the time, and we'll use them next year." As Russia is able to back up its trained people in the third-party nations with surpluses, their effectiveness multiplies. In Des Moines Khrushchev said, "We know that so far as corn is concerned you are the first in the United States. We are competing with you there, and we hope it will prove a useful competition."

The advantages are with the great America. Helping to solve the problems of all countries is part of the process of solving the problems of our own surplus agricultural and industrial production and providing employment for over a million additional American wage and salary earners every year. The Kremlin, on the other hand, weakens itself internally by providing technicians, food, and goods to the uncommitted peoples. Russia needs all that it can produce for her own people for several years to come.

America's current advantages in surpluses are temporary and no lasting role in the world can be built upon them. Russia eventually will develop surpluses as we have. All that will prove is that a surplus is the end result of a productive process. In the meantime we have to prove that the good material life, so created, is merely a foundation for an Age of Excellence, where human dignity and the freedom for self-development are the ultimate purposes of life on earth.

The three E's are in ferment all around our planet. The age-old defeatist ideas that the poor and impoverished must always be with us and that ignorance and illiteracy are unconquerable have died. These processes in development can evolve without a world-wide nuclear conflict into a world welfare society. There is nothing inevitable in the nature of things, however, that says that free democratic institutions will predominate in a developing world welfare society over the enslavement of people to national goals. But dedicated Americans, who understand the processes in development, can influence events in the decades ahead—if they but have the will to discipline themselves to wage a moral war of construction.

EXAMPLE OF WELFARE ENTERPRISE IN WAR OF CONSTRUCTION

During the fifties I worked against poverty and illiteracy and the insecurity and fear that breed on them. I conducted my own campaign on all the continents to facilitate the self-developing countries whose claim to a full measure of equality of opportunity America can no longer refuse to heed. I did my facilitating as a welfare enterpriser. I functioned as a water boy, spreading the know-how of developing clean, healthful drinking and irrigation water from the underground. My competitors laughed at me for spending so much time and money in the early 1950's creating an international sales and service organization, and then sat back waiting for me to go busted.

My competitors were mistaken in their judgment that as soon as President Eisenhower liquidated the Korean War, for which he was elected in 1952, he would also liquidate Point Four, for which he was not elected. I guessed that he wouldn't want to, but if he tried, he couldn't. As America entered the 1960's, the Point Four idea had been appropriated by her welfare enterprisers, who are expanding our international development activities—fast and big. We are accelerating the conversion of America's moral principles into practical programs for "a new birth of freedom; and that government of the people, by the people, for the people, shall not perish from the earth." Our conservatives are being disturbed by the realization that we have to pay a lot of dollars, production, and more taxes to convert Lincoln's Gettysburg Address into reality everywhere. They are beginning to understand that the self-developing countries have a moral right to ask us to facilitate their development, and that we have a moral obligation to respond.

During the 1930's and 1940's I was able to fight against poverty at home, and to fight for more steel capacity so that my country could fight poverty overseas.[5] Over 36 million tons of steel, that could be used to prosecute this war remain unproduced in 1960—a weakness in our economic fabric that must be repaired early in the 1960's. "The American interest is now identical with that of the world as a whole," Lancelot Law Whyte wrote in 1943.[6]

Water, one of these "things" taken for granted in the United States, is a luxury in many countries. How we in Stardrill-Keystone Company facilitated the development of clean, healthful ground water around the world illustrates in a small way how other welfare enterprisers in a bigger way can promote their own business by promoting the welfare of the people of the world who are not American citizens. Beginning in March, 1951 I began to build an organization, and we proceeded to sell, produce, ship, and service Stardrill-Keystone rigs and Acme tools everywhere that our politicians would let us trade. By 1955 we concluded a long-term arrangement with Franks Machine Company, of Enid, Oklahoma, adding rotary drilling machines to our line, and became the first manufacturer to market every type of machine—cable tool, rotary, and reverse circulation—used to drill water wells in every kind of formation,

[5] Harold J. Ruttenberg, "End the Steel Famine," *Harper's Magazine*, February, 1948.
[6] Lancelor Law Whyte, *The Next Development in Man*, Henry Holt and Company, New York, 1948, p. 300.

from 4 to 60 inches in diameter and as deep as 5,000 feet. In 1957 we published our 75th Anniversary catalog, *Drilling Holes,* in which we were able to say,

Stardrill-Keystone's purpose is to contribute toward advancing and improving all methods of drilling. We are interested in promoting the art of drilling, and send our drilling experts to all the continents of the world to:

1. Spread the American drilling know-how and
2. Bring back to the United States and carry from country to country the growing knowledge of drillers of all nations.

When the Russians started to replace us in Syria in 1956-1957 they found Stardrill rigs drilling water wells and facilitated the purchase of more of our rigs to undertake a hydrological survey as part of their Point Four. Their technicians found fifteen Stardrill rigs in Iraq when they abruptly displaced us there in 1958. Jack Allen, our sales vice-president, in 1955 had sold the development board on a program of facilitating the development of village water supply. Oscar Lundberg, head of our world-wide company, signed the order in 1956 for the first five rigs, and stationed a full-time instructor with them to teach the three R's of drilling. In 1958 we delivered ten more rigs to expand the village water supply program with the newly trained Iraqi drillers. But Arvid Lindqvist, our instructor, had to leave in a hurry. Ivan Tovarich took his place, but we shall return.

Clarence Reed, Stardrill's ace captain of the three R's of water well-drilling, is a handsome American. Go to Burma, Japan, Taiwan, the Philippines, Jordan, Spain, and the several other countries where this citizen of Ohio has spread his knowledge and know-how. Ask about him among the ground water people. You'll find an answer to *The Ugly American.* In 1959, for example, Clarence Reed helped conduct a school for over one hundred drillers in the Philippines under the supervision of Joseph Silverstone, ICA water supply engineer. A few years ago Clarence put several rigs to work in Burma. A Burmese trainee at first refused to do the harder work around the rig. He argued that he had freedom now, and before he had freedom all he did was hard work. Clarence picked up a sledge and showed him how. "I've got freedom too," Clarence said, "It's the freedom to work." His new friend got the idea. It's a dynamic one. And it works.

"Harold, they ain't got what we got. They know it. And they don't like it. But they aim to get it, and they don't care whether the white man is wearing a red shirt or a red-white-and-blue one, just so long as he teaches them how to solve their problems."

I sold the Stardrill-Keystone Company in January, 1959, to acquire the undivided time to write this book. The officials of the Koehring Company were puzzled about why it could be bought. Its potential was just being realized, and in another two or three years it might have made me a millionaire. But running your own business in which your all is invested consumes most of your creative energies and physical time.

In the spring of 1958 from atop the thirty-story-high Atomium—the central theme of the Brussels World Fair—the compulsion grew in me to get on with the writing and the completion of this stage of my thinking and synthesis of the United States of America on which I had been working for over fifteen years. In the shadows of this 2,000-ton, 160-billion-time enlargement of an elemental crystal structure—the symbol of this bringing "together the peoples of the world, so that from a confrontation of their efforts may spring a new humanism"—I could see how urgent it was for us all to find our way in the world. I had to speak out—now.

We made a success of a world-wide business venture that my "practical" competitors said was an impractical dream. In 1958 we shipped to fifty different countries on all the continents. Not until 1959 did our biggest domestic competitor even begin to try to imitate our world-wide sales and service organization. Our success has been based on two premises:

1. The continuous development of the U.S.A. is dependent upon the self-development of every other country.

2. The self-development of every country requires that

its economy be integrated into the mainstreams of international trade, a process which the more developed countries, like the U.S.A., must facilitate as an integral part of their own continuing self-development.

"You can ship to Afghanistan, Pakistan, Burma, Thailand, Viet Nam, Korea, Iran, Iraq, Angola, Rhodesia, Bolivia, and what have you," the sales vice-president of our big competitor told me in 1954, "but you'll wind up with nothing. Because all trade with them is based on U.S. aid, and when that ends, as it will, those Latin American, Asian and African countries will drop out of the export picture. There's no future with them. We are sticking to Mexico, Canada, and the more stable countries that have always been an export market. We have to be practical."

Why, in 1959, did his company change its policy, and follow our lead in developing sales in Southeast Asia, Africa, the Middle East, the poorer Latin and Central American countries, as well as in the historic export markets? The answer lies in the realization that every last country on our planet is in the process of being integrated into international trade. The American producers now need the business to employ their people and operate at an adequate profit. We need to develop new markets for our industrial as well as our agricultural surplus.

In the field of water-well-drilling, Stardrill's squad of Point Four drillers has met the Russians on several fronts, and out-drilled them. These encounters renew my faith in our capacity to perform. We can lick the Russians. Just don't tie our hands with amoral concepts about why we are there, or with obsolete moral judgments on any profits we might make while we are there.

DEVELOPING INSTEAD OF EXPLOITING THIRD-PARTY NATIONS

In September, 1959, President Eisenhower took a Lincoln-ian step into Point Four. He told Europe that they, too, have a moral obligation to help the self-developing nations. In his proposal, which was adopted, to create the International Development Association (IDA) with a billion dollar capital he told the emerging peoples of the world: We are your permanent partners in self-development, and we shall use our moral force and economic power to see that our brethren in Europe join us all in this great common effort for humanity.

Douglas Dillon, Undersecretary of State, said that the IDA's purpose is "to increase the total flow of development capital to the less-developed areas and not as a substitute for bilateral assistance from the industrialized countries."[7] Robert B. Anderson, Secretary of the Treasury, on September 29, 1959, told the finance ministers of sixty-eight nations meeting in Washington as governors of the World Bank, the International Monetary Fund, and the International Finance Corporation that the world was faced "not with a dollar shortage but with a capital shortage. . . . The United States will not shirk any part of our responsibility to help supply capital to the less developed part of the world."[8] Then he turned to the West European finance ministers and said, "There must be a reorientation of the policies of the earlier postwar period and a new determination by all the industrial countries to face the common obligation to share in the task of providing capital to the less developed parts of the free world." [9] Edwin L. Dale, Jr., in *The New York Times* (September 30, 1959) reports that Anderson told the European countries "remove [your] remaining controls on imports and payments in dollars, and extend more aid to the underdeveloped countries." Uncle Sam is evoking the inner humanity of Europe into conceding a permanent moral obligation to extend equality to everybody. The exploitation of the former colonial peoples cannot be reimposed in more refined garb. This is the age for codevelopment. The World Bank, for example, has organized over $800 million dollars from the several Western countries to undertake the Indus Basin projects in Pakistan that are a beginning toward settling India-Pakistan dif-

---

[7] *The New York Times,* October 1, 1959.
[8] *Ibid.,* September 30, 1959.
[9] *The Wall Street Journal,* September 30, 1959.

ferences. This is the first large-scale world development project jointly financed by the U.S.A. and its allies.

The capitalism of West Europe[10] will have to be transformed into welfare enterprise. While we have been pouring aid and capital into the self-developing countries, our European fatherlands have tended to drain some of it into their treasuries. While we dropped our tariff, making it easier for the West Europeans to sell over a million of their cars in the United States in the last half of the 1950's—which gave them the margin of difference that enabled them to achieve a greater convertibility in 1958-1959—they have been slow to lower their restrictions on importing American goods for dollars. We helped to rehabilitate them after the war as a moral obligation. We did not do it so that they could exploit the self-developing peoples in Latin America, Africa, and Asia, or to take advantage of Uncle Sam. Dr. Ludwig Erhard of West Germany returned home and told his people:

West Germans must ask themselves whether we have the right to enjoy all to ourselves the steady annual increase of six percent of our national product. . . . Part of this could well be devoted to aid to underdeveloped nations . . . Such aid is the greatest task of the twentieth century. It is high time that European countries begin to share the burden so far carried by the United States. . . . [and] the United States has good reason to demand an end of discrimination against its products in European markets. Liberalization of the trade policies of European countries should be carried forward with more vigor.[11]

France is doing much more in this regard than is West Germany, where Dr. Erhard is having difficulty getting his people to assume their moral obligation toward the self-developing countries.

IDA may well become the international term for Point

[10] The U.S.A. vis-à-vis our NATO allies is outside the scope of this discussion, except to note that the key to our relationships is the unequivocal emergence of general agreement in America on our national purpose in the World.

[11] *The New York Times*, October 4, 1959.

Four in the 1960's. Its basic concept is facilitation for economic growth and not aid for relief. The International Development Association, to which the United States and Europe, Canada, and Japan together subscribed an equal amount, is the first large-scale international development program in the West. It is an affiliate of the World Bank. Properly administered in a world where America rediscovers its national purpose during the 1960's, IDA can become a United Nations agency in the 1970's with Soviet participation. Such a development would be accelerated by U.N. and United States recognition of the People's Republic of China and the integration of mainland China into the mainstreams of international trade. It would enable Japan to further her own development by facilitating the self-developing Chinese mainland.

EQUALITY IN INTERNATIONAL TRADE

Espousing equality is easy. Practicing it costs money, taxes your intellect, and/or expends your emotions. While the Western industrial powers took a step forward with IDA, at the same meeting they stood still and turned a deaf ear to the urgent, unanimous plea from some emerging countries:[12] "Do something to stop the violent fluctuations in prices of raw materials" that are our largest dollar-earning exports. Chile, for example, pleaded for stable copper prices. How can she carry out long-term development projects when her dollar earnings fluctuate widely with the world markets? How can she maintain stable government during the resulting periods of unemployment and starvation except with tanks and guns? How can she service her debts to Export-Import, Development Loan Fund, IDA, while the market prices of her raw materials behave as though we were still in the eighteenth century? The brilliant talent around the rich and powerful spin fine fabrics of economic theory about the market fluctuations of commodity prices that get ordained with concepts of freedom and liberty. They raise all of the practical problems involved and conclude by doing little or

[12] *Ibid.*, September 30, 1959.

nothing, except to continue the hardship to raw material producers which is inherent in "free market" prices.

Something becomes mighty practical by doing it. America and the other industrial countries have to pay the price for devices to stabilize commodity prices on the international markets. The consequent problems will adjust themselves accordingly. Pressures for such devices have to come from the commodity exporting countries. The welfare enterprisers in government service have to facilitate these pressures. The big corporations, particularly the commodity trading houses, will fight to preserve their money-making status quo. U.S. Steel understands why it needs stable steel prices to develop long-range iron ore projects, expand and modernize its facilities and products; its management would go crazy trying to execute its growth development programs with steel prices fluctuating 20 to 40 per cent every year or two. Chile, Burma, the Philippines, Turkey, and the other self-developing countries, dependent upon dollar earnings from commodity exports, are faced with just that problem almost every year. For example, during the 1950's, Gunnar Myrdal reports in his *An International Economy*, the "underdeveloped countries" had to team up with "the countries in the Soviet bloc" to get a decision in the United Nations' Economic and Social Council "to set up a new commission to tackle the price stabilization problem." All of the industrially advanced countries voted against it, and Uncle Sam "declined to be represented on the Commission except by an observer."[13] This remnant of blind and parochial capitalism must be expunged from our body economic and politic. The emerging raw material countries will revolt to enforce stable prices, as our steel and auto industries, for example, have. Stockpiles of ferrous- and nonferrous-bearing ores are an absolute necessity to offset the debilitating effects of "free market" price fluctuations. That's welfare enterprise internationally. Our self-development is tied into the facilitation of economic growth in the

[13] Gunnar Myrdal, *An International Economy*, Harper & Brothers, New York, 1956, p. 253.

self-developing countries to whom an equal opportunity in international trade must be assured.

The struggle for international economic equality for the self-developing peoples during the 1960's will embroil us in one "practical" problem after another. As the decade of the 1950's came to a close, for example, America was concerned about its balance of payments that ran average deficits of $1.5 billion a year since 1950, but rose to $3.4 billion in 1958 and were $3.7 billion in 1959, but in the first part of 1960 dropped to an annual rate of $2.5 billion. The balance of payments and the gold outflow were being used unwisely and unfairly to thwart our Point Four efforts. Our imports in 1958 were fairly stable at $12.9 billion, but our exports dropped by $2.8 billion, from $19 to $16.2 billion in 1958 or by more than the increase in our balance of payments deficits. The 1958 decession caused that. We ran out economy at 80 percent of capacity in 1958. The poorer countries suffered more than the richer ones. They lost more income since 1956 through a drop in their commodity prices and sales volume than they received in World Bank loans. They could not buy as much from us as we have been paying them lower prices for their raw materials, and, worse, buying smaller tonnages. IDA was created to expand our exports to them. They also need stable prices to keep on buying and growing. We are all tied together in these processes of world development. The poorer countries need the richer countries. And we need to develop them as markets to provide jobs and profits in the U.S.A.

PROVING MARX'S PROPHECY WRONG INTERNATIONALLY

The richer countries are getting richer by facilitating the poorer countries to become less poor. If this formula succeeds internationally, as it has domestically in the United States, the Sino-Soviet bloc will become integrated into the international economy as it has been developing since the first trade vessels sailed the seven seas. But if the richer countries become richer while the poorer countries become poorer, the latter will be lost to the Sino-Soviet bloc. Gunnar Myrdal puts the question:

It is a relevant and immensely important question whether Marx's prophecy, which has been proved wrong for the individual nations, may not turn out to be an accurate forecast in regard to the relations between nations.

. . . to prove Marx wrong also in those international relations would require the growth of solidarity among nations on a vast scale. *The concept of the welfare state, to which we are now giving reality in all the advanced nations, would have to be widened and changed into a concept of a "welfare world."* It is probably the only alternative to giving Marx's prophecy its due in the vastly more crucial international sphere, while he has been proven wrong in the national one. . . . I for one would not commit myself to the belief that Marx's prediction of cataclysm, which proven wrong for the national states, will prove right in the international field. The unexpected may happen again. If it happens, the change of attitudes will not come as a sudden dramatic conversion of nations to internationalism but . . . will be rather in the nature of a cumulative process engendered by countless efforts, sustained faithfully over years and decades.[14]

Our domestic victories are insecure until the forms of Marxism that deny the dignity of the self-developing individual are buried. This makes America an integral part of the processes of world development that are becoming the extra supplemental organizing force for running an expanded American economy at full capacity and full employment. This is the chariot to which our horses are tied.

Lancelot Law Whyte, writing in 1943, forecast:

In the development of its own power as the dominant center of the new world, the USA, in order to maintain internal employment and world stability, will barter its export surplus for legal and political rights. This process may be concealed within the operations of an international investment authority. But after a decade of military and economic assistance to Europe, Asia, and Africa the United States will by 1950 find itself—directly or indirectly— the legal tenant of military bases, ports, factories, and plantations in all continents. The rest of the world will have sold a part of its birthright in return for the opportunity to develop, and all countries

---

[14] *Ibid.,* pp. 324-326. Emphasis mine.

will have renounced something to one another in order to achieve a general economic expansion. The exchange of goods for titles which is necessary to lay the basis for that expansion will progressively forge a world unity marked by the fading of the conception of sovereignty and the emergence of one dominant center of world power. So long as the expansion is in the main guided so as to facilitate the development of all peoples, the dominance of one or more centers will not imply domination, and the process equilibrium will be stable.[15]

LINCOLN WINS AGAIN

In May, 1956, I spoke before the NICB (Chapter Ten). An assistant to the president of a steel company came up to me after the meeting and said, "Harold, you've been in industry for ten years, but you still talk like a New Dealer." Another man argued, "That's just a big world-wide WPA you're proposing." To which I retorted, "There is more in common between why we had to facilitate the development of our own people in the thirties through the Works Progress Administration and the cold war than you realize."

I addressed the NICB again in January, 1958 (Chapter Twelve).[16] We were now in the post-Sputnik era, and our domestic decession was still receding. My talk was at the closing luncheon, and the last question from the floor brought the meeting to an abrupt end. "Where is the money coming from for the economic cold war, when the Federal government is already running a deficit?" I replied, "There is another $15 billion to $20 billion tax revenue for Uncle Sam in her unused productive capacity. We can't win the world for democracy running on only five of six cylinders. The greatly heralded American ingenuity has to eliminate the waste of idle men, machines and farms, and this can best be done by integrating our economy more fully with the international economy."

[15] Lancelot Law Whyte, *The Next Development in Man*, pp. 300-301.
[16] "A New Program for Collective Bargaining," *Management Record*, March, 1958, National Industrial Conference Board; "A Wage Program That Could Stop Inflation," *Reader's Digest*, May, 1958; and, "How to Stop Inflation," *New York Herald Tribune*, January 23, 1958.

The audience was not ready to tackle this life-or-death problem facing the great America, and anyway it was Friday afternoon with the clock approaching commuter-train schedules. The chairman adjourned the meeting. Sixteen short months later, I was back at the NICB. After Sputnik made us do some hard thinking about Russia's Point Four program, President Eisenhower appointed several committees to make recommendations. One of these was the Committee on World Economic Practices, chairmaned by Harold Boeschenstein, president of the Owens-Corning Fiberglas Corporation.

While only five years separate the Boeschenstein Report (January 22, 1959) from the Randall Report (January 23, 1954), the contrasting substantive content reveals how fast the developing 1950's raced along. The anti-Lincolnian "We recognize no such right"[17] is repealed with the forthright Lincolnian statement[18] that "the long-term interests [of the United States] are linked with the freedom and economic advancement of other countries. The peoples and leaders of each country must be convinced that the United States' economic program is a part of a two-way cooperation effort. We must make clear that, contrary to Communist and other propaganda, there is a fundamental community of interest between the United States and the recipient country."

These are the words of America's rich and powerful industrial and financial leaders: Henry C. Alexander, chairman, J. P. Morgan & Co.; S. C. Allyn, chairman, National Cash Register Co.; S. D. Bechtel, president, Bechtel Corporation; R. Gwin Follis, chairman, Standard Oil Company of California; Eugene Holman, chairman, Standard Oil Company (New Jersey); Philip D. Reed, chairman, Finance Committee, General Electric Company; Frank Stanton, president, Columbia Broadcasting System; A. Thomas Taylor, chairman, International Packers, Ltd.

[17] Commission on Foreign Economic Policy, Clarence B. Randall, Chairman, *Report to the President and the Congress,* January 23, 1954, p. 9.
[18] *Report of the Committee on World Economic Practices,* Harold Boeschenstein, Chairman, The White House, January 22, 1959, p. 13.

Their report proposes an elaborate series of steps that the Congress and Federal government should take to facilitate the "greater use . . . of the resources of private enterprise . . . [to] encourage balanced economic growth in the less developed areas." They propose to undertake development projects in the self-developing countries where private companies can do so at a profit and without undue risk of their stockholders' capital. Where these two conditions cannot be met, they propose that the U.S. government underwrite a normal profit and/or guarantee an investment against abnormal risk. Their program is to forge "a private enterprise-government partnership . . . to stimulate the investment of private capital and to encourage the participation of private enterprise in U.S. government programs."

To comprehend what these men are saying it is necessary to translate their report into terms that are understandable. When I read a practical report that men issue in the reality of the practical politics of the moment, I ferret out the action advocated from the verbiage in which it is clothed. Listening to Harold Boeschenstein and S. D. Bechtel sell their action program to their constituents did not give me any inside knowledge. They spoke in the same terms of their report. They spoke naturally in the accepted dogmas in which they have been reared. They may resent my translation, but you can learn what these men and America's other welfare enterprisers will be doing in the 1960's by cutting through to the heart of what they are saying.

I paraphrase their report:

Dear Mr. President:

You have over nine billion dollars of interest to pay on the Federal debt each year. To raise this money you have to tax production. We will not tolerate your taxing our wealth. But we are happy to work like beavers to increase production so that you can obtain the increased revenues from taxation to keep our government solvent. You can carry more debt on a higher gross national product, which we can achieve only by running our industrial and agricultural capacities closer to 100 per cent.

Now, Mr. President, we have a problem too. We cannot sell all that we can produce at home. No significant company is selling as much as it can produce. (True also in 1960.) We must ship our industrial surplus abroad. You shipped over a billion dollars worth of surplus food overseas last year and paid five billion dollars in subsidies to farmers. We need subsidies also. But you do not have to reflect much of them in the Federal budget. We will put up the cash for many development projects in the new countries now becoming part of the international market. All you have to do is underwrite them with guarantees. We will not risk our wealth (capital, stockholders' money) in countries or on projects that cannot pay out on time. But we will undertake these projects with the Federal government assuming the risk and spreading any losses among all of the people. This is what you do for the farmers. Do the same for industry.

You have no alternative, Mr. President, because over a million new people are looking for jobs every year and we already have four million unemployed. The farms are not giving them jobs, but in the last twenty years have sent over nine million people to industry to earn their livelihoods, and absorbed none of the increase in population. This trend continues.

Our continuing prosperity (jobs for all, self-development) is dependent upon promoting the prosperity (economic growth) of the less-developed countries.

Time is of the essence, because the Russians and Chinese are disrupting our international markets. They are trying to incorporate the less-developed countries into their bloc where they will then have a monopoly of trade with them. We need them for markets for our own surplus capacities (to facilitate their economic growth).

Frankly, we are concerned with the Sino-Soviet bloc and its "ideology and a political system alien to free ideals and principles (with an) avowed intention to dominate the world." But we don't scare easy, Mr. President, and we can lick 'em. We are willing to pool our talent and wealth with the Federal government. All we ask is that the risk be spread among the poor, the less poor, and us rich fellows. We are all in this together ("To combat the Sino-Soviet bloc, a public-private partnership is essential. Success cannot be achieved by government action alone; it requires understanding, effort and sacrifice by all our people").

And there is profit for all of us in this undertaking. To be sure, we will become richer, and at the same time our poor will become less poor. By helping the poor countries to become less poor, America will become richer. This formula for social-economic progress has worked domestically. We are confident that we can make it work internationally.

NEW MORAL JUDGMENT ON PROFITS

The first and lesser moral question is that of underwriting private profits. Democrats may denounce the Boeschenstein report as plundering of the public purse. This is the old moral judgment on private capitalism. It had validity before income and inheritance taxes. My economics and history professors taught me how "evil" the railroad magnates were in plundering the public purse in the nineteenth century. They got special concessions. They bought state legislatures. But they facilitated the opening of the West and brought the Pacific Coast closer to the Atlantic. True, they profited excessively, but America be-became a two-coast nation thirty to fifty years faster. Their excessive profits and antidemocratic actions (bribing legislators) aroused righteous indignation that facilitated the democratic processes that, step by step, transformed that kind of private capitalism into today's welfare enterprise.

The moral judgment on profits needs transforming too. Profits today are more public than private monies. This changes the moral question. Fifty-two per cent of corporate profits go to the Federal government, and this rate needs to be increased to win the world for self-developing free nations. Another one to three per cent (after Federal taxes) go to state governments. The more profits corporations and individuals earn, the more income can the Federal and state governments take in to provide more individual welfare benefits and community services. The rich could never take it with them, but they could keep it in the family. We tried to tax their inherited wealth and have had moderate success. But the rich have been able to keep control of much of their inherited wealth by putting it into charitable and educational funds, which are largely used for promoting the public or common welfare. For example, the Ford Foundation's efforts in Indonesia can be compared to those of ICA (International Cooperation Administration) itself. A member of Parliament in India told us that he felt that the Ford Foundation's programs were more significant than the I.C.A.'s in his country. In 1946-1948 when I advocated tax concessions for steel companies, for instance, to expand their capacities through accelerated depreciation, my Democratic friends charged me with selling out to the "vested interests." Time has proved the wisdom of this policy. After five years they had to begin to repay the accelerated depreciation, and in the meanwhile America had the benefit of increased steel capacity.

So, too, with foreign economic aid. I am for a policy of facilitating welfare enterprise (privately controlled capital) to join hands with the government (publicly controlled enterprisers) to facilitate the self-developing countries. Private corporations will profit and private individuals will gain. But the real beneficiary at home is the U.S.A. and abroad it is humanity.

THE NEED FOR THINKER-DOERS

The immediate future belongs to the thinker-doer. We need innovators who can devise practical programs that translate into reality the purposes espoused by this book. The role of the thinker is to strength our public philosophy so that America uses its full resources to the end that, as Henry R. Luce has paraphrased Abraham Lincoln on slavery, "Communism must be so stopped from spreading that men can confidently foresee its withering away."

The business of America is development, and not Coolidge-style business with its inherent exploitation. One of our provincial newspaper editors was shocked by his personal observation of communists in action in Venezuela shouting, "The Yankees are stealing our oil and iron ore." Fifty years ago our own people on the Mesabi iron ore range in northern Minnesota shouted the same thing, "The Eastern Monopolists are stealing our iron ore." They taxed the ore as high as they could and with the taxation built for their children the finest public school buildings of their time. This counter-force, which is essential everywhere to remind the exploiter of his exploitation, forced the Easterners, for example, to develop northern Minnesota by building a steel mill in Duluth to process Mesabi ore into iron and steel and to provide a larger employment base for these developing people. So, too, in Venezuela. My visits to Brazil, for instance, impressed me with the urgency of our facilitating the development of more iron and steel producing capacity to provide work and higher living standards for Brazilians. We will sell them more coal and steel machinery.

America's business-for-business policy in Cuba for the last sixty years has produced another revolt there. This time it is a social revolution, and not just a change of palace guard to plunder the public purse for private gain. The Kremlin moved in to facilitate the Revolutionary Government of Cuba to plunder American and other private investments for national gain. President Eisenhower responded with a social and economic development program for Latin America, excluding Cuba, to forestall comparable revolts in other Latin American countries. He and his State Department again proved incapable of proposing an act of "justified creative risk" in Cuba. This would be in the form of proposing to facilitate the Cuban Revolution's agrarian reforms and economic development, which I tried to do as a welfare enterpriser in the early months of the Castro government. The risk is that this would encourage comparable expropriations of American private property in other Latin American countries. But that risk is extant anyway. And we have to codevelop with Cuba. We cannot afford to turn its social and economic development over to the Kremlin by default. President Eisenhower in his Latin American statement (July 11, 1960) called for "supreme human effort . . . (in) the form of social evolution or revolution." His problem and that of his successor is that our State Department is inexperienced in the art of social revolution.

In Venezuela, for example, we should promote the earmarking of government revenues on oil and iron ore primarily for Venezuelan development projects that are vital to the people. In short, the practical program to stop communism in Venezuela is to facilitate the social and economic development of the country in the process of using Venezuelan oil and iron ore. How? That is the joint program for our government and our large oil and steel companies. And if the latter fail to innovate practical means, our government has to do it for them. Our vital need is for practical programs to develop the natural resources of the world without exploiting, or letting corrupt indigenous militiary governments exploit, the people in the raw-material producing countries. America will be most effective in this role by operating through our welfare enterprise organizations, supporting governmental action via guarantees, tax incentives, and government-to-government programs that welfare enterprisers can not do as well.

The role of America in the world is that of a developer. Nowhere have I found much evidence that economic development necessarily will follow along American lines. Our system of welfare enterprise may be unique; certainly not much of it can be exported. Each country will develop according to its own cultural conditions. We are exporting the American Revolution, not the American system. Our job is to facilitate each country's development toward human dignity and the freedom for individual self-development. We cannot afford the luxury of another New Deal type of fight between private and public enterprises as to who does the job. It has got to be done jointly and with the full collaboration of our labor movement, using those people experienced in the art of social revolution. As Charles F. Kettering has said, "We are simply professional amateurs. We are amateurs because we are doing things for the first time. We are professionals because we know we are going to have a lot of trouble." And this applies equally to the leaders of industry, finance, labor, and government. The sobering fact about Cuba is that no leader in any of these groups came up with a practical program to make the Cuban Revolution unnecessary, and no one has come up at this writing with a practical program as to how the U.S.A. can establish mutually beneficial relations with Cuba again. Of course the dominant view is that we have no such obligation. The promising nature of President Eisenhower's mid-1960 Latin American program is that America now acknowledges that its leaders do have such an obligation.

As Latin America is the major emergent area where government-to-government programs have been subordinated to private investment, welfare enterprise has an especial responsibility to answer the genuine challenges by innovating practical programs, like joint government and savings and loan association home mortgaging financing, to make the Latin American countries *safe for democracy*.

POINT FOUR YOUTH CORPS

The one concrete proposal that William James advanced to implement his idea of a moral equivalent of war was

a conscription of the whole youthful population to form for a certain number of years a part of the army enlisted against *Nature* ... the military ideals of hardihood and discipline would be wrought into the growing fiber of the people; no one would remain blind as the luxurious classes now are blind, to man's relations to the globe he lives on, and to the permanently sour and hard foundations of his higher life. To coal and iron mines, to freight trains, to fishing fleets in December, to dishwashing, clothes-washing, and window-washing, to road-building, and tunnel-making, to foundries and stoke-holes, and to the frames of skyscrapers, would our gilded youths be drafted off, according to their choice, to get the childishness knocked out of them, and to come back into society with healthier sympathies and soberer ideas. They would have paid their blood-tax, done their own part in the immemorial human warfare against nature; they would tread the earth more proudly, the women would value them more highly, they would be better fathers and teachers of the following generation.

As I write these words, my daily radio, both before and after the morning news, is urging me to write to the local Civil Defense office to find out how to prepare a fallout shelter for my family. I do not like the resignation of defeat implicit in this advice. I have not written yet. Have you? I would rather have the radio urging me to write my Congressman and Senators to formally declare a world-wide war for construction, and to Pass H.R. 9638, an amendment to the Mutual Security Act, in the words of Henry S. Reuss (Wisconsin) who introduced it, ". . . to provide for a study looking toward a Point Four Youth Corps of young Americans willing to serve their country in public and private technical assistance missions in faroff countries, and at a soldier's pay." The late Senator Richard L. Neuberger (Oregon) introduced an identical measure—S. 2908—in the Senate on January 26, 1960.

The objectives of the Point Four Youth Corps will be—

(A) To make additional technical manpower available to United States agencies and to private agencies carrying out economic, medical, educational, and community development programs in underdeveloped friendly foreign countries;

(B) to assist in broadening the understanding by the peoples of other nations of the ideals and aspirations of Americans, through close contact with young Americans participating in the Point Four Youth Corps; and

(C) to offer our young people an opportunity to serve their country in a stimulating way, while broadening their understanding of the problems facing other peoples and nations, and thereby helping them better to understand American policies and purposes abroad.

This Reuss Bill passed Congress, but no money was appropriated for it, and the International Cooperation Administration hoped to find a private foundation to finance the study.

Two programs have already set the pattern for a large scale Youth Corp. The International Farm Youth Exchange (IFYE) program is fostering understanding among the youths of over fifty Asian, European, Latin American, Pacific, and Middle Eastern countries. The other "inbound-outbound" program is for high school students and is sponsored by the American Field Service International Scholarships Program. Each year hundreds of students from over thirty countries of the free world study in America for one year. In return, American students of like age and schooling spend their summer vacation with foster families abroad. What has proved practical and vista broadening for several hundred students can be equally beneficial for several hundred thousands. It is only a matter of organization and money. This proposal is designed to provide an international doing and learning experience to make world developers out of young Americans.

PRESSURES FOR WAR OF CONSTRUCTION

We consider now, in the words of the original author of the Youth Corps back in 1910, the prospects for "the state of public opinion that would" require a draft of America's youth to fight its first nonkilling-and-being-killed World War. "Such a conscription," James wrote, "should get toughness without callousness, authority with as little criminal cruelty as possible, and painful work done cheerily because the duty is temporary, and threatens not, as now, to degrade the whole remainder of one's life. I spoke of the 'moral equivalent' of war."

During the Korean War the internal conflict of the Amer-can people was brought out in the open. The stimulus of "fighting communism," upon which the politicians relied almost entirely during the 1950's to organize American collectivity, was not enough to get Americans to sacrifice butter for bullets to fight the Korean War. As we have seen, our politicians and enterprisers had to expand productive capacity (accelerate annual rate of growth) to produce both butter and guns to wage war in Korea. A working family whose head was employed in our Beaver Falls factory illustrates this internal conflict. His wife, two sons, and one daughter were all able to get good-paying jobs (means steady overtime pay) during the Korean War in which one son and one son-in-law had to fight. I will call them the Stillmans. The single-household annual income was over fifteen thousand dollars. They were effective consumers of the products of Madison Avenue. The mother, Irene, a woman in her late forties, expressed the conflict in discussing the 1952 elections with me, "Joe would kill me if he knew I was going to vote for Eisenhower," she confided.

"Stevenson would make a better President," I argued.

"Yeh, I guess so. He talks real good and would be good for the working man," she agreed, "but I'm scared. Danny is out there fighting and Mary's husband is on his way to Korea. They might get killed. Joe says not to worry. He came back okay in the First World War, and our Eddie didn't get hurt in the Second World War. But," she hesitated, "I'm scared for Danny and Mary. I guess that's the way a mother feels."

The idea that Stevenson could also bring the Korean War to an end was one that I just could not sell her. She was voting for Ike and, she whispered, so Mary and Eddie might also. However she agreed that her husband and I were right about Stevenson and left me with this comment: "If we could just keep our jobs with overtime pay, and not have to worry about losing them, without Danny and Mary's man being in danger of getting killed in Korea, I'd vote for Stevenson. We won't all be able to keep our jobs and big pay after Ike ends the Korean war over there, but at least Danny and Mary's man will be safe."

This family's internal conflict is the internal conflict of the American people. When Khrushchev personally proposed total disarmament to the United Nations in 1959, he touched the vital chord of inner conflict that is stretched tense in the bosom of all America's households. The fear of what such a proposal would do to jobs and profits got expressed in charges of insincerity and propaganda. Of course, our economy can be reconverted to nonkilling production to replace the cut in our $42 billion defense program that disarmament would cause. But we could not do so without an economic equivalent. We cannot reconvert existing employment and capacity now used for armaments, let alone utilize our idle manpower, growing work force and capacity, just producing for Americans. We must find the economic equivalent in a moral equivalent to war.

We tax ourselves for the same reasons that we buy life insurance—out of fear; in this case fear of the Kremlin bombing us the way we bombed the people of Hiroshima and Nagasaki. The proposals to end the cold war and to disarm cause, in the words of James, "the fear of emancipation from the fear regime . . . fear regarding ourselves now taking the place of the ancient fear of the enemy." I can visualize a public opinion emerging out of this fear to support the Youth Corps and war of construction. "Taking human nature as a whole, its wars are its best protection against its weaker and more cowardly self, and mankind cannot *afford* to *adopt* a peace-economy," James found.

James's call to fight a nonkilling war is the practical way to put an end to killing-and-being-killed wars. I revive his moral equivalent of war because a half century of history finally has made it current.

James's distinguished student and successor at Harvard, Dr. William E. Hocking, as I read him, is saying that the U.S.A. and U.S.S.R. are joint developers of "The Coming World Civilization." He writes:

The West is only beginning to realize its potential property in the unlosables of the East. These processes can neither be stopped nor undone; the lines that have "gone forth into all the world" cannot return to their origin. The making of a single civilization is contained in the two concepts, the universal and the unlosable, plus the simple existence of the arts of unlimited human communication. . . . For the first time our entire world space is permeated with ideas which, as Locke said about truth and the keeping of faith, "belong to man as man and not as a member of society." . . . In giving birth to the universal, the West has begotten something that can never again be private property. . . . The era of "the civilizations" being past, what we now enter is either the era of civilization or the era of universal desolation.[19]

[19] William Ernest Hocking, *The Coming World Civilization*, Harper & Brothers, New York, 1957, as excerpted in *This Is My Philosophy*, ed. by Whit Burnett, Harper & Brothers, New York, 1957, pp. 295-296.

The public opinion to support the Youth Corps and a nonkilling war to make the world safe for democracy[20] is all bottled up inside the bosoms of our 180 million people. Irene Stillman's plea for an America in which she and her husband Joe and her sons all have good-paying jobs without the fear of unemployment and war is the plea of America. She is only too willing to have her Danny and Mary's husband drafted to fight in a war of construction in Korea, Indonesia, Iran, Brazil, Bolivia, Cuba, southern Italy, Spain, and everywhere else where "our Danny and Mary's man will be safe."

A newspaper story about Crawford Greenewalt, president of E. I. Du Pont De Nemours, says that he "quotes William James to suggest that if there were a moral equivalent to the effort of an all-our war we would produce vastly more than we do today."[21] There is. We have found it during the 1950's; in the 1960's we shall be embracing it formally and fully. The direct federal budget cost need not be more than five billion a year. Welfare enterprise will and can carry the bulk of the cost with adequate government guarantees, loans, and credits. We can pay for this kind of war with increased production in the 1960's as we did in the 1930's and as we did to fight the 1939-1945 and 1950-1953 wars. Greenewalt has observed how we would increase production through "a moral equivalent to an all-out war." Our job is to evoke his inner humanity to using a big chunk of such increased output to wage the war of construction, and to have his fellow industrialists call off the inhuman campaign of threatening the American people with inflation. The problems of stability and growth are tough enough without using the natural fear of inflation as a tactic to hold back America from asserting its national purpose in the world.

How do we get Senators and Congressmen to legislate the necessary guarantees, credits, and loans for private industry and to vote the initial funds and levy the necessary taxes for these

[20] No American criticizes Woodrow Wilson's objective; it was his failure to make the world safe for democracy that we mourn.

[21] Charles Lucey, "du Pont Head Calls for Unlimited Cash for Pure Research," *The Pittsburgh Press*, January 4, 1960.

and government-to-government programs? There is no problem facing them that they can solve without first solving the problem of sending the output of our surplus agricultural and industrial capacities and excess manpower around the world. The anti-Communist reasons for stirring ourselves are just as real now as before Khrushchev. To release the spiritual energies of 180 million Americans we also have to stir ourselves for prohumanity reasons that have stirred Americans since Jamestown, Plymouth Rock, and Ellis Island.

DAVENPORT'S SEARCH AND YOURS AND MINE

I reject Louis M. Hacker's prophecy that "the future historian undoubtedly will say that the 1950's marked the peak of American power."[22] To be sure, our peak will come, but not until after we have developed the Age of American Excellence that will set the standard for the world in the twenty-first century.

"The martial virtues must be the enduring cement," James observed, and "although originally gained by the race through war, are absolute and permanent human goods." I answer in the affirmative to his question, "Why should men not someday feel that it is worth a blood-tax to belong to a collectivity superior in *any* ideal respect?" To solve our dilemma of democracy we have to formulate practical measures to organize the collectivity of our people to serve the power of democracy without losing the freedoms for self-development of dignified human beings who are ends-in-themselves.

In 1960 the dilemma of the Great American Democracy is all enveloped in this basic question: Is the devoted collectivity of a people the exclusive power of a totalitarian system of government? I repeat: Any American who believes that the collectivity of the American people cannot be organized within the framework of civil liberties and personal freedoms is a licked American. Lincoln did it to save the Union a century ago. We have

[22] Louis M. Hacker, "A Historian Previews the Sixties," *Saturday Review,* January 30, 1960.

done it in four overseas wars since. Each time civil liberties and personal freedoms were risked and in the 1914-1918 and 1939-1945 wars temporarily abridged. But after the Civil War Negroes began to participate in some of these freedoms, and they emerged out of the 1939-1945 war with more effective social-economic-political expressions of freedom than they had when they went into the war. During the 1950's the world-wide pressures of the emerging peoples were a significant factor in the development of still more meaningful expressions of personal freedoms for American Negroes. These same pressures, as we have seen, are also working for a moral equivalent of war. They will get translated into the equivalent of a War Production Board, the World Development Board (WDB) into which the Lincoln-centennial administration will be organizing the several international aid and loan agencies. Whether the equivalent of the Office of Price Administration and War Labor Board also will be created will depend upon the speed with which the wage-price, pace-setting industries develop wage-productivity collective bargaining. Welfare enterprise will play the same role through the WDB in the War of Construction that it plays in our defense program through the Pentagon. This is America.

Russell W. Davenport's search is yours and mine. "Our idea of freedom," he wrote,[23]

does not seem to fit either the needs or the ideals of most of the people of the globe. There is something lacking in it that people want, something that they need, something that must sound in our words if our doctrine of freedom is to ring true. And we had better find out what that "something" is. . . . This book is a search for that something . . . it is a search for an attitude. Our aim is to try to open up a path for others to follow who are more skilled than we, or better equipped, to carry on the search.

I hope that in these pages I might also open paths for others to follow, as Davenport did for me.

A fresh, new, distinctive creature, who did not exist before

[23] Russell W. Davenport, *The Dignity of Man*, Harper & Brothers, 1955, pp. 25-26.

Columbus, travels the world today. He is not an exploiter; he is a developer. He has developed a powerful nation out of the North American wilderness; he is in the process of developing it into a great nation by using his power to facilitate the development of the peoples in all other lands. He is an American.

INDEX